i

Audiovisual Media and Libraries

Audiovisual Media
and Libraries

Selected Readings

Emanuel T. Prostano

1972

Libraries Unlimited, Inc.

Littleton, Colo.

Library of Congress Card Number 72-89111
International Standard Book Number 0-87287-053-7

LIBRARIES UNLIMITED, INC.
P.O. Box 263
Littleton, Colorado 80120

To

Joyce, Steve, Lori

TABLE OF CONTENTS

MORE COMMUNICATIONS TECHNOLOGY

MEDIA EVALUATION

INTRODUCTION

Audiovisual media have long been a part of library collections. Some types of AV media have been relatively commonplace, such as record and film collections in the public library. Again, there are those libraries—"the innovators"—where all audiovisual forms applicable to learning are automatically incorporated into the service pattern. Formal educational institutions in particular are representative of the latter type and are also cited as the leaders in the development of unified media programs.

A basic, continuing criticism of libraries has been their reluctance to house and utilize media other than printed resources. This appears to be a criticism which has some validity. Some of the reasons posed for not incorporating the range of audiovisual media into libraries relate to a lack of funds, space, and trained personnel. Perhaps the high value placed on books as opposed to other formats is also a factor.

The terminology employed by the library profession does little to alleviate the situation. While use of "print and nonprint" or "book and nonbook" may be an adequate means of differentiating between the printed format and other forms, it does tend to cast a cloud over forms other than traditional library resources. Although no effort is made here to mandate terminology in the field, the term "media" has been suggested for some time as a common denominator. *Webster's Third New International Dictionary* cites media as the plural of medium, the means "through or by which something is accomplished or carried on."[1] The 1969 school media standards provides another definition of the term media—"printed and audiovisual forms of communication and their accompanying technology."[2] As you may observe, my preference lies in this direction.

THE AUDIOVISUAL FIELD

Though the audiovisual field may be considered an entity in itself, it generally functions in an institutional framework other than its own. In very modest institutions, varied audiovisual forms may simply be used in carrying out the goals of the institution. In a more complex situation, audiovisual service may enjoy equal status with a library or may be a department within the library. On the other hand, audiovisual service may be the prime focus of an institutional support system which merely incorporates a library as one program element.

There are those who cite "change" as the only factor providing continuity in our society. We know that educational institutions and libraries are rapidly becoming more oriented toward change. This is also the situation in the audiovisual field. It has expanded its concepts and framework to accommodate changes in our technological society. While the term "audiovisual" is still commonly applied, we can note major changes in the field. For example, the name of the national organization has changed from Department of Audiovisual Instruction (DAVI) to Association for Educational Communications and Technology (AECT). The change was designed to focus attention on the advances in modern educational technology now in the purview of the organization.

1. *Webster's Third New International Dictionary.* Springfield, Mass., G. & C. Merriam, 1969. p. 2322.
2. American Association of School Librarians and Department of Audiovisual Instruction, *Standards for School Media Programs.* Chicago, American Library Association, 1969. p. xv.

In the educational setting, AECT focuses on the Domain of Instructional Technology developed by Kenneth Silber.[3] Instructional technology means "1. the organization and the 2. application of 3. resources—men, materials, devices, procedures and ideas—in a systematic manner in order to solve instructional problems."[4] Resources are central to the concept and are called instructional system components (ISC's). Application refers to the developmental process which must act on ISC's to turn them into an instructional system. This process consists of six instructional development functions: 1) research-theory, 2) design, 3) production, 4) evaluation-selection, 5) utilization, and 6) support-supply. Organization relates to the management of personnel and data.

Thus we find that the audiovisual field, like the library field in general, is in the process of change and redefinition. When we discuss technology in any of its ramifications, we are talking about aspects of modern audiovisual programming.

THE COLLECTION

In library science, we expect students to use an extensive approach to learning. That is, we expect wide reading and the gathering of information from various sources. Library literature is really not bursting with writings about audiovisual media. Also, it is difficult to ferret out literature which relates—assuming one is aware of what does relate. This collection is designed to provide a comprehensive overview of audiovisual media utilization in libraries.

Readings were selected on the basis of significance to the field and the degree to which they illuminate specific aspects of audiovisual media utilization. Because the field is very fluid, only articles of recent vintage have been included.

The collection provides: an introductory section dealing with some philosophic considerations and an overview of technological innovations; sections dealing with varied traditional audiovisual forms and utilization practices; sections devoted to the major technologies destined to change libraries significantly in the future—microforms, computers, and communication systems; and a section dealing with the evaluation and selection of audiovisual media. In brief, the collection provides the reader with an opportunity to gain a better understanding and appreciation of what has been the neglected half of library science.

The volume should be useful in graduate and undergraduate library science programs where there is interest in expanding the range of interest of students. It should also be of interest to the professional in the field who wishes to gain new insight into the ramifications of library science or desires to apply new information to a practical work situation. The instructional technologist (audiovisual specialist) and other educators who are interested in library operations should find the collection useful.

My thanks are extended to those authors and publishers who allowed their material to be reprinted here. I would also like to thank Joyce S. Prostano for her assistance in reviewing the work, and Elaine S. Mazeika for typing the manuscript.

E. T. P.

3. Kenneth Silber, "What Field Are We In Anyhow," *Audiovisual Instruction* 15:21-24 (May 1970).
4. *Ibid.*, p. 24.

A NEW LOOK AT THE AUDIOVISUAL FIELD

*The works included in this section are designed to provide a
generalized introduction to the domain of audiovisual media
and technology. While the nature of the material does not allow
for a logical progression from article to article, each article does
provide a forecast of new directions for libraries and, in most
cases, a philosophic perspective.*

THE MEDIUM WAY*

By Louis Shores

American education has a new *learning mode.* In two words, it can be
identified as *independent study.* But there is also a third word equally useful in
the identification of the new learning mode, and that word is *library.* One can see
how crucial these elements are to the success of America's educational commitment by recalling Winslow Hatch's comment, "The degree to which students can
study independently is one measure of quality in education." (2)

In the new learning mode, the student has his own individual work bench,
called a *carrel.* Here he works with the *generic book*, in all of its varied formats,
under the direction of a bibliographically sophisticated faculty. As far as higher
education is concerned, this mode reaches its ultimate degree of sophistication
in a teaching method known as the *Library-College.*

The trend to independent study is a concomitant of the national commitment to universal education. As more students enter our schools and colleges,
the educational challenge of quantity is second only to the educational challenge
of quality. We are now confronted by the widest range of individual differences
ever. The classroom teaching mode is no longer able to cope with the spread of
talents that meets as a group for cramped exercises of recitation and note-taking.
At long last, we are being convinced that something must be done about *individual
differences.* That something is independent study tailored to the talents of the
individual student.

As librarians, we can no longer avoid the implications of this trend toward
independent study. For years we have celebrated our support of the classroom.
But if the classroom is soon to become secondary to the carrel, what then will
we support? Will we merely continue our traditional role of supplier—a role that
has largely been one of acquiring, processing, and circulating the materials of
instruction, while occasionally making a pass at learning through something we
have called Reference, and more recently, Information Science? Or will we
accept the challenge hurled at us by Chancellor Branscomb in his classic study
for the Carnegie Corporation, and published under the hardcover title *Teaching
with Books.* He wrote in 1940, as some of us will recall, "To sum up, it may be
said without hesitation that the fundamental need of the college library is to
develop a distinctive program of its own." (1:9)

---

*Reprinted by permission from *Library-College Journal*, 1:10-17, Winter 1968.

The opportunity is here for the library in the schools, as well as in the colleges, to develop a distinctive educational program of our own. The national commitment to universal education, the widening range of individual differences, student revolt against the classroom lockstep, and an inept groping by faculty colleagues who know little about exploiting a mushrooming independent study movement, are all factors in a situation that demands leadership from libraries. Because of the nature of this dilemma, and because its solution calls for a new dimension in academic librarianship, it is more important than ever that our profession abandon its ancillary complex, its supportive role, its devotion to management and housekeeping, and assume educational leadership.

The reason is simple. For the first time in the history of education, instructional materials are so many and so varied that individual differences in students can be matched with individual differences in media. These media make independent study feasible. They render the classroom mode uneconomical and ineffective as a primary educational method.

But media learning requires a new breed of faculty. It requires teachers who not only know their students, but who know their media as well. Despite Dr. Branscomb's expose of college faculty ineptness in teaching with books, we all know many classroom teachers in schools, as well as in colleges, who are library-minded. But we know, also, that the percent of librarians who know books and libraries is much higher than it is among classroom teachers. So, to begin with, we librarians are in a better position to teach in this new learning mode called Independent Study, than any of our colleagues in educational work. The only question is how many of us are willing to *library teach* rather than to *library manage*?

Before we answer this question, let's dispose of the pragmatic one. I refer, of course, to the problem which many call the "grass roots approach," the "feet on the ground policy," or any of the other shibboleths that gain political fortune in pedagoguery as well as in demagoguery. Who will acquire and accession; classify and catalog; charge out materials; collect fines on overdues; read and revise shelves; check periodicals, documents, continuations? And on and on. I agree that these questions must be answered. I want a neat, efficient, quiet, well-organized library, as much as anyone. But I do not want it at the expense of the high educational role we have long denied our profession.

The manner in which I would attack these practical questions concerning library housekeeping has already been set forth in various writings on current library management. For example, two of the most important means now at our disposal are machines and technicians. Our mechanical heritage has made us more susceptible to the dramatics of automation than to the prosaics of semi-professionals. With frenzy, we are buying hardware and installing it, often without bothering to justify it until some later date. Not so long ago, I visited a library with print-out catalog, computerized serial records, systems-studies galore, and serious consideration of LDX (long distance xeroxing) with remote consoles already under demonstration. I asked, "How is the innovating going?"

"Confidentially," she whispered, "it takes longer and it costs more, but we've doubled our library budget, and the President escorts more visitors, personally, to the library than he ever did before."

Of course, there has been much unnecessary automation. But by far, most hardware has relieved professional librarianship of much of the routine that has contributed to the unfavorable features in our professional portrait. For instance, I believe the print-out book catalog will inevitably replace our 3" by 5" files. It will absorb a large share of the routine processing on which professional personnel dissipate much of their effort, and it will free us for creative literature searching and bibliographic description. Through offset printing, we will be able to furnish selected indexes to any part of the collection by subject, level, and format; furthermore, we will be able to provide this material in any arrangement desired by a specialist, no matter what his purpose. The only remorse I see about this aspect of computerized technical processing is on the part of those of us who have committed millions of dollars to reclassifying by LC, when we at last understand that a simple ID number is easier for the computer, and that any broad classification for the physical book, such as the Dewey Third Summary, is adequate.

We have been somewhat less receptive to the idea of positions at a technician level with semi-professional competence, although the present high ratio of professionals to clericals on our library staffs should give us real concern. Some of us dread another library education articulation problem which could be caused by the proposed junior college technician program. Only now, after many years of resistance, have we finally correlated the NCATE undergraduate and ALA graduate programs. But some of us in library education do not yet see the correlative opportunity in the junior college program—an opportunity that could result in ridding ourselves of many of the techniques that keep library science from gaining full graduate and senior division respectability.

And some of us in library practice fear that many of the technics we have enjoyed will be taken from us by a whole new class of semiprofessionals. It is disadvantageous both to the library and to librarianship for professionals with master's degrees, and above, to continue to devote so much time to these necessary but semi-professional tasks. Nor does such devotion enhance the professional image we hope to use in recruitment. Within recent months, some of our most promising graduates have written of disenchantment with library practice, simply because of the disproportionate time required for routines that could more effectively be performed by technicians. Despite the New York State conclusion (4) of several years ago (and to me the conclusions did not seem to follow the findings), there has been a solid movement for a junior college technician program, and at least one state plans to launch such a program in its community junior colleges. (6)

Assuming that machines and technicians will inevitably relieve the professional librarian of many, if not most, of the technics we have undertaken in the past, what then will he do? For one thing, he will become a full partner in research. He will not only *retrieve* information for the scientist, but interpret it as well. What is more, he will carry on a part of the investigation, and in some instances make the discovery, or come up with the invention that will deserve the Nobel prize.

For another thing, the librarian will become a full partner in education. He will not only support the classroom, if there still is a classroom, but he will provide an even more effective learning locus in the library carrel. No longer will the librarian slavishly follow a course of study constructed by others. Instead, he

13

will be in the vanguard of curriculum development, presenting colleges and schools for the first time with a phenomenon of content following the library, rather than *vice versa*. From a long experience and an extensive training in comparative education, book selection, and curriculum development, I can say unqualifiedly that I would rather trust the education of the next generation to a method of teaching that makes such use of librarians than to most schemes that have heretofore been tried.

Let me particularize on two major aspects of our professional role in the new learning mode of independent study. Without knowledge of books and libraries there can be no independent study. Had the Monteith experiment (3) proved nothing else, it still would have served a useful purpose by demonstrating that both faculty and students lack the type of library sophistication required in the new independent learning mode. Consequently, the highest priority must be assigned to developing means whereby the next generation of teachers and students will have a sophistication in library use that goes beyond anything that has yet resulted from orientation periods or separate freshman courses.

To accomplish a new dimension in library-use instruction, we will first have to be sure that we ourselves are adequately reoriented. I am not taken by new terms such as "Learning Resources Center," when used as a substitute for the word *Library*. Such captions serve little purpose except as a dramatic label to entice financial support from school boards and college presidents who themselves have not been library-minded in the past.

Before you shake your head and insist that a Learning Resource Center is something different from a library, let me recall that Florida pioneered the "Instructional Materials" concept as well as the "Materials Center," both forerunners of what now passes as a Learning Resource Center. The Library School of Florida State University was the first ALA accredited graduate school to require audiovisual competence of all its graduates. The literature will attest to my own personal crusade for a unity of materials concept, a campaign which dates from the first audiovisual course ever offered in the South, back at Peabody in 1935. My book, *Instructional Materials,* was probably the first textbook for teachers to treat the whole range of educational media, from textbook through television.

What I must insist on at the outset is that we reorient ourselves to consider all formats in the whole range of instructional materials as part of the *generic book*. In our professional vocabulary, henceforth, the term "non-book materials" must be banished as it has been for some time among Florida Instructional Materials Specialists. In our concept, the film must become a book in the same sense that the hardcover is considered a book. This, of course, means that certain preconceptions will have to be overcome, and this may not be too easy, for if we place our reluctance with audiovisual media in historical perspective, it may be that we will appear in a light similar to the conservatism of a fifteenth century monastery librarian who declared, shortly after Gutenberg's first imprint: "This is a true library. Here one will find only handwritten manuscripts, and not any of those machine-made reproductions that some have the audacity to call books."

There is a basic educational-philosophic concept in the generic book, which Marshall McLuhan, in my opinion, has only partially exploited. The educational concept may be stated most simply by the following: If learning is fundamentally

communication between learner and environment, then the format of the medium
of communication may influence learning. In the past, our library classification
schemes have considered subject as the all-important approach to knowledge.
More recently, the level of difficulty, measured essentially by vocabulary, has
been an important consideration. But now, for the first time, and probably as a
result of McLuhan's spectaculars, we have begun to realize that medium format
may be as important in a particular learning situation as either subject or level.

Many examples from my experience, and yours, could be drawn to illustrate the superiority of films, transparencies, tapes, field trips, globes—or yes, even
hardcover print—when teaching a particular subject at the mental age of the
individual student concerned. Botany teachers who have used time-lapse photography know how much more effectively 16mm motion pictures communicate
plant growth than almost any other format. And for communicating nuances
of pronunciation, what can compare with tape recordings of Latin American
children's voices in homey conversation. But don't sell print short, as McLuhan
does. The hardcover, the magazine, the government document—they still communicate messages that all other formats, when taken together and laid end-to-
end, cannot do. And as for fact-finding, there are certain system designs in basic
reference books that our Information Science colleagues might well study if they
with to improve retrieval efforts.

So we separatists—we audiovisualists, information scientists, and librarians
alike—must first of all reorient ourselves in the generic book. But those of us who
believe the film, or the flat picture, or the tape, or the peep box, like Duz, does
everything, need to rediscover the power of print. And the Information Scientist
who believes passionately that the System is the thing, might well spend a few
hours away from key-punch and computer re-examining encyclopedists' struggles
with information retrieval. But above all, a librarian with my mechanical ineptness needs to disillusion himself that the term *audiovisual* means electronic specialism, or even the annoyance of replacing a burnt-out bulb. What audiovisual really
means is an extension of the means of communication between learner and environment; consequently, the librarian must make himself as knowledgeable in
these other formats of the generic book as he now is with those which are lumped
together under the heading of print.

Once we ourselves have this reorientation, the first element in our new
professional role as librarian, audiovisualist, information scientist, or media
specialist will be to sophisticate the next generation in the use of tools for independent study. We must do this in a more imaginative way than we have taught
the use of libraries and instructional materials in the past. Dramatically, we must
present the whole repertoire of formats, generally at first, and then by subject
and level. We must somehow convince teacher education that it is just as important to teach media *per se* as it is to teach these media incidentally to subject, to
level, to method, and to what not. So a major part of our professional attention
shifts from management to teaching—teaching the tools of independent study, to
a new generation of students, and to a new breed of teachers.

The second major aspect of our new educational role is to introduce a new
gestalt into curriculum development. Since World War II, at least, we have experienced a concurrent though comparatively mild effort to balance our rage for
specialism with that of generalism. The colleges called it general education. In

15

the curriculum it resulted in the substitution for such specialized beginning courses as chemistry, physics, and geology, with an integrated course known as "physical science," or "phy sci"; for botany, zoology, physiology with "bi sci"; for sociology, political science, economics, with "social sciences"; and for literature, art, music, philosophy, with a general course called "humanities." Although the movement was at first given a hard time by the specialists, it finally became accepted in many, if not most, institutions of higher education.

The time has now come for the next step in *gestalt*. C. P. Snow called our attention to the schism between the two cultures of science and humanities. I agree with him that the schism exists, but I disagree with his opinion that scientists are more aware of the humanities than the humanists are cognizant of the sciences. But however that may be, I am in agreement that the time has come for a general course, or division, in our curriculum—one that cuts across the sciences and humanities and draws the social sciences and all its applications into an overview of knowledge.

From the nature of our pedagogues' and specialists' curricula, you would gather that the account in Genesis should be corrected to read, "On the first day, God was a chemist and created the elements; on the second day, He was an economist and created the means of production, consumption, and distribution—if not exchange itself; and on the third day He was a musicologist and created the sounds of the spheres." Certainly, the student who moves from a chemistry class to a session in economics, and then to a class in art appreciation has such an order of creation confirmed for him every Monday, Wednesday and Friday during the academic year. The time has come to show God's universe as a whole, for the unity it unquestionably is. And no one can do this better than the faculty who work with the generic book.

The librarian or media specialist is by nature a generalist. From time immemorial he has maintained his neutrality among the disciplines, serving them all impartially. Furthermore, through his classification of knowledge, the librarian has done much with the class called "generalia." He has had a major influence on the encyclopedia, the medium which is concerned with presenting a summary of the knowledge most significant to mankind. By the nature of his competence, the librarian is equipped to participate in work of the curriculum as no one else can participate. Such competence stems from his expertise with an area which, for want of a more distinguishing term, we may simply call "Knowledge." As I see it, every curriculum from "K through 14" (since junior college is basically general education) should have an overview at the beginning, and a capstone at the end. These curricula should give relationship and perspective to the hallowed and predatory courses, subjects, and disciplines, that we have for so long celebrated academically.

Not only does the librarian have the content for such an area from his practice in general book selection, but he has also a method—the forerunner of independent study—which we call professionally by such terms as *browsing, reader advisory,* or *book listing.* These professional methods of ours are the very heart of teaching in the independent study learning mode.

Throughout this nation's gigantic effort in education, innovation is bubbling. At the center of experimentation is the trend to independence in learning. Some 100 colleges, like Antioch and Stephens, Elmira and Florida

Presbyterian, Oklahoma Christian and Jamestown are in the vanguard of the development now known as the Library-College, i.e., a college which is completely a library and in which the carrel has replaced the classroom as the center of learning. Uncounted high schools like Ridgewood, Illinois, and numerous elementary schools like Shaker Heights, Ohio, are trying to see how far pupils can study independently with no teacher supervision except guidance. The librarian or media specialist must, of course, continue to support the classroom teacher who carries on conventionally. But we have a special responsibility to those classroom teachers who are working with honors students, as well as with small groups in seminar-type situations, who wish to develop independence of the classroom. And above all, we owe ourselves a try at our own brand of education. We must accept Chancellor Branscomb's challenge, and see if we can come up with an education of our own, an education which can meet the most daring educational undertaking the history of the world has even known—the higher education of all the people.

Because I believe ours is a profession of destiny, I have faith that we will make of this new learning mode a way to a better education for the next generation.

REFERENCES

1.   Branscomb, Harvie. *Teaching with Books.* Hamden, Conn., Shoe String Press, 1940.

2.   Hatch, Winslow Ropen, and Ann Bennett. *Independent Study.* New Dimensions in Higher Education, No. 1. Washington, U.S. Department of Health, Education, and Welfare, Office of Education, 1960.

3.   Knapp, Patricia B. *The Montieth College Library Experiment.* New York, Scarecrow Press, 1966.

4.   New York (State) University. Deputy Commissioner of Education's Evaluation Committee on the Experimental Library Technician Program. *Report.* Albany, University of the State of New York, State Education Department, New York State Library, 1962.

5.   Shores, Louis. *Instructional Materials: An Introduction for Teachers.* New York, Ronald Press, 1960.

6.   Shores, Louis. *Statement on Junior College Library Technician Programs.* ALA Education Division Newsletter, No. 60 (December 1966), 4-5.

AV TASK FORCE SURVEY REPORT*

By C. Walter Stone

The Audiovisual Task Force Survey was authorized by the American Library Association during the summer of 1967 and was launched formally during September of that year. Its purpose was "to study needs for a membership organization within librarianship and a national office staff which could provide advisory and coordinating services relating to audiovisual services provided by libraries. . . ."

The chief stimulus which caused development of the survey proposal and its initial sponsorship by the Audiovisual Committee of ALA was an opinion expressed by increasing numbers of individual members of ALA and by groups associated with the library profession that ALA itself has not been meeting adequately the information needs of professional librarians concerned with development of audiovisual services. Further, there is too much uncertainty in the field respecting what such needs are and which organizations or agencies can or should actually offer librarians help.

The basic plan of the survey called for sponsorship of five (or six) regional conferences to which would be invited a variety of individuals including persons judged prominent in developing new media services by libraries or other agencies and who were known to have sufficient educational background and work experience to view the major problems posed from a national perspective. It was also intended that meetings be held with the executive secretaries (or their deputies) of several key professional organizations concerned with provision of educational media services, e.g., DAVI, NAEB, et al., and that a follow-up questionnaire study be conducted to elicit recommendations directly from the field. A draft of the questionnaire was checked with conferees and a revised edition sent to the field in the fall.

Because response to the questionnaire was limited, in March 1969 a follow-up letter was mailed to 308 individuals. Some 104 replies were received and their contents were then analyzed. As a final part of the survey effort, Dr. James Brown, dean of Graduate Studies and Research at San Jose State College and nationally-known specialist in fields of educational communication, authored a brief paper on roles played by professional associations and headquarters staffs working in the fields of educational communication and information services generally. Following completion of the procedures described, this Final Report has been compiled. And it is now urged that the recommendations presented be forwarded to appropriate units of ALA for action.

The first part of the report summarizes chief findings obtained from survey efforts and the major recommendations offered. While information was obtained from many individuals and organizations during the course of the survey, any errors of interpretation or of presentation should be attributed to the survey chairman. The second part of the report, as written by Dr. Brown, responds to a charge given him to set forth his own opinions, beliefs, and recommendations.

Full statements concerning Task Force expenditures and related materials including the questionnaire and copies of field letter responses have been filed with the Chairman of the ALA Audiovisual Committee, Mr. John Moriarty, director of libraries at Purdue University.

*Reprinted by permission from *American Libraries,* 1:40-44, January 1970.

During the fall, winter, and spring of 1967-68 a series of regional meetings was held in Atlantic City, Denver, Seattle, Berkeley, Miami, and Kansas City. To each of these meetings were invited a number of individuals (usually ten to fifteen) representing various media service interests and including specialists in the professional education of both librarians and audiovisual personnel.

Growing out of the six regional conferences, individual interviews, returns from a "trial" questionnaire, and responses to the field letter were the following conclusions and recommendations.

Identified more frequently than any other needs for assistance which could or should be provided by one or more professional (media) organizations were the following, listed in order of priority.

1. Recruitment and *improved training* of personnel who will exhibit more favorable professional attitudes toward development of A-V services by libraries.

2. Regular gathering, compilation, and publication of more complete and reliable *information about audiovisual materials* appropriate for library acquisition and distribution.

3. Gathering, compilation, and publication of more complete and reliable *information concerning items of equipment required for effective use of audiovisual materials* in libraries and by library patrons.

4. More concerted and productive *efforts to promote the interest of librarians in audiovisual services* and to explain the importance of such service to the various library clienteles served.

5. More help with development of *special services which utilize audiovisual materials and equipment* including those established for hospital patients, disadvantaged groups, special education programs, etc.

This rank order listings of needs, while it does indicate priorities, does not show the strong emphasis usually present in any discussion of needs in the field for better-trained personnel and more favorable professional attitudes. A majority of those consulted believe that the education offered currently by professional schools responsible for career preparation of librarians, audiovisual service personnel, and educational broadcasters et al., does not provide the background needed, nor does it instill the attitudes required for optimum service. Both conferees and correspondents suggested that a major role could and should be played by the American Library Association itself, working through the Library Education Division and other units, to encourage improvement.

The lack of detailed and reliable information concerning A-V materials and equipment was (with few exceptions) identified as a second major problem to which professional association efforts should be addressed. It is felt the problem will not be resolved by the available media indexes, guides, or other publications issued currently because normally these lack evaluations. Respecting equipment, it is hoped that the Educational Products Information Exchange may prove a fruitful source of technical standards and, that concerning materials, something like the *Educational Media Index* (issued first by McGraw-Hill) can be published in an edition very much more complete and accurate than was the original.

Also needed urgently is a profession-wide effort mounted under auspices of such an organization as ALA which can stimulate both public and professional interest in the provision of needed audiovisual service and elicit commitments from librarians to develop those special A-V service programs which may assist instruction of the retarded, the disadvantaged, the homebound, et al.

Stated by specialists as unresolved questions in the field were several pertaining to the need for clear definition of audiovisual library service as an area of professional responsibility. Those consulted and interviewed asked, for instance, many questions relating to the future place of microforms and of computer-stored information. Also—"Does the library role begin when independent use and study are involved as distinguished from formal classroom or group utilization?" The lack of answers to such questions of definition, of guiding principles, and of philosophy for development of audiovisual service by libraries was cited repeatedly as a handicap.

In considering these matters, a consensus derived from the regional "conversations" as well as from individual interviews was to the effect that the library function may be defined satisfactorily for agencies which offer or assist formal instruction as "provision of the full range of recorded communication and information services needed to sustain the instructional and research efforts of the clientele(s) served." A-V service responsibilities of those performing the library function in behalf of such agencies may well include *production* and/or reproduction of information; *research* pertaining to the effectiveness of materials in terms of their educational or information value as well as studies of service operations as such to determine their efficiency; maintenance of *demonstration and display* services; *counselling and training* activities to insure that both those who administer use as well as patrons may understand fully optimum ways of making use of modern audiovisual materials; and finally, *use of modern computer technology* not only for data processing functions but also information storage as well as direct instructional service. Once this range of activities had been discussed, agreement usually came quickly regarding A-V responsibilities.

To sum up, a librarian's responsibility for developing audiovisual services was expressed by a majority of those consulted as mandatory, requiring full and regular library management and/or administrative cooperation in the distribution of both graphic and photographic materials, sound recordings and other broadcast products including program material on videotape as well as computer-based instructional aids. (As one footnote to the foregoing statement regarding definition, it can be said that regional meetings often began by focusing on problems cited in professional literature covering administrative issues encountered frequently in defining audiovisual materials and services and audiovisual "library" activities. The key to solution of this problem was to give primary attention to functions as distinguished from media forms and formats. Once the functional approach had been adopted, assignment of responsibility for the administration of A-V service by libraries was no longer questioned and administrative decisions regarding organizational structure and operations tended to become regarded as matters best answered in terms of local institutional logic or expediency.)

Listed below are ten recommendations. The listing constitutes a summary statement of the A-V aims, objectives, and activities in behalf of which survey results suggest the American Library Association should now work.

1. Continuing development and refinement of both qualitative and quantitative *standards* for audiovisual collections and services for all library types (taking into account not only more traditional activities, but also problems of coding, cataloging, financing, provision of adequate facilities, etc.).

2. *Publication* (or encouragement—some of which is now beginning under

ALA auspices)* of needed guides and reviewing media (preferably organized under broad subjects) concerned with audiovisual equipment, materials, and related test efforts (e.g., those conducted by the Library Technology Project) both by ALA itself and by its various membership units, as well as through organizations and government agencies. (A case in point is recent development by the American Association of School Librarians and the Department of Audiovisual Instruction of the NEA of joint *Standards for School Media Service Programs*.)

3. Fostering (through sponsorship individually or in cooperation with other agencies as appropriate) local, state, regional, and national discussions, *training* activities, planning, and legislative effort necessary to insure sound development of audiovisual library service for provision of institutes, workshops, conferences, seminars, and publication activity. Especially to be encouraged is development of a *national cataloging service* for audiovisual media. The lack of compatibility among various types and systems of equipment as well as materials themselves was also identified as a continuing national problem (e.g., in relationship to the production and uses of videotape). Adoption of suitable technical standards and specifications was also urgent.

4. Work should be undertaken to improve the preservice, inservice, and "retread" educational activities of library schools in behalf of audiovisual service, and real "teeth" should be put into this effort by requiring that ALA *accreditation procedures* take audiovisual training programs more directly into account. Considering the need for certification of special classes of personnel working in audiovisual library service departments—technicians and technical assistants, for example—ALA should encourage provision of more *scholarships* in the field, and the Library Education Division might well be urged to set up a special subgroup of that organization for educational media specialists.

5. More adequate reflection of the needs of qualified librarians and others working in the field by setting up a *new office or center within ALA* staffed appropriately and housed in the national headquarters office in Chicago. It should be the responsibility of this office to maintain *national clearinghouse functions* in behalf of the library profession covering audiovisual library service matters and to provide a secretariat for any membership group activities. Whether the last should result from the efforts of a new division or those put forward by existing units as the consequence of creating a new membership group, the goal is the same. Available also from a headquarters office should be *consultation and expert advice*. The office staff should be asked to report to the profession regularly (drawing upon the talents of outside agencies and specialists as needed) the status of audiovisual work being done by and through library endeavors and should maintain a *continuing inventory of both the objectives and accomplishments of other associations, of relevant legislation, and experimental programs in the field worth watching and/or which might be visited by professional personnel.* It is assumed that such an effort might be maintained with the help of the U.S. Office of Education, the Department of Audiovisual Instruction, the National Association of Educational Broadcasters, and, in particular, the Educational Media Council. Especially to be encouraged in the same regard is *more*

---

*To be commended is the recent announcement by ALA that full-time personnel are now being employed to review audiovisual materials for the *Booklist*.

work at the state level in behalf of state library and school library specialists associated with state departments of education.

6. Needed urgently and on a continuing basis is *improvement of communication and more regular means of coordinating audiovisual projects and programs launched and/or maintained by existing ALA offices, committees, projects, and divisions.* Again, it is assumed that the headquarters staff effort proposed above would meet this responsibility. (In 1966, no one person within the Association really knew what was going on in the rest of the organization insofar as A-V activities were concerned.)

7. *Active promotion of A-V library service interests* and improvement of the image of those performing such services among librarians, educational administrators, and boards of trustees as well as the general public should be undertaken to create a climate of opinion more favorable for support of audiovisual services. The full range of public relations media and techniques should be considered in developing such promotional efforts, and no opportunity should be lost to indicate their importance.

8. There should be encouraged throughout the country the identification or *setting up of selected libraries as demonstration and display agencies* (not unlike the school library projects and demonstration programs supported with Knapp Project funds). Until and unless those having direct administrative responsibility or who are interested in audiovisual library service have opportunities to see what can be done and to appreciate through personal observation the nature of a truly well-staffed and equipped facility, it will remain difficult for many to develop and maintain the necessary levels of interest and understanding.

9. Encourage and/or jointly *sponsor on a continuing basis necessary research and special studies* pertaining to audiovisual library service interests, e.g., a) efficiency of service operations as such, b) effects of newer media, c) manpower requirements (which might be derived from "task analysis" studies), d) resolution of major information retrieval problems which continue to plague the field, and e) provision of service to special groups, e.g., the disadvantaged, taking into account those opportunities, obstacles, and practices considered optimum.

10. Encourage both libraries as institutions and librarians as individuals to interest themselves in audiovisual materials as historical documents (e.g., *oral or visual history*) and in the many sources of help and valuable information or direct educational aid which might be extended to the retarded, to hospital patients, to foreign-born, and to remedial study groups.

The ten recommendations given by no means exhaust possibilities for strengthening audiovisual library service. They do, however, spotlight areas of inadequacy in present ALA organizational efforts and suggest avenues for improvement.

If there is a single and dominant lesson to be learned from results of the survey, it is represented in the lack of identity and personal recognition presently accorded to and felt by librarians serving all types of library clienteles and a general lack of appreciation given roles which can be played effectively by audiovisual media to help meet instructional, informational, or general enrichment service needs. One consequence of this problem was establishment in 1967 (and consolidation in 1968) of the Film Library Information Council (FLIC) by a group of individuals associated for the most part with public libraries and who were responsible for maintaining 16mm nontheatrical motion picture collections. In 1968 the FLIC group broadened its constitution to include all types of library interests and sought a home within ALA as a part of the Public Libraries Division.

The existence of the FLIC organization, originally outside of ALA, serves, however, to document the continuing need for identity, recognition and appreciation as well as for information and help, needs which also were *not* being met for librarians by organizations outside of ALA.

In considering the recommendations written into this report and specific steps which should be taken soon, it is important to take into account the need for active promulgation of the new *Standards for School Media Service Programs* (mentioned previously), developed by AASL in cooperation with DAVI. Also, the special A-V equipment testing program developed by the Library Technology Project under a grant from the Council on Library Resources (covering 16mm projectors, tape recording and playback units, slide projectors, and filmstrip projectors) should be renewed and its operations expanded on a continuing basis perhaps in cooperation with the Educational Products Information Exchange (EPIE), an organization also identified earlier, although its impact and long-term potentials are not yet known.

As of January 1969, uncertainty continued regarding publication of a revised version of the *Educational Media Guide.* There are increasing efforts by various publications serving the field, for example, the school section of *Library Journal*, to introduce A-V materials on a cross-media basis. A growing number of institutes and workshops held at regional, state and national levels and concerned with instructional resources offers further documentation of mounting field interest and activity. As examples, review the proceedings of a conference held at Monte Corona, California, by the State Department of Education during the summer of 1967, covering new media generally. An institute held by Drexel in the spring of 1968 on the "Role of the Computer in School Library Service" attracted applications from three times the number who could be permitted to attend. And preconference activities of recent years sponsored under auspices of the American Association of School Librarians concerning instructional technology represent additional cases in point.

Also to be noted are stepped-up activities of ALA audiovisual committees (including preparation for ACRL of a manual on audiovisual services for college and university librarians). A partial inventory of A-V activities sponsored by all units of ALA was undertaken during the annual conference of the Association held in San Francisco during June 1967, and a report is on file.

Finally, in looking ahead one additional point should be made. The accelerating advance in both the design and the development of modern communications technology has resulted in a growing tendency to erase the lines which separate the various media forms and formats. Recent evidence of such a change is represented in microtext reproduction of computer-stored information by the 3M Company. One can also observe that conference themes and meeting schedules of such organizations as the National Association of Educational Broadcasters and other media service groups are conducted increasingly in terms not just of radio and television (the priority interests of NAEB), but of the total media field. The implications of this shift in emphasis are obvious for librarians. The day when the library responsibilities began and ended with acquisition and distribution of print or near-print materials has long since ended. And among library groups which have suffered most from ALA failure to respond to the changing nature of modern communications technology and, hence, to library responsibilities involved, are those concerned with formal instruction notably at the junior and small four-year college level as well as for the public at large.

In closing this report (by taking a look at the national scene) it may be said that as of mid-1969 the chief problems affecting development and use of modern audiovisual media and other forms of instructional or information technology differ from those of ten years previous chiefly in matters of degree. American education and society still are plagued on all levels by the lack of qualified teachers and of other professional personnel trained to make optimum use of instructional and information media. Despite billions of dollars invested since "Sputnik" in educational and instructional innovation, there is still among too many librarians a lack of certainty regarding optimum contributions which can be made to the processes of education through use of newer communications media including graphic and photographic materials, recordings, educational radio and TV, programmed instruction, and computers.

Another debilitating problem is represented in the continuing lack of a national information system capable of affording in convenient format listings and guides to the resources which are now available to assist instructional or information processes. Local, state, regional, and national reservoirs (or "banks") of A-V media and equipment must be developed as must the creation of sufficient numbers of new demonstration and display centers to which those interested may be referred to see at first hand benefits which may be accrued from effective use of modern communications technology.

A-V media distributive systems and mechanisms are generally clumsy, if not obsolete. Yet, looking ahead about ten years, there is little doubt that electronic interconnection will make it possible for American libraries, schools, colleges, and universities as well as business, industrial, and government agencies to switch back and forth among themselves to provide virtually any type of educational communication or information service desired. Such services may be expected to employ computers extensively both for storage of basic information as well as for control of its distribution. And, despite the cost, a growing demand for improvement of basic "library" service across the nation will hasten the advent of such interconnection. Such, indeed, may be concluded from reading reports issued recently by the National Advisory Commission on Libraries:

> Of greater potential importance for future libraries than any past technical innovation will be utilization of high-speed digital computers and their associated information-handling equipment, for the employment of computers in libraries has already led to high hopes for improved access to information resources in spite of the exponential growth of knowledge. Computers will most likely be applied to library operations in three successive stages. The computer has already demonstrated its usefulness as a rapid and efficient counting device for the control of such library functions as acquisition, circulation, serial records, and binding as well as for general business

operations; this is the first stage. Second, we are witnessing the initial successful attempts to apply the computer to bibliographic operations. The third and most exciting stage of computer involvement which we are only beginning to approach is the interaction between the library and the on-line computer community in which a time-shared central computer is used as a general intellectual tool by many users working simultaneously at different terminals in a network. Development work is now in progress on the transmission of bibliographic data in such networks and on the more formidable problem of storing and transmitting the full text of documents.

In the course of time, different local networks will be interconnected and we shall see the emergence of regional, national and international information transfer networks. What we know today by the term "interlibrary cooperation" will be superseded by a much more fluid pattern of providing access to distant users without preventing concurrent access by local users. The evolution of these networks is the brightest promise of the new technology for libraries. . . .

FOUR A-V WONDERS BOARDS WILL BUY IN THE 70s*

No more pencils, no more books, no more teachers' dirty looks. The better part of that old ditty—which youngsters still sing to celebrate school's end—resounds with truth right now. The reason, of course, is educational technology. Pencils and textbooks (lecture halls and chalkboards, too) still will be around when the Seventies aren't, but the decade ahead almost certainly will see schools and industry speed up their efforts to supplement the standbys with faster, more efficient tools geared to these complex times when more students must be taught more information than ever before.

Already, technological tools in use in schools across the country range in complexity from simple cassette tape players to extensive audio/video/computer systems costing nearly $1 million. All have been developed by U.S. industry to help schools improve educational methods and do a better job of passing along information to their students.

Obviously, not every school district or classroom needs even the full range of hardware available today. But the people in charge of school districts—board members and administrators—do need to know what new educational technology is being developed and what tools are available if they are to make intelligent decisions about putting the knowledge and hardware of technology into daily use.

As education enters the decade of the Seventies, four prominent trends in the use of technology for education are evident:
1. cassette audio tape recording
2. simplified videotape recording
3. random access audio/video systems
4. computer assisted instruction (CAI) systems.
Let's take a closer look at each of these trends.

CASSETTE AUDIO TAPE RECORDING

In a short period of time, cassette tape recording seems destined to become as integral a part of schooling as are textbooks. Cassettes permit students to obtain recorded lesson material from the library or other school source, and to record lectures and other classroom material as well.

A cassette, by way of review, is a small plastic case housing a reel of 1/7-inch-wide magnetic tape and a take-up reel. The tape is wound from reel to reel completely within the plastic case, eliminating tape handling and threading. The tiny cassette, slightly longer and wider than a deck of playing cards and about half as thick, is inserted into a cassette player/recorder for listening and/or recording educational or entertainment programs.

Among advantages of cassette recording in education: Schools can provide a wide range of recorded lessons or supplementary material on magnetic tape for convenient listening by students. Students either can listen to the material at school or can take home the cassettes for playback on the same machines they use for listening to popular music. This type of learning experience allows the

*Reprinted by permission from *American School Board Journal*, 158:45-47, November 1970.

student to proceed at his own pace in absorbing lesson material, playing the tape as many times as he wishes, and rewinding the tape to concentrate on especially difficult portions of the lesson.

By using a cassette with blank tape and an inexpensive recorder and microphone, the student also can record classroom material for later study. Blank cassettes can be erased and reused hundreds of times.

Another advantage: Cassette lessons can be produced to allow a student to record his responses to questions. Or cassettes can be programmed to activate a slide projector that will give the student an audio and visual learning experience. New high speed cassette duplication techniques permit economical production of countless copies of lesson material for distribution to large numbers of students.

Cassette audio recording combines both economy and simplicity. Cassette players may be purchased for less than $20, and blank tape costs less than $3 for 60 minutes of recording time. Cassettes are as easy to use as a radio and require no special training for the user.

Many school districts, especially in large cities, already offer cassette check-out programs through school libraries. Expect the trend to become increasingly popular—and necessary.

SIMPLIFIED VIDEO TAPE RECORDING

Among the first consumers of closed circuit (nonbroadcast) television were educators, a fact that accounts for the widespread use of this medium in school districts today. Systems range from a simple camera linked to a television set to sophisticated systems incorporating dozens of video tape recorders, cameras, and other equipment for the production and distribution of high quality educational programs.

The introduction by industry of compact video tape recorders in 1966 vitalized the use of closed circuit television in education. For the first time, schools were able to preserve their best lectures and best visual material on magnetic tape at a reasonable cost. Video tape recorders range in cost from $1,500 for simple units to $20,000 for those with more sophisticated production accessories. Some 65,000 of them have been placed in service throughout the world in the last four years (more than half the units are in use in education).

On the horizon is a new generation of video tape recorders, featuring greater simplicity and economy, factors that promise expansion of the use of the devices in schools. Simplified cartridge loading will enable teachers and students to operate the new recorders without tape handling and threading. Recorder and camera systems weighing less than 20 pounds and costing in the $1,000 range are virtually certain to bring video tape recording into the individual classroom.

The simplified cartridge recorder/players also will permit fast and efficient distribution of television programs produced on the production video tape recorders now used by schools. Capable of color recording and playback, the new recorders will be on the market sometime next year.

Another development destined to make possible wider use of video tape in education is high speed contact duplication. It will enable schools to produce any number of copies of a program in far less time than is currently possible. The first video duplicators (used in broadcasting) duplicate 60-minute programs in only six minutes and are able to make five copies of a program at one time.

RANDOM ACCESS AUDIO/VIDEO SYSTEMS

Certain to gain growing acceptance within the foreseeable future are random access audio/video systems that give students almost immediate access to recorded program material.

These systems combine high speed audio duplication, video and computer technologies to permit new speed and flexibility in learning. The first such system is in operation at Oak Park and River Forest High School, Oak Park, Ill.

Random access systems are designed to facilitate individualized, self-paced instruction. They fill the need to present instructional material to the student automatically, on demand by the student, and at a pace dictated by the student's grasp of the material. Random access systems relieve the teacher of the task of presenting repetitive lectures, freeing him to counsel, guide, motivate, and inspire the student.

That the trend clearly is toward such educational concepts—and the adoption of hardware and systems to implement the concepts—is shown by the fact that between 600 and 700 dial access audio systems have been installed in schools since 1966.

Random access differs from more conventional dial access equipment in that the student receives the lesson from the beginning. In dial access systems, students calling for a program already in use must wait until the program is completed or begin listening at the point the lesson is in progress. Simply put, random access is more efficient.

Video lesson material (related to the audio material) also can be relayed to the student at his own console under a random access setup. The number of students who can take advantage of programs within the system is limited only by the number of consoles. Random access systems provide high speed audio cassette duplication, permitting the student to record the lesson on his own cassette recorder in seconds and play it back at home or elsewhere.

Other advantages: The computer that controls functions of the random access system can be used to establish a dialogue with the student, much as in computer assisted instruction systems. Also, students can receive audio material from the master program bank by telephoning into the system from remote locations.

Designed for schools, districts and even larger educational entities, random access systems range in price from $100,000 to approximately $1 million for an audio/video system with a liberal number of student terminals. Larger systems can serve an entire state or other wide geographic area.

COMPUTER ASSISTED INSTRUCTION SYSTEMS

This newest of educational technology concepts currently is undergoing considerable experimentation, mostly at the university level. In essence, computer assisted instruction (CAI) is a method by which a student receives lesson material from a computer and directs his answers and questions to the same computer.

Benefits of CAI are that the computer, unlike most teachers, has infinite patience and permits the student to progress at his own pace; a properly programmed computer can dispense virtually unlimited knowledge; and, fortunately or otherwise, many students relate better to a machine than they do to a human.

Disadvantages of CAI include its high cost, need for standardization of computerized programs, and its limited format. Current systems use a teletype input/output device at the student terminal, which limits replies of the computer to printed words. Audio/video systems give the student a much wider range of responses.

CAI, largely funded by the federal government at this time, still is in its experimental infancy and may yet be an important contribution to education in the decade that is just beginning.

TRENDS IN LIBRARY TECHNOLOGY*

By Joseph Becker

Much has been said and even more has been written about the use of computers in libraries. Computers have been applied to almost every standard library housekeeping function, such as serial records control, acquisitions, circulation control, book catalog production, technical processing, etc. They have served as catalysts in encouraging far-reaching programs such as MARC at the Library of Congress. Over the next few years MARC will gradually develop into a bibliographic data bank of immense proportions. Production of similar magnetic tapes by bibliographic centers in other countries will provide a critical mass of world-wide bibliographical data, the implications of which are so new that we hardly know how to study their ultimate effect on information dissemination practices among libraries. The MARC communications format has become an international standard. The British National Bibliography is recording its cataloging data in this tape format, and other countries are following their lead. The Italian National Bibliography will reportedly henceforth be recorded this way as part of a project called ANNA (Automazione nella Nazionale di Firenze); and at the National Diet Library in Japan, the J-MARC (Japan MARC) program is beginning. In time, magnetic tapes will probably be exchanged among all national libraries, first no doubt by Boeing 747 and later by satellite communications.

The ability to use standard communication channels, such as telephone lines, for the exchange of computer data means that libraries can go "on-line" with a computer rather than having one on the premises. Both the Los Angeles and the Bethesda, Maryland, offices of my company, for example, are subscribers to the General Electric Time-Sharing Network; and both offices can call up the GE computer, in Ohio, and interact with it via a terminal, using a very simple conversational computer language. We use the computer this way to simulate library operations, such a book ordering and personnel management for clients, and also to prepare our internal payroll and accounting reports; but the same procedure could be used by libraries if, for example, they wanted to telephone LC for the latest MARC records on a particular subject or communicate with a book jobber's computer to order books by standard book number.

COMPUTER TECHNOLOGY

What will the marriage of computers to communications mean to libraries in the long run? There is no easy answer to this question. It is still too new and there is no hard information on which to form judgments. However, this advance in technology provides a larger leap forward in interlibrary communications than anything before, and thus it is certain to accelerate the development of resource sharing programs among libraries and speed the interconnection of data banks, reference centers, and information networks.

Within recent years considerable advances have been made in the manufacture of small computers—mini-computers—which may be programmed to

*Reprinted by permission from *Special Libraries*, 62:429-434, October 1971.

perform a limited number of specified functions. These machines are far less expensive than their large-scale, general purpose antecedents, yet they possess the power to execute medium-scale library routines on an almost tailor-made basis. Library interest in the mini-computer is just beginning to emerge; however, it heralds an important trend because of the implied reduction in the cost of computer operations in libraries.

TELECOMMUNICATIONS TECHNOLOGY

A second relevant technology of importance is telecommunications and, in particular, the Touch-Tone telephone, especially because of its new capabilities in the areas of educational communications and information transfer.

In many ways the Touch-Tone telephone is similar to the familiar dial telephone—both rely on audio input and output. However, there is a major difference—only the Touch-Tone telephone enables a user to transmit analog information to a digital computer.

It does this by emitting different frequencies of sound for each number represented by the twelve pushbuttons on its keyboard. When a Touch-Tone telephone is used to call a distant machine—a computer, teletype machine, or key-punch machine—it is able to transmit numerical information *after* the telephone connection is established. And, when this numerical or digitized information is received by the distant machine, it can cause it to function by remote control. Originally there were only ten pushbuttons on a Touch-Tone keyboard; but in 1968 the Bell System assigned two more buttons—an asterisk (*) and a pound sign (#). These two new buttons are codes to increase a user's remote control of the switched telephone network and also a computer. For example, the pound sign is a standard signal which can activate a series of different programmed computer functions—START, STOP, SKIP, ADD, etc.—and the asterisk can serve as a separator to distinguish between different elements or fields of a data record such as author, title, collation, etc. This means that the two signs, plus the ten digits, allow the Touch-Tone telephone to manipulate data automatically in a distant machine in a number of different ways. It has been designed so that it will eventually accommodate up to sixteen pushbuttons in order to permit transmission of the letters of the alphabet, as well as numbers and punctuation, and to feature additional remote controls.

Many advantages accrue when a Touch-Tone telephone is used as an input/output terminal in an information system. Its greatest advantage, however, exists in its dual usage—it can function as an ordinary telephone and as a data terminal. This dual usage is important because the cost of the Touch-Tone telephone can thus be shared by both functions. If in the accounting all costs are deferred for its primary use as a telephone, then it essentially becomes a free input/output terminal. Other advantages include: immediate availability, quick and easy installation and replacement, free Bell System maintenance, quiet operation, no additional power requirements, and no supplies to keep it functioning. Its two disadvantages at present are the inability to produce a printed record of what is sent over the Touch-Tone keyboard and the availability of a limited character set.

The Touch-Tone telephone now comes optionally equipped with a new card reader. The dialer cards are plastic of a certain thickness and approximately credit card size, and each card can be pre-punched with up to fourteen digits of information. Several companies are in the business of converting old credit cards into new dialer cards which are not only embossed, but are also punched for use in a Touch-Tone telephone. Although the cards were originally intended to be used for frequently called telephone numbers, they are also being used to code frequently used instructions pertaining to computer and other machine operations. For example, researchers assigned to Project THEMIS at the University of Houston actually use Touch-Tone telephones connected to a computer to write and debug programs. And some blind people have learned to write computer programs by making use of the Touch-Tone telephone and a voice answer back computer.

The Touch-Tone telephone is also the forerunner of the Picture-Phone now in operational use between certain large U.S. cities. The Picture-Phone possesses all of the characteristics of the Touch-Tone, but in addition it can provide a television picture of the person called, of printed data, or a display of selected output *from* a computer. Together they represent a powerful information team. The Touch-Tone terminal remotely controls the selection of information, while the Picture-Phone displays the information for individual use. Companies such as RCA and Westinghouse have demonstrated allied communications technology which can be used to find and activate a single home television set for the display of requested information. This is equivalent to telephoning a TV set.

During the next few years, the various communication carriers in the U.S. will be upgrading their inter-city lines in order to increase their network capacity to carry computer and picture data, as well as voice. CATV (Community Antenna Television) systems are rapidly finding their way into American homes, and recently the Federal Communication Commission handed down a ruling which authorizes private companies to compete with AT&T in the development of nationwide data transmission networks. As this occurs, wider use will undoubtedly be made in libraries of devices such as the Touch-Tone and Picture-Phones. Use of the telephone as an information retrieval terminal is already evident with dial telephones. For example, if you are a general practitioner living in the state of Missouri, you can telephone a certain number that will gain you access to 1,000 pre-recorded five- to six-minute messages on various specialized medical practices and procedures. Eventually Touch-Tone telephones with remote controls will enable the caller to interrupt a message, repeat or replay a portion of the message, or activate a juke box type of mechanical device to pick and play one or more audio cassettes of the caller's choice. Should data banks of audio information on many different subjects be kept by libraries, each person with a Touch-Tone telephone would have his own library terminal. This challenges our ingenuity to find new user services that will motivate the caller to utilize the full range of library resources in support of his information needs—not only audio information, but also printed materials, the newer media, computer controlled data banks, etc. The Touch-Tone telephone development is, therefore, particularly important to the profession because it is a user-oriented development.

Some libraries are also investigating the use of Touch-Tone telephone systems for circulation control. By using a mini-computer, a voice answer back unit, and machine readable book and borrower cards, it is practical to enter transactions into a computer by telephone and, on demand, receive a voice response about the loan or reserve status of a given book.

Touch-Tone and other developments in telecommunications technology are certain to prompt librarians and information scientists to re-evaluate user services. The Touch-Tone terminal is the one device which can place all information users "on-line" with the library.

MICROGRAPHICS TECHNOLOGY

In the past ten years the field of micrographics has advanced very rapidly. Today, images of the printed page can be made at very high reduction ratios. "Ultrafiche" are images which are reduced at ratios above 100:1; "superfiche" employ reduction ratios under that number. Today, holographic and laser recording techniques can write a line on film one or two microns wide; one micron is equal to .000039 inches. This is so tiny that a very high-powered microscope is required to even see the intelligence.

Micrographics technology has reached the limits of photoreduction and, therefore, emphasis in the future is likely to be on the use of microfilm as supporting information systems rather than as compact storage media. Within the past year, for example, a number of companies announced special microfilm information systems geared to supporting reference and technical processing functions in libraries. Encyclopaedia Britannica and the National Cash Register Company both advertised the availability of new microbook collections; and Nicholas Spence, the Public Printer, indicated his intent to publish U.S. government documents in microfiche form.

Many commercial organizations and professional societies offer microfilm equivalents of their printed indices and data banks. *Chemical Abstracts* is a good example. The development of COM (Computer Output to Microfilm) machines has made this service possible. COM machines are special purpose devices which project computer output directly onto unexposed film according to pre-programmed instructions. Thus, for example, one company now uses MARC tapes to produce updated microfilm images of LC catalog cards. It then sells this film to library technical processing departments. The trend toward information systems on microfilm for reference and technical processing purposes can only continue to expand. Today, the speed at which computers can logically cumulate information and generate microfilm is much faster than the time it normally takes for conventional printing, and that is what makes the difference. As long as this advantage persists, the application of micrographics technology to reference and technical processing functions will steadily increase. Whereas microfilm was at one time thought of only as a space saver in libraries, its primary use in the future is more likely to be as an integral component of some information support system.

As microfiche collections in libraries grow larger, the means for making copies of a fiche as easily as we can copy the printed page will emerge. Thus, we can expect to see fiche-to-fiche duplicating machines and portable microfiche readers as popular in the libraries of tomorrow as the Xerox copy machine is today.

AUDIO-VISUAL TECHNOLOGY

Advances in audio-visual technology are happening so quickly that it is difficult to keep abreast of them. Leading the list of new developments is the color video cassette. This new technology makes it possible to record television for individual use. Until now, television has been part of mass media communication reaching thousands of home sets at once through scheduled broadcasting. The video cassette, however, permits segments of television to be recorded at very high density and duplicated in quantity so that TV-replays are available at one's own convenience. A number of companies, such as RCA, AMPEX, CBS, Motorola, Telefunken, and SONY, are keenly aware of the potential implications of this development for the recreation and educational markets; consequently, they have been competing to introduce the first workable system.

SONY has a public exhibit hall in its building on the Ginza in Tokyo where it demonstrates its video cassette system and associated equipment. A number of devices comprise the system. First, there is the cassette itself. It is the size of a standard book, approximately 7" by 9" and 1" wide. Inside, there is a ¾" magnetic tape which records up to 60 minutes of color television. Because the tape is magnetic, it is erasable and reusable. The spool of tape is enclosed in a tamper-proof container which incorporates mechanical features for automatic threading. The tape records TV images and two parallel sound tracks which can be used either for stereo music recordings or for dual language recordings.

To use the video cassette requires playing equipment. The SONY player is about the size of a standard hi-fi amplifier. A flick of the finger loads the video cassette into the player. Four controls, similar to those on an automatic microfilm machine, are available: *start, stop, fast forward,* and *rewind.* There is also a switch for each or both sound tracks. These give the user great flexibility for individual viewing and listening. The viewing machine itself can be any standard television set, not just those manufactured by SONY. A wire connects the player to the set at its antenna terminals or through a special plug. No elaborate or costly intermediate machine is required.

The video cassette of today will undoubtedly be the audio-visual book of tomorrow. In fact, SONY very wisely decided to place its video cassette in a plastic box that looks like a book and can be processed and shelved like a book.

A particularly intriguing item was the new machine which SONY exhibited for the production of video cassettes. At the front end there is a "mixer" which accepts various audio-visual formats—2" by 2" slides, ¼" audio tapes, audio cassettes, video tapes, film strips, and sound movies—and transfers them one at a time or in combination to a master video tape which in turn can produce hundreds of video cassettes simultaneously. This is an extremely important development because it provides a way to transfer the multiplicity of extant or new audio-visual materials to a single format for individual use. The video cassette serves as this common denominator.

Mr. Morita, President of SONY, encouraged me to make a video cassette to test the programming capabilities of the "mixer." The cassette I made contained a ten-minute segment of live video in which I explained the SONY system in front of a slide backdrop of Mt. Fuji and to the accompaniment of traditional Samisen music, a 20-minute segment featuring a set of thirty 2" by 2" slides and ¼" sound tape on which I had prerecorded my consulting report, and a five-minute segment of 16mm color film with English and Japanese sound tracks. The conversion process through the mixer worked smoothly. A SONY player connected to a regular GE television set displayed the results. Duplicates of the video cassette remained in Tokyo for local viewing and another was sent to Bangkok for special viewing there.

It will probably take several years to introduce the color video cassette into the mainstream of educational audio-visual materials. But it does have major implications for libraries.

CONCLUSION

No discussion of technology can be complete without mentioning something about the effects of technology on the printed book and the printed word. To do so, I quote from a recent book by Ben H. Bagdikian called *The Information Machines: Their Impact on Men and the Media.* Unlike many authors, Bagdikian does not succumb to the worship of technology; to him, a machine is an instrument and he believes that it is man that gives it its moral and social tone.

He is also especially alert to the issue of competition between the printed book and the media. "Whatever other cultural change this generation has seen, and whatever the growth of electronic media, the ability to read and the power to reason abstractly has never been higher." He goes on to challenge Marshall McLuhan by commenting, "Print is neither dead nor dying. It is being forced to make a place in the family of communication for a new way of transferring information and emotion. . . . The new medium is disrupting and even revolutionary, but it leaves the alphabet and the document still indispensable to the efficient use of the eye and brain and to the demands for human rationality."

For a century or more, American librarians have been diligently devising ways and means to make man's thoughts and deeds available to posterity. Today, man's inventiveness has given us new instruments for extending and distributing the flow of knowledge. Somehow in the next decade we must find a way to incorporate these new technologies sensibly into the mainstream of our activities.

THE FUTURE MIXED MEDIA LIBRARY NETWORK*

By John Meany

Amid the swirling tides of invention, it is becoming possible to discern the outlines of library applications which will almost surely develop over the next decade to form a mixed media network for information interchange.

This is small consolation, however, for librarians everywhere are wondering which new developments are likely to win out in the competitive market and, thus represent the best present investment. The fact is that we have always had a very mixed media system for information interchange, including, at present or at some past time, such media as messengers, mail, TXW, print, offset, xerox, and COM.

Therefore, we may expect the presently intersecting and cross-pollinating media to be the components of a mixed media system that is at once richer, more redundant, more wasteful, more surprising and confusing, and more inevitable than any unmixed system could be. Everything today seems to be pointing toward the enormous potential of linking such media together into a flexible mixed media system for information interchange: the design flow is right for such a move, the availability of distribution media is prospectively enormous, and the national policy is encouraging. The implications of this type of system for information interchange may be grouped generally under economic and administrative headings.

The economic implications are far more than monetary for they include that basic economy of means which is a key principle in the attainment of efficiency and quality of performance. A mixed media system necessarily implies, by the very survival of the mixture, that each element has a certain irreducible advantage to offer. Even before we reach complicated questions of transfer and cross-media reinforcement, or the possibilities of contrapuntal media utilization in instruction, for example, there is the simple and obvious fact that if each medium is used precisely in the area of its greatest specific advantage, there will result an overall efficiency of operation, which should produce the highest quality result at the lowest cost in effort and money.

From another point of view, this matter of efficiency and economy of operations in mixed media systems might be said to imply a principle of subsidiarity: in general, using the simplest means available for a given end and, thus, avoiding situations in which relatively simple material is transmitted over relatively complex media merely because such media are available. The classic example of the thing to be avoided is what happens sometimes on instructional television—often a lecture is transmitted by television, although the fundamental requirement of the material is for a merely verbal statement for which an audio transmission would be adequate.

A mixed media system also clearly implies a relatively miscellaneous set of equipment at local institutions. It requires us to forego the utopian dream of the single black box that can do everything. We will need to acquire the specific

*Reprinted from the *Drexel Library Quarterly*, 7:153-159, April 1971, by permission of the publisher. ^c1971.

equipment which will enable us to tap the data banks in which we are interested. It means that our libraries will need more kinds of listening stations, more viewing and display devices for tapes, microforms, slides, 8mm cartridges, EVR or SelectaVision cartridges, videotapes, etc. It means that our libraries will continue to expand their functions as sound and picture depositories—or, at least, as access points for these.

Having multiple media existing and functioning concurrently will also mean greater redundancy among them. The same still pictures in color may be available in both photographic and magnetic devices, and the same motion pictures in both film and EVR cartridges. However, such overlapping may also lead to more highly individualized uses and greater flexibility and creativeness in user adaptation.

MIXED MEDIA NETWORKS

On the administrative side, such a mixed media network will present more persistent problems of access, indexing, and control at the local level, but at the same time, it will have the advantages of greater autonomy and decentralization. If it is valid to draw a parallel between the electric power grid and the information network of the future, we may conclude that a somewhat greater total reliability is to be anticipated in the relatively decentralized structure.

The fact that the mixed system will not depend on any startling breakthroughs, but will include many media with which we are presently familiar, offers some assurance that the mixed system can be introduced to its users with less difficulty and resistance and, possibly, be more readily accepted and more extensively used than a totally unfamiliar system. While it is true that media will not be used unless they are made available, it is unfortunately not so certainly true that making media available will necessarily lead to their effective utilization. Mass transit authorities have often found that merely providing a cheap, efficient and fast transport system is no guarantee that people will use it in sufficient numbers to make it pay. In the media field, also, we have seen broadband telecommunication networks linking campuses together over wide areas. For years, we have assured scholars of their availability for library facsimile transmissions, however, they go on transmitting television lectures almost exclusively. Obviously, even the most modern media do not escape the elementary facts of human inertia and habit. However, the mere convenience implied in making more means available to more people at the local level should eventually lead to a greater total utilization.

The kinds of utilization will also change. New and unforeseen uses must be expected to emerge. The mixed media network will not simply lead to the accomplishment of the same old tasks in new and better ways. It will lead to the discovery and addition of new goals on top of the old ones—just because the new ones suddenly appear to be possible.

A mixed media situation challenges its administrators with a complicated bibliographic, indexing, and control process. They will have to know where the pictures, films and tapes are; how to get to them; what is in them; and how to index them. Something radical is implied in all of this. We know how to index books, but how does one index pictures? Do we index them by a verbal description of what they contain, or by a truly pictorial representation—or by some combination of the two?

Along with the technological interface between media, we need to develop what we might call transmedia analogs. And here we are up against the ancient problems of synaesthesia. The ears and the eyes of men represent two senses with certain areas of radical and, perhaps, irreducible difference, although we reduce them physiologically to similarly transmitted impulses in our nerves. There are interesting experiments with television grids projected onto the skins of blind men in order to enable them to feel a kind of vision, and yet the sound and the picture fringes of our libraries continue to present us with enormous problems of day-to-day bibliographic integration. There is not much advantage in delivering the typewritten card by means of facsimile printout a hundred miles away, if the necessary visual indexing is not on the card.

MANAGING MIXED MEDIA

The prospect of living indefinitely with a mixed media system should bring us to face certain needs which are inherent in such a situation—needs which include four areas: standards, new research, depositories, and demonstrations.

The Need for Standards

There should be a comprehensive study leading to the design of improved standard setting procedures for the United States. Something is radically wrong with present procedures, which have allowed us to enter the helical scan videotape morass. Apparently we are unable to extricate ourselves from it, unless by default to foreign systems. We need to pinpoint the reasons for our difficulties and the steps needed to solve them and to prevent their recurrence in future developments. Granted that we want to protect the great advantages of the free enterprise system and competition, we may also need to give more direct protection to our common good. We are finding this to be true in other areas—environmental pollution, for instance. There it seems that a great many competing industries operating in our free enterprise system have somehow failed to take adequate account of our common good. Where so many are so intent on their private profit, it may be that the common good does not automatically accrue without someone to speak for it. We are likely to find that fact to be equally true in the field of technical standards.

We might learn much from a careful study of our recent history in the matter of standards. How could the long-playing record war have been avoided? Is it true that the American electronics industry has simply shown little interest in arriving at standards for helical scan recorders, because each industry giant is naively confident that his system will win out in the end, or at least box off a large enough segment of the market to be profitable? Is it true that fear of the federal antitrust authorities inhibited many industries from having conversations with others about standards? Have the American National Standards Institute and standards-generating agencies such as the Society of Motion Picture and Television Engineers been crippled by inadequate funds to get the job done?[1] If it is true that our standards are necessarily industry-generated, is it not still possible to achieve a stimulus role for government, something less arbitrary and indirect than the present buying power of the Department of Defense? If we can revise our copyright law to be more in harmony with the international scene, can we not harmonize our standard setting procedure with the international practice?

The study of such questions ought to call upon the expertise of many agencies: the American National Standards Institute, the Society of Motion Picture and Television Engineers, the Department of Justice, the Department of Commerce, National Bureau of Standards, Library of Congress, American Library Association, the National Commission on Libraries and Information Services, the Corporation for Public Broadcasting, the National Institutes of Health, the National Institutes of Education, the U.S. Office of Education, the Department of Defense, Electronic Industries Association, the Information Industries Association, and many others. The study might be undertaken by almost any of these, or by others, such as the Rand Corporation, on contract.

The Need for Research

When it becomes apparent that competitive industry has allowed an interface gap to develop in some area, there ought to be an agency in a position to stimulate the design and, perhaps, partially to subsidize the manufacture of new interface devices.

We also need additional research to develop designs and recommended practices for catalogs and machine readable indexes of media materials. Before we can have the logical starting tools for networking, we need to design these tools. They should be developed as compatible extensions of standard bibliographic tools, thus insuring integration with central catalogs rather than isolation as special media resources.

There are already beginning what are certain to be two most interesting pilot prototypes for a national information network: the Bell picturephone development[2] and the *New York Times* Information Bank.[3] Here are many of the parallel problems and techniques to be mastered: TV-computer interface, alternate CRT and TV use of a picture tube, two-way interaction, switching, directory publication, standardization, evolution through processes of consumer experience and demand, and computer storage and retrieval of a significantly large data bank. The *New York Times* bank will give computerized access to news and editorials in full text and abstracts—eventually even to photographs, bibliographies and references—of the *New York Times* itself as well as a selection of materials from more than 60 other newspapers and publications. Information utilities may be born as a spinoff of such developments. All of this experience needs to be studied and applied through the persistent review of a national agency. Perhaps the new National Commission on Libraries and Information Services is the proper agency to undertake such research, subsidy, and review functions.

We have recently seen in the space program a striking demonstration of what industries can accomplish when they are given adequately defined goals: film, radio, and TV technology combined to do what was regarded as impossible until very recently—putting high resolution pictures of the moon and Mars into digital form, transmitting them over narrow band widths for very long distances, and then reconverting them to pictorial form, thus transmitting live color television pictures from the surface of the moon with low-power, compact devices of small weight. After such achievements, it appears that the library networking problem requires only adequate specification and definition and an operating authority backed by adequate appropriations to get the job done. A national network of libraries might be set up and run quite efficiently by an organization equivalent to NASA. The only problem with this is that libraries are much closer to the sensitive nerve of our nation than is the surface of the moon. A national library network operated by a government agency would surely raise fears of thought control, and this fact has clearly been taken into account by Congress when it set up the new National Commission on Libraries and Information Services as an independent agency rather than as a component of HEW. The actual operation of network services is better left to decentralized and regional units.

The Need for Depositories

We need stimulation and subsidy for comprehensive and interconnected regional network depositories. The original conception of the regional educational laboratories and the operational experience of the ERIC centers would be pertinent parallels here. Not only would geographical regions be served by the decentralized units, but these should also ideally be committed to dividing up the total task into specific areas of specialization. Thus each regional unit would be the national depository for specific subject areas, and the nation at large would be flexibly served by the interconnections between all regional units.

The Need for Subsidies

We need a subsidy program for selected mixed media publication and for demonstrations and pilot operations using mixed media—a program with a built-in provision for disseminating information and for providing access points to them. The depository mentality is practically hopeless today; not only is the volume of past publications and writings too great for local assembly, but the rate of increase of new publications makes the task even more futile. Even if it were possible to start now with computerized textual input, it would be impractical. The really successful library of the future may have relatively little on its shelves. Yet it will have the firm and grateful support of its clientele because it will have an efficient staff and automated procedures which provide quick access to any material desired—access varying from viewing screens with immediate printout capability to prompt physical delivery of an entire hardbound volume.

CONCLUSION

This is the goal of the library process—access, a peculiarly American reality. Max Lerner once told of being asked by some Russian intellectuals to summarize American in one word. He chose the word "access"—we know that men are born with unequal abilities and advantages, but we believe that they

40

have equal rights to acquire the education that will enable them to develop their innate, human potentials to the fullest. Libraries as access will be very directly serving this goal.

FOOTNOTES

1.   "Symposium on Video-tape Recording Standardization," *SMPTE Journal* 7 (July 1968): 737-46.

2.   Donald Janson, "Picture-telephone Service Is Started in Pittsburgh," *New York Times,* July 1, 1970, p. 1.

3.   John Tebbel, "Libraries in Miniature: A New Era Begins," *Saturday Review* 54 (January 9, 1971):41.

AN OLD STANDBY: 16mm FILM

The 16mm film has been the old standby of public libraries. It has also been a mainstay as an audiovisual medium in educational circles. Today, we can add the 8mm silent and sound film as leading contenders in the field. The introduction of filmmaking as an innovative input in schools and libraries leads to a forecast of continued expansion of the use of this medium. Articles in this section provide varied views of the field and represent diverse aspects of utilization in libraries.

FEATURE FILMS IN YOUR LIBRARY*

By Paul Spehr

Do you have Fellini in your library? Bergman? Welles? Eisenstein? How about Georges Méliès, John Ford, or, for that matter, D. W. Griffith? You do? You have books by and about them . . . and even published copies of their film scripts? Why don't you have their movies? Not possible? Well, perhaps one can make it so. My point is that it *is* possible, desirable, and at some time in the future it will be mandatory for university and public libraries to serve movies to interested scholars.

The straws are already in the wind. In colleges and universities all over the United States (and in all the rest of the world, for that matter) students are taking up the study of film almost as fast as the courses can be added. In fact, the supply of teachers is far behind the demand. In 1969, the American Film Institute surveyed the situation in the United States and determined that there are now 219 institutions of higher learning offering some sort of film course and 51 offering degrees (5,300 students were working toward degrees). This may not seem to represent enough of a flood to cause you to remake your library collecting habits, but it does represent a significant trend. The American Film Institute estimates that this constitutes an increase of 85 percent in the past five years. High schools, too, are beginning to offer film courses.

Course changes and student enthusiasms do not constitute just cause for revising long-range growth programs and changing next year's budget. The factor which makes this a development of uncommon importance is the intrusion of cinema into the exclusive world of art, culture, and intelligence.

The young people flocking to cinema courses in college, struggling to express themselves with camera and splicing cement, are convinced that the film is an integral part of cultural expression. To those in the embattled older generations, this may not appear as a truism and may require some justification. The American cinema developed as a part of cheap, popular entertainment and it continues to maintain this tradition. Sometimes lost in the midst of this flood of popular diversion are unique examples of a new, contemporary art form, one that

*Reprinted by permission from the April 1970 issue of the *Wilson Library Bulletin.* Copyright ᶜ1970 by The H. W. Wilson Company.

43

is so new that it is still trying to define itself and is frequently far too apologetic for its existence. Anyone who regularly attended the films of the sixties or is going to film society screenings of older "classics" knows that there is little to be apologetic about. The increasing number of "serious" film makers are creating art, culture, and intellectual communication of the most vigorous and far-reaching sort.

The ever-increasing tide of students is now searching for film material to study in the traditional way that they have learned to study other intellectual disciplines. They find that films are difficult or impossible to find without expensive trips to Washington, New York, Rochester, or even to London or Paris. The alternative is to persuade some film society to book the desired film or take the chance that a shrivelled and chopped version will appear on the local TV tube.

It is not that public and university libraries have no film programs. Of course these programs exist and in come cases have been very active for years. The scholar's problem is that the program is not really oriented to the film as film (or cinema, or art, or whatever term you prefer). The basic emphasis of such programs is on the film as an auxiliary material—on the film as supplementary matter to biology, physics, community relations programs, etc. Public library (or state educational system) films are selected because they are good films about something or because they are good for somebody (children, old people, poor people, black people, or all people). This is not an evil situation in itself. The audiovisual programs have a place within the institution, but it is sad that selection of films of cinematic merit is given such perfunctory treatment within the selection system.

A shift in emphasis in your film program will inevitably bring you face to face with two problems which I am sure have already occurred to you. The first is the high costs of such a program, and the second is the extreme difficulty of purchasing the films.

MONEY MATTERS

Costs are inevitable in the motion picture field. Even if it is possible to purchase films at the minimum laboratory costs, a half hour of 16mm film will cost at least $40 for a black-and-white sound film and about $80 for color. A feature-length film will cost from $120 to $500. The costs for 35mm film run much higher (it may comfort you to learn that for a public library 35mm film is probably impractical). If there are even minimum profits involved, the cost of purchasing films reaches levels which panic administrative officers and other executives of the exchequer. If you add the cost of projectors ($500 for the bottom of the line), film cans, film handling, and inspection equipment, it is no wonder that the salaries of audiovisual librarians remain low. Money has to be saved somewhere along the line!

Costs of this nature must be carefully planned for and realistically met. Far too often, planners avoid the total required and begin from halfway. This results in half-way growth by a process of attrition, a system which punishes both user and librarian. If the full costs are recognized, it will become obvious that the costs will have to be shared by large, interlibrary programs (metropolitan, regional, etc.). Such programs, carefully considered, can seek additional funds from foundations or government, and provide full, rather than partial service.

44

UNAVAILABILITY, OR, THE FILM FLAM GAME

The matter of obtaining films is an equally thorny problem. At present, practically no "theatrical" films are available for sale to public libraries. There appear to be two factors responsible for this situation. First is the limited demand on the part of libraries, which means that the potential for sales is small. Second, and far more basic, is the tradition of exclusive ownership which has been the keystone of the marketing system of the American motion picture industry. Screening copies of theatrical films are very rarely sold on the open market. Distribution depends on lease and rental to the exhibitor, and reissue for purposes other than theatrical showing usually is done by very restrictive contract— the owner of television rights may not rent for 16mm exhibition and the owner of 16mm rights may not display on television. Such contracts ordinarily prohibit resale. Therefore, no matter how desirable it might be to own *Citizen Kane, Persona, Dr. Strangelove, 8½, On the Waterfront, La Chinoise,* or some other contemporary cinema gem, they just don't appear on the market.

It appears unlikely that this situation will change immediately, but there are some factors which offer hope for increased film availability. The well known Hollywood companies had been owned by the same management since the time they were founded, usually fifty or more years ago. In recent years, these companies, one after another, have been passing into the hands of large investment corporations. New management and new competition from TV and foreign sources have forced the industry to search for new ways of sustaining itself. It seems likely that the management must inevitably respond to new market demands.

Evidence of response to new demands appears in the form of the growth and expansion of distribution companies renting 16mm films to students and to film societies. Several major Hollywood companies have founded 16mm subsidiaries or have expanded existing operations. Two pioneer companies in this field, Brandon Films and Contemporary Films, have been purchased by larger corporations that promise more expanded operation.

This response to new demands comes despite a particularly sensitive reaction on the part of the nation's theater owners who have, for the past twenty-five years, faced perplexing problems of deteriorating theaters, increasing competition from television and foreign films, increasing costs, and the by no means crucial but rather frustrating demands from film enthusiasts who desire older films but cannot agree which ones they want to see. These exhibitors, always the most conservative part of the industry, became more protective as they felt more vulnerable. They had a particularly strong reaction to what some exhibitors felt was undue competition from the student and film society movement, and the reaction came at a time when these groups were beginning a period of significant growth. This has meant that the past fifteen to twenty years have seen rather strong pressures to inhibit the availability of films desired by the small groups of cinema enthusiasts and by students.

The new 16mm film distribution companies offer more films than ever before; however, rental films have specific and stringent restrictions placed upon their use, and rental rates have risen sharply. More significant to the librarian is the confusion which confronts the potential film user who is finding it more and more difficult to locate the film he wants.

45

LIBRARY SERVICE TO FILM ENTHUSIASTS

As an immediate improvement in library service to film scholars and enthusiasts, information about film sources needs to be expanded in almost every library. An excellent basic reference tool is James Limbacher's *Feature Films on 8 and 16 Mm* (New York, Educational Film Library Association), a book all too often missing from library shelves. This should be supplemented by catalogs from the major theatrical distributors and film periodicals serving both film enthusiast and film scholar. A list of some of these catalogs and journals is appended.

There are two things which can bring the library directly to the scholar's service. First is an effort on the part of the professional organizations in the library field to reach the organizations of the commercial movie industry—the producers, distributors, and exhibitors—to develop a precedent and program for library service in films. This has never existed before, with the exception of films made for educational or promotional purposes. The librarians should approach the industry with a proposal to use the feature film as a scholarly reference tool, serviced to individual film scholars, in a program quite devoid of any other use, particularly exhibition of the films. It should be stressed that such a proposal would be unique in the film field. Proposals for public screenings always raise the fear, however remote, of commercial competition. The appeal made by the librarians to the film industry should be one which would raise the industry from showmanship to scholarship. This is exactly what the young film students feel is necessary.

Regional depository collections of film classics might be developed and made available to member libraries, where scholars could view the films on small screen viewing machines such as the Moviola Library-Reader, or adapted film editing machines such as the German Steenbeck machine. These machines permit the scholar to control the viewing of films himself—stopping and starting at will and re-running if desired—while assuring privacy of viewing and a minimum of wear and tear on the films.

Separate programs geared to audience viewing might be developed, so long as it was clear that they had nothing to do with the service being provided to the film scholar.

A proposal for regional libraries providing this service was made at the time the American Film Institute was founded in 1967. At the present writing, no specific proposal has been forthcoming from them, but they do have a program for promotion of educational activities. It would seem most logical that this program, if it is developed, should find a home in the institutions best geared to serving the multiple needs of the scholar—the university and public libraries. Otherwise, the programs will come about but will develop as separate libraries, unrelated to collections of books, periodicals, and manuscripts which the scholar has a right to find in one location.

The second factor which can improve library service to film scholars is the training of film librarians. At the present time, film training and library science are separate disciplines, frequently unavailable at the same school. Only students with individual initiative can obtain training in both fields and almost no effort is made to relate the two. Furthermore, should the library science student prepare

46

himself for work with films, there is little or no possibility that there are jobs waiting for him. It seems axiomatic that if any program to provide the film scholar with library service is developed, it must be done by well trained professionals who have a background in the history, aesthetics, and some of the technology of the motion picture field.

Trained film librarians, given a well planned and carefully developed program, can answer the needs of the generation of students who are now coming to the libraries in search of their world of knowledge, their new dimension of communication. They have a right to expect that their intellectual demands will be met with intellectual resources.

MOTION PICTURE DISTRIBUTORS

Catalogs may be obtained from the following companies or organizations that sell, rent, or lease feature-length motion pictures. Some distribute interesting short films, too. I have also included some distributors of experimental or underground films.

Audio Film Center, 34 MacQuesten Parkway South, Mt. Vernon, N.Y. 10550.

Blackhawk Films, Eastin-Phelan Corp., Davenport, Iowa 52808.

Brandon Films, Inc., a subsidiary of Crowell Collier and Macmillan, Inc., 221 West 57th Street, New York, N.Y. 10019.

Canyon Cinema Co-operative, Room 220, Industrial Center Building, Sausalito, Calif. 94965.

Center Cinema Co-op, 540 North Lake Shore Drive, Chicago, Ill. 60611.

Cinema 16/Grove Press, Cinema 16 Film Library, Inc. 80 University Place, New York, N.Y. 10003.

Columbia Cinémathèque, Columbia Pictures Corp., 711 Fifth Avenue, New York, N.Y. 10022.

Contemporary Films/McGraw-Hill, 330 West 42nd Street, New York, N.Y. 10036.

Continental 16, a division of the Walter Reade Organization, Inc. 241 East 34th Street, New York, N.Y. 10016.

Walt Disney Productions, 800 Sonora Avenue, Glendale, Calif. 91201.

Em Gee Film Library, 4931 Gloria Avenue, Encino, Calif. 91316.

Embassy Pictures Corp., 1301 Avenue of the Americas, New York, N.Y. 10019.

Film Classic Exchange, 1926 South Vermont Avenue, Los Angeles, Calif. 90007.

Film-Makers' Cooperative, 175 Lexington Avenue, New York, N.Y. 10016.

Films Incorporated, 4420 Oakton Street, Skokie, Ill. 60076.

Fleetwood Films, 34 MacQuesten Parkway South, Mt. Vernon, N.Y. 10550.

Ideal Pictures, 34 MacQuesten Parkway South, Mt. Vernon, N.Y. 10550.

International Film bureau, 332 South Michigan Avenue, Chicago, Ill. 60604.

Janus Films, 24 West 58th Street, New York, N.Y. 10023.

Mogull's, 112 West 48th Street, New York, N.Y. 10019.

The Museum of Modern Art, Department of Film, 11 East 53rd Street, New York, N.Y. 10019.

The Newsreel, Box 302, Canal Street Station, New York, N.Y. 10013.

Radim Films, 220 West 42nd Street, New York, N.Y. 10036.

Rogosin Films, 144 Bleeker Street, New York, N.Y. 10012.

Trans-World Films, 332 South Michigan Avenue, Chicago, Ill. 60704.

United Artists 16, 729 Seventh Avenue, New York, N.Y. 10019.

Universal 16, a division of Universal City Studios, 221 Park Avenue South, New York, N.Y. 10003.

Warner Brothers-Seven Arts, Inc., 16mm Non-Theatrical Division, 666 Fifth Avenue, New York, N.Y. 10019.

CINEMA PERIODICALS, A SELECTED LIST

The periodicals listed here include a variety of approaches to the cinema. Some deal with film as an art form, others as leisure, education, trade, or commerce. All of them, with the exception of *Cahiers du Cinéma*, are English-language publications.

AFI Education Membership Newsletter. The American Film Institute, Education Department, 1815 H Street, N.W., Washington, D.C. 20006.

The American Cinematographer. 1782 North Orange Drive, Hollywood, Calif. 90028. (Monthly.)

Box Office. 825 Van Brunt Boulevard, Kansas City, Mo. 64124. (Weekly.)

Cahiers du Cinéma. 63 Avenue des Champs-Elysées, Paris 8, France. (Monthly.)

Canyon Cinema News. 5313 Rosalind Avenue, Richmond, Calif. 94805.

Cinéaste. 27 West 11th Street, New York, N.Y. 10011.

Cinema. 9667 Wilshire Boulevard, Beverly Hills, Calif. 90212. (Quarterly.)

Cinema Journal (Journal of the Society of Cinematologists). Radio-TV-Film Department, William Allen White School of Journalism, University of Kansas, Lawrence, Kansas 66044 (Attn. Richard D. MacCann).

Classic Film Collector (formerly *8mm Collector*). 734 Philadelphia Street, Indiana, Pa. (Quarterly.)

Daily Variety. 6404 Sunset Boulevard, Hollywood, Calif. 90028. (Daily except Saturdays, Sundays and holidays.)

Film Comment. 100 Walnut Place, Brookline, Mass. 02146. (Quarterly.)

Film Culture. G.P.O. Box 1499, New York, N.Y. 10001. (Quarterly.)

The Film Daily. 1600 Broadway, New York, N.Y. 10019. Also publishes *Film Daily Yearbook.* (Daily except Saturdays, Sundays and holidays.)

Filmfacts. Box 213, Village Station, New York, N.Y. 10014. (Semimonthly.)

48

Film Heritage. Box 42, University of Dayton, Dayton, Ohio 45409.

Film Library Quarterly. 101 West Putnam Avenue, Greenwich, Conn. 06830.

Film News. 250 West 57th Street, New York, N.Y. 10019. (Six times per year.)

Film Quarterly. University of California Press, Berkeley, Calif. 94720.

Film Society Review. 144 Bleeker Street, New York, N.Y. 10012. (Monthly, Sept. through May.)

Film World and A V Newsmagazine. 672 South Lafayette Park Place, Los Angeles, Calif. 90057.

Films and Filming. 75 Victoria Street, London SW1, England. (Monthly.)

Films in Review. 31 Union Square, New York, N.Y. 10003. (Monthly except summer, when published bimonthly.)

Filmmaker's Newsletter. 80 Wooster Street, New York, N.Y. 10012. (Monthly, except summer.)

The Hollywood Reporter. 6715 Sunset Boulevard, Hollywood, Calif. 90028. (Daily, except Saturdays, Sundays and holidays.)

The Independent Film Journal. 165 West 46th Street, New York, N.Y. 10036. (Biweekly.)

Journal of the Society of Motion Picture and Television Engineers (SMPTE). 9 East 41st Street, New York, N.Y. 10017. (Monthly.)

Journal of the University Film Association. c/o Mr. Robert W. Wagner, ed., Motion Picture Division, Department of Photography, 156 West 19th Avenue, Ohio State University, Columbus, Ohio 43210.

Motion Picture Daily. Quigley Publishing Co., Rockefeller Center, 1270 Sixth Avenue, New York, N.Y. 10020. (Daily except Saturdays and Sundays.)

Motion Picture Exhibitor. Jay Emanuel Publications, 317 North Broad Street, Philadelphia, Pa. 19107. (Weekly.)

Motion Picture Herald. Quigley Publishing Co., Rockefeller Center, 1270 Sixth Avenue, New York, N.Y. 10020. (Biweekly.)

Sightlines. Educational Film Library Association, 17 West 60th Street, New York, N.Y. 10023.

Take One. P.O. Box 1778, Station B, Montreal 2, Canada.

Variety. 154 West 46th Street, New York, N.Y. 10036. (Weekly.)

LIST OF FEATURE FILMS

The list of feature films which follows is not intended to be a list of "all-time-great-classics." Several standards have been applied to determine appropriate titles. Among these standards are: artistic merit, historical importance, popularity, and critical acclaim. A few are personal favorites. Several are films which I do not really like, but others are ones I am enthusiastic about. A number of titles are included because they represent types or important trends, and if your mind says to you that another related title is better than the one I have included, please feel free to mentally substitute it. The list is terminated in the early 1960s.

A Trip to the Moon. Georges Méliès, Star Films, 1902.

The Great Train Robbery. Thomas A. Edison, 1903.

His Trust and *His Trust Fulfilled.* Biograph Co., 1911 (director, D. W. Griffith).

The Birth of a Nation. D. W. Griffith and Epoch Producing Corp., 1915.

Intolerance; a Sun-Play of the Ages. D. W. Griffith, 1916.

Shoulder Arms. Charles Chaplin, 1918.

The Cabinet of Dr. Caligari. Ufa-Decla Bioscop, 1919. Released in the U.S. by Goldwyn Pictures Corp., 1921.

The Toll Gate. William S. Hart Co., 1920. Paramount-Artcraft.

The Last Laugh. Ufa Films. Released in the U.S. by Universal, 1925.

Nanook of the North. Robert J. Flaherty and Pathé Exchange, Inc., 1922.

Battleship Potemkin. First Studio of Goskino, 1925. Released in the U.S. by Amkino, 1926.

The Freshman. Pathé Exchange, 1925.

Greed. Metro-Goldwyn-Mayer Pictures, 1925.

The Gold Rush. Charles Chaplin, 1925. Released by United Artists.

The General. Joseph M. Schenk, 1926. Released by United Artists.

Sunrise. Fox Film Corp., 1927.

Secrets of a Soul (Geheimisse der Seele). Ufa, 1926.

The End of St. Petersburg. Mezhrabpom-Russ, 1927. Released in the U.S. by Arthur Hammerstein Enterprises, 1928.

October (The Ten Days that Shook the World). Sovkino, 1927. Released in the U.S. by Amkino, 1928.

Storm Over Asia. Mezhrabpomfilm, 1928. Released in the U.S. by Amkino, 1930.

The Passion of Joan of Arc. Société Générale des Films, 1928.

The Wedding March. Paramount Famous Lasky Corp., 1928.

Variety. Produced by Ufa, 1926. Released in the U.S. by Famous Players-Lasky Corp.

The Jazz Singer. Warner Bros. Pictures, Inc., 1927.

All Quiet on the Western Front. Universal Pictures Corp., 1930.

The Blue Angel. Ufa and Paramount-Publix Corp., 1931.

Frankenstein. Universal Pictures Corp., 1931.

Kameradschaft. Nero Film A. G., 1931.

Scarface. Howard Hughes, 1932. Released by United Artists.

King Kong. RKO Radio Pictures, Inc., 1933.

Gold Diggers of 1933. Warner Bros. Pictures, 1933.

Queen Christina. Metro-Goldwyn-Mayer Corp., 1934.

Top Hat. RKO Radio Pictures, Inc., 1935.

Modern Times. Charles Chaplin, 1936. Released by United Artists.

The Spanish Earth. Contemporary Historians, 1937.

Snow White and the Seven Dwarfs. Walt Disney Productions, 1937.

Grand Illusion. Réalization d'Art Cinématographique, 1937. World Pictures Corp.

Ninotchka. Metro-Goldwyn-Mayer, 1939.

The Wizard of Oz. Metro-Goldwyn-Mayer, 1939.

Stagecoach. Walter Wanger Productions, 1939. Released through United Artists.

Gone With the Wind. Selznick International and Metro-Goldwyn-Mayer, 1940.

The Grapes of Wrath. Twentieth Century-Fox, 1940.

Citizen Kane. Mercury Productions, 1940. Released by RKO Radio Pictures.

Shadow of a Doubt. Universal Pictures Co., 1942.

The Magnificent Ambersons. A Mercury production. Released by RKO Radio Pictures.

Desert Victory. British Ministry of Information, 1943.

The Miracle of Morgan's Creek. Paramount Pictures, 1944.

Open City (Roma, Città Aperta). Excelsa Films, 1945-46.

To Have and Have Not. Warner Bros. Pictures, Inc., 1945.

La Belle et la Bête. André Palvé, 1946. Released in the U.S. by Lopert.

Les Enfants du Paradis (Children of Paradise). Tricolor Films, 1946.

Shoeshine (Sciuscià). A.L.F.A. Cinematographica. Released in the U.S. by Lopert, 1946.

The Postman Always Rings Twice. Metro-Goldwyn-Mayer, 1946.

Great Expectations. Cineguild. General Film Distributors, 1947.

Home of the Brave. Screenplays II Corp., 1947. Released by United Artists.

Monsieur Verdoux. Chaplin Studios, 1947. Released by United Artists.

Paisan (Paisà). Organization Films, 1947. Released in the U.S. by Mayer-Burstyn.

Odd Man Out. J. Arthur Rank. A Two Cities Film. General Film Distributors, 1947.

Symphonie Pastorale. Gibe Film for Pathé Cinema, 1948.

Hamlet. Two Cities Films, 1948. Released in the U.S. by Universal-International.

Key Largo. Warner Bros. Pictures, Inc., 1948.

Louisiana Story. Robert J. Flaherty, 1948. Released through Lopert.

Yellow Sky. Twentieth Century-Fox, 1948.

The Heiress. Paramount Pictures, Inc., 1949.

The Bicycle Thief (Ladri di Biciclette). DeSica Productions; S.A.F.A. Studios. Released in the U.S. by Mayer-Burstyn, 1949.

The Third Man. London Films, 1949.

The Treasure of the Sierra Madre. Warner Bros. Pictures, Inc., 1948.

Sunset Boulevard. Paramount Pictures Corp., 1950.

Lavender Hill Mob. Ealing Studios, 1951. Released in the U.S. by Universal Pictures.

Tales of Hoffmann. London Films, British Lion, 1951.

High Noon. Stanley Kramer Co. Released by United Artists Corp., 1952.

Rashomon. Daiei Kabushiki Kaisha. Released in the U.S. by RKO Radio Pictures.

The Robe. Twentieth Century-Fox, 1953.

From Here to Eternity. Columbia Pictures, 1953.

Marty. Hecht-Lancaster Productions. Released by United Artists, 1954.

On the Waterfront. Horizon Pictures, 1954. Released by Columbia Pictures Corp.

La Strada. Ponti-deLaurentis. Released in the U.S. by Paramount Pictures Corp.

Around the World in Eighty Days. Michael Todd Co., 1956. Released by United Artists.

Pather Panchali. Presented by Edward Harrison, 1958.

The Seventh Seal (Det Sjunde Inseglet). Svensk Film Industri, 1957. Released in the U.S. by Janus Films.

Paths of Glory. Bryna Pictures, 1957. Released by United Artists.

The Defiant Ones. Lomitas Productions, Inc., and Curtleigh Productions, Inc., 1958. Released by United Artists.

Breathless. Produced by Georges de Beauregarde. Released in the U.S. by Films-Around-the-World, 1961.

The 400 Blows (Les Quatre Cents Coups). Les Films du Carosse et Sedif. Presented by Zenith International, 1959.

Ballad of a Soldier. Mosfilm. Released in the U.S. by M. J. P. Enterprises and Kingsley International, 1960.

L'Avventura. Cino del Duca. Released in the U.S. by Janus Films, 1961.

My Life to Live (Vivre sa Vie). Union Films release presented by Pathé Cinema Corp., 1963.

Hiroshima Mon Amour. Argos-Daiei-Pathé Overseas Production. Released in the U.S. by Zenith International, 1960.

THE ENTERTAINMENT FILM IN EDUCATION*

By Bosley Crowther

As a critic who has seen an incredible number of entertainment films, I have buoyed myself in the knowledge that film is a language, indeed an art, which charges minds with concepts and emotions that no other medium has been able to provide to the same degree. I have also been racked by the awareness that it has conveyed trash and trivia in such abundance that the cultural atmosphere has been as polluted by this debris as our rivers by urban and industrial wastes. And since entertainment, though a pastime and an escape, is also a form of experience, no matter how good or bad, it leaves a dent on the psyche just as all experience does. This influence upon the shaping of personality, in the last analysis, is what education does.

The critic must therefore be quite as concerned with the cultural values of a movie as he is about the quality of pleasure it may stimulate. I'm sure this is the attitude of most film critics today. Indeed, the entertainment film is now so widely accepted as art as well as popular diversion that it is being challenged by social thinkers to perform as such. They acknowledge it as the most extensive 20th century art or literature.

The film's qualities as visual and not verbal literature, as a medium of pictorial stimulation that can reach the heights of drama and poetry, commend it to educators not only for instruction, but for the enrichment it can give our lives. This may sound awfully lofty to schoolteachers who have had to endure the monosyllabic enthusiasms of their pupils over an old Gangbuster movie on TV. Yet there is an abundance of excellent old film literature available for showing to, and study by, pupils that will belie the trash. Pupils may also be encouraged or even assigned to watch some of the better revivals when they come up on TV, as they do regularly, and discuss these films in class or in small groups. The large reservoir of film classics available through the rental library, through the larger libraries that major film companies are now setting up for their older products, or even to be spotted regularly on TV, makes easier the job of the teacher determined to use this great 20th century literature.

TWENTIETH-CENTURY VISUAL LITERATURE

If for no other reason, acquaintance with this visual literature as an academic necessity is virtually compelled by the fact that much of our language and our metaphorical allusions are colored by film literature these days. Who quotes from Shakespeare or Tennyson or even Edgar Guest? Conversation is peppered with allusions to plots of movies, personalities of stars. Language derives from *Laugh-In* and wisecracks on TV panel and talk shows.

But it is really the quality material of film that should be used most profitably in educating our modern youth. And to this end, educators should become

---

*Reprinted from *School Library Journal*, April 1970, published by R. R. Bowker (a Xerox Company), copyright ^c1970, Xerox Corporation.

as knowledgeable and fluent in entertainment films as they are in the area of teaching films and textbooks. The great John Grierson of the Canadian National Film Board once said, "The problems of education should be approached along the lines of our actual and active interests." And certainly films and all they convey are of actual and active interest to our young people.

In following this pursuit I commend to you the excellent handbook *The School and The Art of Motion Pictures.*[1] It contains a long listing of memorable visual literature, where it may be obtained, and how it may be used. There is also the very helpful book, *The Film Viewer's Handbook.*[2] Though this is primarily a guidebook to setting up and running a film society or a film club—which could be and should be an adjunct of every good library in the country today—it is equally useful to educators who want to use available film classics.

I cannot begin here to indicate any more than the broadest possibilities and pitfalls in using visual literature. The areas and categories are many, and your chances to explore social and historical experience through film are infinite. This is true of the pursuit of films *as literature*, not as supplementary material in the study of, say, history or geography.

Just consider the literature of the American Western, with its poetry of action and its elaborations of myth. There is an exciting invitation to enjoyment and study and an opening awareness here. Or the excellent films based on Shakespeare, like Laurence Olivier's *Hamlet* and *Henry V* ("Hank Frank," as the college students called him). Or the recent Zeferelli *Romeo and Juliet.* Or one version of *Hamlet* made by the Russians which took the whole scene out of doors and made it a roaring, racing, magnificent medieval melodrama. These films can do so much to deepen the comprehension of Shakespeare that it is amazing they aren't used regularly in all schools where Shakespeare still is read.

Some teachers continue to show old Paul Muni biographies, films like *The Life of Emile Zola,* and *Pasteur,* and *A Song to Remember,* based on the life and music of Chopin. There is a vast reservoir of classics and films not so classical but still excellent to use for stimulation, enlightenment, and, I think, education.

Though the significance of this body of visual literature to the educator, and all of us, is that much of it is of lasting quality and still viable today, we must remember that our films before 1960 were made, with few exceptions, under the restraints of statutory censorship in many states and under the controls of the film industry's own production code. Which means that we're held rather firmly within the limits of middle-class respectability. For this reason, and also for the reason that film fashions and techniques do change over the years, some of the older films do look stilted and dated today—especially to youngsters accustomed to contemporary modes. That really does not matter too much, however, if we can recognize their historical context. This itself is educational.

I must remind you, too, that the body of our visual literature embraces and projects in its substance a great deal of fantasy. Not the fantasy of Walt Disney or *The Wizard of Oz,* but the fantasy of the standard Western, or the social romance, or *Gone with the Wind.* Some of it has become so rooted by virtue of comforting thought in its repetition that it is now accepted (or it was until recently) as truth.

The camera can convey so strongly the illusion of reality by virtue of the reproductive accuracy of motion photography that the substance of fanciful creation comes across as reality. Dreams, when the dream stuff seems actual, and the happy ending, seem thoroughly probable.

It is amazing, to some of our older people, that much of our film literature was the projection of forms of myth. But I was astonished recently when some younger film critics proclaimed confidently that the utter fiction and fantasy of the contemporary film *Bonnie and Clyde* might be regarded as accurate documentation of the 1930s and of the actual bandits Clyde Barrow and Bonnie Parker! I'm not going to open again the controversy I got into over *Bonnie and Clyde* as a critic. I can only say that *Bonnie and Clyde*, which was embraced and accepted by the younger people as a magnificent display of the irony and pathos of the lives of two romantic losers, was enjoyed as greatly as if it had been truth.

In education, as in life, we must be aware of allowing ourselves to be deceived with the seemingly substantial illusions we find comforting and convenient to believe. It is part of a teacher's preparation not only to disabuse himself of the illusion before discussing these matters with the young, but to discuss just these things.

THE "COPULATION EXPLOSION"

What of the visual literature today? We have seen the liberation from censorship restrictions, from restrained implications of sexual excitement and activity, such as we had, say, in *Gone with the Wind* when Clark Gable very gently kissed Scarlett O'Hara on the cheek, or when at the very end he uttered the expletive "I don't give a damn" and that was regarded as probably the most profane word one could say on the screen. The liberation from censorship restrictions to the utmost candor in the depiction of sexual behavior—to the point of outright pornography—have made this a whole new ball game, as the TV language-swingers say. We are viewing films on the screen today that suggest and convey beyond question "the copulation explosion," as my friend Louis Untermeyer so aptly put it. The "copulation explosion," in films as well as in other media, has made for some startling and historic material on the screen. I'm sure that the Swedish *I Am Curious (Yellow)*, which has been challenged in so many states and indeed was held up for a long time by customs because it does show explicitly the performance of acts of copulation—I'm sure that this film, now being seen by millions of people, will stand up as an item in the visual literature of the 1960s just as forcibly as will *The Sound of Music*, let us say. (Incidentally, *The Sound of Music* is even more popular than *I Am Curious*. Regardless of all the presumed interest in seamy movies, *The Sound of Music* is still the most popular film that we have had on the screen in all time—and this includes *Gone with the Wind*.)

The fact is we are seeing today films that can be regarded with great appreciation as expressions of the attitudes and of the difficulties of modern youth—films such as the very popular *Easy Rider* or *Goodbye, Columbus* or *Medium Cool*. Films like this are presenting the youth hangups, and the youth urges, and the youth anxieties clearly enough for us to understand that this is being expressed to us in motion pictures as well as in any other medium. They certainly should go down as part of our visual literature for future generations to see. But there are other films being presented of such a nature that I do question whether they are sufficiently honest, sufficiently accurate, and sufficiently acceptable—by our conventional standards, at least—to be offered as education for the young.

I realize that one of your great problems as audiovisual specialists is how to find materials that can be presented in the courses you are trying to develop in, say, sex education. This is a great problem, and I can understand fully how it can be one of such delicacy and difficulty today that your attempts to move forward in this area are probably being restrained very much by non-professionals who don't understand the difference between enlightenment and repression.

But in this area there are still many films which can be used, and I do suggest that films like *Goodbye, Columbus*, for instance, might very well be used for study by the young. *The Graduate*, a fine picture, much more poignant and sad than many realized, could also be excellent for the education of the thinking of young people about their own alienation from the establishment world.

Other films are dubious. We are witnessing a considerable influx, particularly from Europe, of avant garde films, in which artists present their experience, their personal statement, much as an abstract painter might offer an expression of a distinct feeling on a piece of canvas. These films also contain a great deal of fragmentation, indications of the alienation of individuals, the withdrawal of individuals, confusion and ambiguities, disorganization. Many of them, of course, express straight anarchy.

I think it was Michelangelo Antonioni, the distinguished Italian maker of *Blow Up* (tremendous expression of the hangups and indeed the fantasy problems of young people today), who himself has been accused of putting ambiguities into his pictures, who said: "The rule is, of course, that every movie should have a beginning, a middle, and an end, but not necessarily in that order."

We also have the underground films, exemplified most familiarly by Andy Warhol, who turned to films because they let him expand some of his pop-art inclinations. Some have used the film simply as a cynical exultation of vice and corruption. They have shown, most frankly, not only explicit indications of sexual aberration, degeneracy, drug-taking, but have gone even more deeply into rather humiliating aspects of human corruption. I don't think that this is going to prevail in our film culture. We are going to have an exhaustion of interest in these films simply by the repetition; it becomes monotonous. I also think, though I don't welcome this by any means, that we are finally going to have a return to some form of control, perhaps of statutory censorship of the sort that we have had before and that many of us fought hard to have eliminated.

We may also have through our educators a more clear, frank, open discussion of films of this sort, discussion of what is happening in our *culture*, not just in our films, but in other areas. If we can have more discussion; if educators will turn to this form of literature and recognize it for what it is and the older and more adult ranges of student contemplation; if we recognize these things for what they are, we can help towards a cooling-off of the curiosity and the excitement, the morbid interest of people in this sort of entertainment, if such it is.

Technically, the entertainment film is going to go into ranges much further and go into technical forms of presentation much broader than any we have known so far. The multiple screen, the multiple image, the wrap-around device, the use of other areas than simply a blank screen in an auditorium for the projection of motion pictures, will be used.

We should also see a film that will be entertainment of a sort but will also be instructional, or inspirational. The Learning Film Corporation, with which I'm associated, is trying to combine a type of film that will be both educational and entertaining, exciting on a higher level than is usually possible by the ordinary film made for educational purposes alone, because more production and larger values and finer writing indeed are put into such films.

I think we're going to see great expansion by the major film companies in this area. This is certainly a consideration of all the major producers today. We all have our 16mm facilities now which in years back would have been unheard of, or scorned, by most of the presidents of the major companies. But now all are trying to move in this direction and are opening up as much as they can the facilities to provide schools, film societies, and libraries, particularly libraries as such, with visual literature.

What can be done with film to stimulate and excite people? To use this language of our day, the visual language, the fact that young people think, that young people work, that young people express themselves with their own little hand-held cameras, with their own little 8mm and 16mm cameras, in order to say for themselves and their own friends that there appears what they think and feel? The fact that this is so extensive is a clear indication that this is the way we are going to communicate in the years ahead.

We're going to communicate with pictures, with sound, sound associated with pictures, but in all sorts of combinations that probably are not even realized by educators or technicians even today. You, as educators, are great opinion-makers in this area. What you say, what you decide, will determine the education—and entertainment—of the future.

REFERENCES

1. David Mallery. *The School and the Art of Motion Pictures.* Boston, The National Association of Independent Schools, 1966.

2. Emil G. McAnany, S.J., and Robert Williams, S.J. *The Film Viewer's Handbook.* Glen Rock, N.J., The Paulist Press, 1965.

THE PICTURE BOOK PROJECTED*

By Morton Shindell

Though I work largely in the audiovisual field, I have long been convinced that no medium speaks more directly and intimately to a child than a book. My conviction dates back to the years when I read to my own children. At first my own imagination, like that of most adults, had long since atrophied, and my reading was a fairly mechanical process of sounding the words and glancing at the illustrations.

But my children, like children everywhere, literally felt what the author was saying. For them the characters jumped live off the pages–there was no doubt in their minds that here's where the action was. Their eyes were glued to each picture as they listened. "Tell it right, Daddy," I'd be admonished if I changed a word or missed a sentence in a book they knew. Cathy, then a pre-schooler, invariably made me wait as she counted the eight eggs that Mrs. Mallard sat on in *Make Way for Ducklings*, just to be sure, each time we read the book, that all the eggs were still there. The Hallowe'en after we read *Jenny's Birthday Book*, my Jeanie chose to dress up as a shy little black cat.

Gradually, I, too, was stirred by my own children's pleasure, and through books we came to know more of one another. Expressing the thoughts and feelings of authors and illustrators helped us say things to each other that we never could have articulated on our own.

I was amazed, too, at the children's involvement as they handled the books, turned the pages, and pored endlessly over their favorite parts. In choosing stories I was always responsive to their requests, for they knew, inevitably, which books they wanted read night after night, and which they had had enough of the first time around.

From our reading together, I slowly became aware of the structure that underlies many story books and helps to sustain their interest. Many develop like a three-act play: they build up, taper off, and then repeat this ever-heightening pattern to a climax. (*The Little Red Lighthouse, The Story About Ping,* and *Little Toot* come easily to mind.) Though written as prose, the words of many picture books read like poetry which one effortlessly commits to memory after only a hearing or two. There is a fascination for children in the sound and flow of words, the cadences of books like *Time of Wonder* or *Millions of Cats*, the alliteration of names like Mike Mulligan and Norman the Doorman.

As I look back, I realize that while reading to my children I was discovering something that youngsters seem to know intuitively: the special qualities that make books a unique medium of communication–especially picture books.

The book is an intimate, direct conversation between an author and the person who reads or hears his words. It never hurries anyone. It makes no demands until it is picked up and read. You can choose to browse through the front, the back or the middle. And when it is well designed, the book is a pleasure to touch and invites handling.

*Reprinted from *School Library Journal,* February 1968, published by R. R. Bowker Co. Copyright ᶜ1968, R. R. Bowker.

Above all, the book is intended for an audience in close proximity, and for a situation in which time is not a factor. Often the picture book is for a single pair of eyes, or a reader closely half-circled by at most six or eight children.

But precisely because of its format and intimacy, the book's "message" is for only a few at one time. I became acutely aware of this some years ago when attending a public library story hour. About 30 youngsters were assembled on a carpet in front of the librarian, who was telling *The Tale of Peter Rabbit*. She obviously enjoyed the story and told it well, but like most teachers and librarians who are not storytelling specialists, she would first read a page of text, then hold the book toward the children so that they could see the picture. The children became restless, first as they were deprived of the sight of the picture while the librarian read, then as the flow of words stopped while she held the book high so that those in the back row could see.

As we talked later, the librarian seemed almost apologetic about the success of her story hours. "A year ago, only 10 or 12 showed up regularly," she explained. "Now the community has grown so that there are usually 30 or more." But she was obviously finding it hard to keep the attention of a much larger group.

Her experience is not unique. Yet many teachers and librarians, faced with this dilemma, blame themselves and feel that they, personally, have limitations as storytellers. They are not at fault—except perhaps in the failure to recognize the limitations of the picture book.

For the book is not a "group" or "distance" medium. Its words were never intended to be orated to a vast audience, and its illustrations were created for children to examine at leisure, down to the minutest detail. Even if a storyteller knows the book by heart and can show the pictures without first having to unwrap himself and turn the book around, only a few children in a larger group will see well enough to really appreciate a picture.

ICONOGRAPHIC FILMING

It was when some perceptive librarians pointed this out to me that I began to produce sound films. Wanting them to be as faithful to the book as possible, I developed what is known as the *iconographic technique*. Unlike animation, where hundreds of pictures are drawn to impart motion to an illustration, it is only the camera that moves in iconographic photography. Hovering over the enlarged projection of the page much as the child would examine it, concentrating always on the picture as it was originally drawn, the camera probes for the essence of each idea that went into the total composition of each picture. By varying light intensity and perspective, by emphasizing one detail and then another, by moving in a deliberate direction at a controlled speed, the camera is made to release the mood and action that the illustrator captured in the pages of his book.

When the pictures are completed, a recorded sound track comprised of the telling of the story, an original musical score, and sound effects, is placed in careful juxtaposition to the pictures. In making the recording to accompany the filmed illustrations, I tried to emulate the approaches and impact of superior storytellers I had heard while learning my craft. But I soon discovered that a richer concentration of elements was required to compensate for the fact that the sounds *my* audience heard would emanate from an impersonal loudspeaker, rather than the lips of a live human being.

In recording a story, the director must explore the text for the nuances of mood and action that the author so carefully framed his words to express. Once these are understood, pace, intonation, and characterization flow almost intuitively as new techniques, superimposed on the storytellers' performance, revitalize the words. To evoke the emotional harmony of an intimate story hour experience, we introduce background music and subtle, muted sound effects to heighten the mood and action. At each step, care is taken not to intrude upon, but only give expression to, the communication in the book.

A STATIC BUT FLEXIBLE MEDIUM

These films opened books up to many parents who had never seen them before, to professionals in workshops or classes, and to television audiences. Teachers and librarians were intrigued by the way the enlarged, projected illustrations could involve large groups of children. But many, being skilled storytellers themselves, rightfully wanted to remain part of the act, not just part of the audience. They began to ask me about the feasibility of turning off the sound track and telling the story live while the pictures were being projected. Some of them had tried it but were frustrated by the inexorable pace of the film. A medium had to be improvised to put the storyteller in control of the medium, rather than the other way around!

Ten years later it has become obvious that filmstrips were the solution. But the concept of the "filmstrip" had first to be broadened. For in those days the pictures in a filmstrip were always horizontal on the screen, while the text was almost always a condensed caption, superimposed in two or three lines below each frame.

The format created special problems for anyone who wanted to transpose a literary work to the screen with fidelity. The vertical illustrations in a book like *Andy and the Lion*, for example, could not, I felt, be distorted to accommodate themselves to the horizontal proportions of the screen, and paring the text to fit the medium was unthinkable for me. Hence the innovation which today is commonplace to most librarians, and accepted for a "filmstrip": pictures photographed on the frames just as they appear in the book, but with the text now deleted; and the complete text printed in a separate booklet, which is keyed to the filmstrip by a tiny reproduction of the picture alongside the words which it accompanies. In this way, the right words are always with the right picture, with almost no possibility of confusion.

Although the screen projection is much larger, this type of filmstrip is still a direct reproduction of the pictures in a book, so that filmstrips come closer to retaining the author's intent than any medium except the book itself. They can be stopped or started at will, and frames, like pages, can be skipped or turned forward and backward. In a darkened room the filmstrip rivets the child's attention even more than the pages of a book, and it has the advantage of reaching far more children listening to a story than could comfortably be assembled around the book itself.

Of course, communication through a filmstrip does lose some of the close feeling that comes only from direct contact with the book or its reader. But the enlarged pictures, in turn, take on even more life than their originals.

BREAKING THE SOUND BARRIER

So part of the gap was bridged: larger groups could get into the pictures. But those who were farthest away from the storyteller still couldn't always *hear*; even if they could, the attempt to project the mood of a story to children way back in the classroom or library distorted the normally intimate storytelling situation.

Now the question came: "Can't you provide us with the sound tracks from the *films*? We could use them in conjunction with the filmstrips in our classrooms and libraries." So we took the recordings already made and reproduced them as phonograph records, two stories on a side of a 12-inch LP, simply because that was the number that fit the best. At first, people ordered these records to accompany the filmstrips they had already acquired or for listening libraries. In time, the natural affinity of the recorded sound to the filmstrip and its text booklet became apparent as the number of requests mounted for these elements in combination. It was from this phenomenon that sound filmstrip sets derived, not needed, perhaps by the expert storyteller, but useful for many teachers and librarians and for children, whether they could read or not, to use alone in the library. The multimedia cycle was complete.

None of these media duplicate the child's private pleasure in holding his own book, yet they can also transmit with integrity and fidelity what the author and illustrator have to say. The medium you choose—reading a book, showing a film or filmstrip, having children listen to records or tape, or combining the various media—should depend on the number of children you are trying to reach at any one time, the surroundings they will be in, and the talent, materials, and equipment available to you.

Each of these techniques has its own traditions, peculiarities, advantages— and disadvantages. Each must be considered with an eye to the circumstances under which it will be used. The choice is easy when you understand the factors involved and the unique qualities of each resource you can use. Through electronic and mechanical means, given materials artfully prepared, you have at your disposal many ways to share with the rising tide of eager children more of the thoughts and feelings that you, yourself, have discovered between the covers of good books.

FILMS ON DEMAND*

By Lynne Hofer

Mrs. Hofer is cofounder of the Young Filmaker's Foundation, started in 1968 by Rodger Larson, Mrs. Hofer, and Jaime Barrios to help support youth-made films. Some 80 short films by young people aged eight to 21 have since emerged from the Film Club, the foundation's storefront workshop (funded by the Helena Rubinstein Foundation) on New York City's lower East Side. The YFF also trains potential teachers, programs youth-made films for screenings at libraries, schools, museums, and for TV, and negotiates commissioned films for students from various New York State film workshops.

Readers desiring more information should get in touch with the author at the Young Filmaker's Foundation, 310 West 53rd Street, New York, N.Y. 10019.

"When I visited Moviebox, I knew there had just been an audience because there was a pile of peanut shells. . . . As I watched, two teenage girls came in, took one look, and left. They came back to stay with friends and plates of French fries and ketchup."

This is one of the first reactions by a library that used Moviebox, a special program designed to solve both a library and a film programming problem: how do you set up a small theater in a library so that you can have open, unscheduled, and accessible film showings that still don't disrupt normal library procedures? Billed as the "smallest movie theater in town," Moviebox turned film showings into a special event for young people.

The experiment marked the convergence of several needs. The New York Public Library was concerned about a growing number of school truants who were using library facilities. It also wanted additional programs that could be used after school, when many teenagers came into the branches, and that would attract previously uninterested youth. At the same time, Barbara Haspeil, of the New York State Council of the Arts, had long wanted to make student films easily accessible to viewers. The Young Filmaker's Foundation was asked to design a program for teenagers comprised of films made by young people, and take it on tour to eight branch libraries, three in the South Bronx, one of New York City's poorest sections.

During past summers, our foundation had already been presenting outdoor screenings of youth-made films in streets and playgrounds, using a Volkswagen bus and a large, portable screen. Could we create something for the libraries that would be as simple and flexible as outdoor movies? A cartridge format was the obvious selection, and this was made easy by Fairchild's offer, to lend us two Mark IV Super 8 cartridge-loading rear screen projectors. But we also wanted this setting to have a special quality of self-containment without rigidity, and

---

to make it absolutely clear that the movies were the total creations of young people in terms of script, direction, shooting, and editing.

So we set the projector in a three-sided frame of aluminum poles and panels—a box, seven feet square at the front, four feet deep, and three feet square at the back, giving an illusion of depth and definition while taking up a remarkably small amount of space. On the side and top panels, we mounted photographs of young filmmakers in action at the Film Club, the Movie Club at Henry Street, and the Film Workshop of the Studio Museum in Harlem. The entire structure could be dismantled in half an hour, placed on top of a car, and moved on.

Surprisingly sturdy, the Moviebox survived its ten weeks of transit and indoor use without a scratch. The projector survived, too, except for the bulbs which had to be changed often because of continuous viewing each afternoon and some mornings. Librarians were shown how to do this themselves each time the Moviebox was installed, and were given a supply of bulbs, an extension cord, and a replacement projector for backup in case of a possible breakdown. Wayne Bartow, who transported the Moviebox, gave the minimal technical instruction necessary, plus background on filmmakers and workshops to the librarians and viewers. Because of his special experience as a film teacher, he could relate to the young people and involve them in assembling and placing the Moviebox.

Our aim was to make this as different as possible from the traditional film program. Jacqueline Lavalle of the Hamilton Fish Library has commented on the old problems:

> We have found on a number of occasions that when showing films in the traditional manner (*i.e.*, darkened auditorium, symmetrical arrangement of chairs, etc.), many children and young people are intimidated by these conditions and are reluctant to enter the auditorium, but will peek from the doorway. The darkened, silent auditorium ("don't trip over the cord," "don't walk in front of the screen") contributes to their reluctance to disturb, make noise in front of all those people or, even worse, have to *leave* before the movie is finished. Many children have parents waiting for them at home or have limited time to spend in the library. The Moviebox removes all these conditions, and the proof was evident as it continuously played to a "full house."

One advantage of short films in the cartridge format was the possibility of seeing a favorite several times. The younger teenagers asked repeatedly to see *Flash*, a 10-minute sci-fic film by José Colon of the Film Club which tells about an alien boy from another planet who saves the earth from an outer space invasion. The "Flash cult" seems to have followed Moviebox from one library to another, as teens repeatedly asked for it, and other favorites like *The Museum Hero* by Alfonso Sanchez (commissioned by the Metropolitan Museum of Art), and *Crime Never Pays* by 13-year-old Orson Montanez.

We felt films like these would have particular meaning for people in the poor neighborhoods where they were shown. We also wanted to show the great variety in youth-made films today. Working with the Youth Film Distribution Center at 43 West 16th Street, in New York, we could choose from over 100 16mm films. They had, of course, to be reduced to Super 8 and combined in 20-minute programs—color films on one cartridge, drug-oriented films on one cartridge (so that individual librarians could use it with discussion if they chose), films aimed specifically at entertaining children, on one cartridge. Finally, films originally shot with reversal film stock could not be combined with films that were shot with negative film stock. Thus we had to omit many possibilities.

Because the project was experimental we sought different kinds of locations for each library, and we also looked for different attitudes on the part of librarians. But for our first tryout, we looked especially for a relaxed atmosphere, close community ties, and many participating young people. The results were a pleasure.

Ideally, I felt that Moviebox should be used as easily as a free pinball machine, with the viewers changing cartridges, regulating the volume, and exercising a kind of proprietorship over the whole operation. Realistically, this would work in some libraries but not in others; what one library called "a tremendous week in terms of order" was seen as chaotic in another. Though the operation of cartridge-loading projectors is incredibly simple, some librarians felt they couldn't trust this operation to children. Often they were amazed when a 12-year-old impatiently snatched a cartridge from the hesitant hands of an adult and ran the show.

Sometimes we placed Moviebox in the center of a library, at other times in a corner. Where it didn't work was where it was *removed* from the mainstream of library activity. In two libraries, where we put it in glass-enclosed rooms, separate, but visible from the main room, people often hesitated to enter during a showing and peered in but didn't participate. This detracted from our purpose— to provide a free and unstructured way of using film. Also, most complaints about noise and disruption of normal activity came from precisely those branches where the operation was the most contained and separate. The closer we got to a kind of "street show," with people coming and going as they chose, no doors or partitions, the more the staff and viewers liked the project. In an open, sympathetic atmosphere, Moviebox elicited a joyous and wholehearted reception.

With an initial collection of only seven cartridges, we were sure that a one-week visit in each library would be more than enough. However, the two libraries where Moviebox stayed for two weeks reported greater interest during the second week. Viewers brought back friends, became familiar with the films, and the library staff relaxed about the technical aspect. Breakage and damage were nonexistent.

Since Moviebox was used mainly in neighborhoods where most young people were black and Puerto Rican, films made by black and Puerto Rican teenagers were chosen. Viewers and librarians alike approved this programming:

> A great way to spend a rainy Saturday.
> I liked it because they are using Puerto Ricans.
> In the city things happen that way.
> It gives you a chance to see short movies that you wouldn't believe a teenager made.
> Moviebox provides an excellent means of serving nonreaders, reluctant readers, and readers who want a change from books sometimes.
> There were first the older teens, many of whom we had never been able to draw into the branch for other than night jazz and drama

programs. They came singly, or in small groups of three or four and sat and viewed all the programs very seriously. Many came back bringing friends with them. They usually came in between 12:00 and 2:00 p.m. This was very unusual, for they had never come into the branch at that time before. . . . Second were the after-school juvenile and junior high school groups who came in *en masse* after school. . . . This was the most consistent group, coming back day after day during the period Moviebox was here. . . . Third were the school classes, and other groups who had received our posters and came either as a formal class visit or after school.

One film, *A Park Called Forsyth*, was asked for repeatedly by a young girl who referred to it as the *West Side Story* of the Lower East Side. She sensed immediately that the film was a somewhat nostalgic portrayal of the gang warfare of the Fifties. An adult viewer thought it anachronistic, without perceiving that the filmmaker was recapturing some of the teenage history and mythology of his neighborhood.

One librarian thought the entire program was inappropriate and that it appealed to a minor segment of her readers:

> The subject matter is another point of concern. Many of our readers simply did not relate to it. The most enthusiastic audience I observed was a group of our black truants who hung around especially to see the films. They seemed to really enjoy them and reacted the most vocally to them. But they are a minor segment of our teenage readers. We have no Spanish-speaking readers to speak of. Many of our white kids were simply disinterested.

This may be, in fact, an unconscious endorsement: We are reaching youngsters who were heretofore unresponsive to library resources.

Staff attitudes—*e.g.*, criticisms about noise, technical quality, or lack of educational content—were often echoed by the teenage audience. *Staff*: "Sound effects enough to drive staff out of their minds after first day." *Young reader*: "I was glad to see it go because I was getting a headache from all the noise." In contrast, the same programs at another library elicited from staff: "Young and old alike never tired of watching the films. . . . The music sound track really turned the kids on." Here teenagers' responses often referred to the sound tracks and, in fact, many of them got up and danced to the music.

Three films depicting teenage drug experience were seldom shown. *Glue Sniffer* tells about a young man, seeking to escape his surroundings and problems through glue sniffing, who finally imagines he is climbing a tree in the country and falls from a tenement roof. *The Potheads in Let's Get Nice* is a montage which effectively captures the hallucinatory nature of marijuana smoking. In *Tomorrow Never Comes*, a young man, distraught over the sudden death of his girl friend, is initiated into the drug world by a friend. After a total exploration of the drug scene, he finally sees his friend as a devil. The New York Public Library adopted a policy of showing these films only when an authority on narcotics was present, thus severely limiting the use of the cartridge. Yet one librarian reported:

> I do feel that in this neighborhood the children are exposed to a great deal more pressure to try narcotics than the short films could

have exerted, so it might have been very salutary to have shown the cartridge, even without an authority, and get the reactions of the viewers.

Later she explained that, at night, from the second-floor windows of the library, she could see several people shooting up. Since any young person in the neighborhood would see the same thing, she thought it unrealistic to think the films could show anything her kids didn't already know. Though a few librarians were concerned about exposure to the content of these films, most felt that any information and airing of the problem was helpful.

In retrospect, there are certain things that might be changed or emphasized: I would have twice as many programs and stay in a library at least two weeks; I would place Moviebox only in libraries where it could be located in the open— easily visible from the front entrance; I would preview all films with the staff, going into the background of the filmmakers and discussing some reactions and prejudices that viewers have expressed. Finally, I would urge that the operation of Moviebox be carried on as much as possible by the young adults, and that it be seen primarily as entertainment to be sampled briefly, casually, and repeatedly, an organic part of the different pleasures a library offers.

MEDIA MIX: UTILIZATION/PRODUCTION

This section might well have been called a "mixed bag." Media represented in the articles include: slides, tapes, transparencies, and the 8mm filmloop. The focus of the articles ranges from design and production applications to the utilization of a cross-media approach to library orientation. The primary purpose of the selection is to present diverse views about a variety of media forms applicable to many library situations.

SYSTEMS FOR INDIVIDUAL STUDY*

By Eugene Fleischer

Various kinds of individual study systems have received attention in the press over the last few years, and the recent cutbacks in federal aid, especially for equipment, make it important for your school or district to consider the alternatives carefully. Which system is best for your needs? Some teaching methods adapt better to one kind than to another, and some may not be compatible at all.

Basically, your alternatives are in terms of heavy duplication of small, simple collections on tape or cassette, to the more centralized but limited loop transmission systems, to the completely centralized dial access. As sophistication increases, the price tag escalates. Somewhere along the line may be the most practical method for your school.

Your major decision—to centralize, provide individual materials and equipment in duplicate, or have some combination of these—depends on your own desires, needs, and resources—and especially on the needs of the user. Take stock of these before you consult with manufacturers or write bid specifications. If your collection is small or concentrated, it would be cheaper to duplicate individual items heavily than to set up a dial access. You could then let the student take home his material on tape or cassette (perhaps with the equipment, too, since cassette recorders can be purchased so cheaply today), control his own pace of learning and review, and keep him from competing for space and for a particular item in the library. If the collection is large in scope, however, you will have to account for the staff time involved in circulating materials.

Largely because of this last factor, the centralized efficiency of a dial access system is likely to appeal to the library administrator's eye—less clerical staff (though you need a technician to service the students in all but random access systems, and have equipment to maintain besides); less risk of damage or loss, and central control. However, the limitations of dial access system are seldom spelled out. Sometimes the material (for example, teachers' lectures, which might well be mineographed) does not warrant the heavy investment; you do need a maintenance staff; and you must allow the space and equipment for use by many students. With just a few carrels, a few students can tie up the system.

*Reprinted from *School Library Journal,* February 1971, published by R. R. Bowker (a Xerox Company), copyright ᶜ1971, Xerox Corporation.

Before consulting with manufacturers and writing bid specifications, take stock of your own desires, needs and resources. Numbers alone may mislead you. If all teachers, for example, require all students to dial in all their lectures, the resulting statistics will be staggering. It may be easier and cheaper to give lectures in traditional classrooms, or to show closed-circuit televised lectures in auditoriums. A small automated system serving some of the student well is better than a large system serving all poorly.

When you discuss your specifications, consider which features are best suited to the needs of the user. Every school situation has its own needs, and the choices of systems and equipment are wide (see *Audiovisual Market Place*, Bowker, and the National Audiovisual Association's *Audiovisual Equipment Directory* for listings of manufacturers). There is also a great variety of software commercially available, primarily in lecture and language lessons. The quality of these vary and some editing may be necessary. (This may be difficult—as in duplication, copyright problems may occur.) The *SLJ Audiovisual Guide* provides a subject and format listing of new materials.

There are, however, several basic *types* of systems to consider for transmitting instructional materials to individual students for class assignments, enrichment, development, or recreation. (I will not discuss those specifically for language labs.)

INDIVIDUAL CHECKOUT

The easiest way to transmit information to the individual student is through standard playback devices. School designed phonographs and tape recorders, as well as some portable television sets, have jacks for hardware. These can be mounted in carrels or checked out from a central place to be used in carrels or other designated areas. The student comes to the checkout desk, requests a program, and signs a control sheet as he receives the disc or tape (and equipment, if it is centrally housed).

Such a system can allow varying degrees of student independence. Portable equipment can even be taken home for use. The student can listen at his own rate, stopping and reviewing when necessary, a particular convenience for listening to class lectures.

The hardware collection can be small or large, depending on your needs and finances, although you will have to duplicate software more often than with a central system. But recording and duplication are inexpensive and relatively easy if you have the equipment. Portable reel or cassette recorders can tape classroom lectures for future review, or recordings designed for special purposes. Lessons can be edited and converted from one format to another, *e.g.*, an audiotape of musical selections can be made from other tapes and be narrated by the music teacher.

The system can be expanded, without an increase in selectivity, by connecting several headsets to each player with an inexpensive "mixer" or distribution box. Thus, several students can hear the story, lecture, or exercise at once. Of course, they must be at the same table, and they cannot control the material independently.

The individual checkout system is relatively cheap and easy to handle.

Portable players are simple and dependable. When one breaks down, it can be replaced without disrupting the whole system. In a small system with low traffic and circulation, the regular staff can supervise and your local repair service can handle maintenance. The largest investment is in the actual purchase of materials, which can be transferred within a school or a system and duplicated in large numbers easily.

CASSETTES

Although the operational principles are the same, cassettes add definite advantages to a listening system. These narrow audiotapes are on reels, sealed in compact containers. They can be recorded, played, and handled without your actually touching the tape. They are inexpensive and come in several lengths— 30, 60, 90, 120 minutes—but all in the *same* container. Because of this fixed size, a fixed speed (1 1/8 ips), a compatible track, and an erase-proof feature, the cassette has become an important standard in school and home tape recording. Many producers of audiovisual materials are now using cassettes. Simple duplication equipment can make several cassette recordings from a master in minutes.

Some advantages of cassettes over open reels are: no tape handling, increasing tape life; easy use by young children; and track compatibility, so *any* cassette can be played in *any* monaural or stereo recorder or player. The disadvantages are: higher original tape cost; fixed lengths, often wasting tape; and the cost of converting from open reel equipment.

If an individual listening system is what is needed, cassettes may be the best answer. Portable players with all the forward and rewind functions can be bought for under $25 (recorders cost from $20 to $150). Because of the popularity in home equipment, compatibility, easy duplication, and difficulty in "defacing" the programs, cassettes and players can be circulated as easily as books. This has been tried in some districts with success, as has the leasing of cassette players to students for a nominal annual fee.

LOOP TRANSMISSIONS

A "wireless" system enabling a number of students to listen to a simple program can be installed for a few hundred dollars. The output signal of a tape recorder or phonograph is radiated from a loop of wire taped to the walls of a room, and the students listen through "wireless" headsets. Without dangling wires, they can sit or move freely. But students are limited to one program and controlled by one operator (though for certain applications this may be desirable).

The loop principle can be used for up to eight programs from a single tape. Several tracks can be transmitted on separate frequency bands from a specially designed track tape player, like several radio stations broadcasting simultaneously. The student's "wireless" receiver has a selector to choose any one program and delete the rest.

Less expensive than dial access, this still achieves a student choice of audio programs sent from a central source. You don't need duplicate copies, equipment is compact, and the student is not tied to a carrel.

The main disadvantages are the limited number of programs and the timing. All programs start at once and cannot be controlled by the student.

CENTRALIZED SYSTEMS

The initial cost of a central system is high, depending upon its complexity, but the most convenient. There is no need for heavy duplication or extensive storage space and little danger of loss, theft, or mishandling since the student uses only a headset, a dial, or perhaps a TV monitor. Terminals can be put in media centers, laboratories, classrooms, study halls, etc.

Group listening or dial access is best for presenting *uninterrupted* information. The teacher may want the student to feel the total effect of a scene in a play, a classroom experience, or to take a timed test.

An automatic system requires only casual checks to see that everything is running properly, handle trouble calls, and answer availability questions. If you need detailed records of use, headsets can be kept at the central control center and students can sign in to use the system.

But a central system can lead to problems in priority scheduling and programs will need changing periodically, teachers must be consulted for their selections, and the actual tapes must be placed on the decks.

All electronic equipment is subject to malfunction and sophisticated systems need the attention of a technician. Routine maintenance prevents costly major breakdowns. (Your office or home telephone doesn't require much maintenance—it may work perfectly for a year at a time, but the Bell System keeps a very large staff of maintenance men to take care of these rare problems.) A technician would spend about 1/4 to 1/3 of his time on maintenance and repair of a dial access tape and television system; the rest could be spent on maintaining normal circulation equipment, such as projectors, saving costly repair bills. In any case, the cost is no higher than maintaining a comparable portable collection.

CENTRAL MANUAL SWITCHING

The simplest and least expensive way to provide a large number of single copy sources with remote access is through a central manual switching system.

A bank of tape decks is manned by an attendant who receives requests from students by wire, mounts the desired programs, and manually interconnects the two (programs can also be assigned in this way at an instructor's request). Besides being cheaper than automatic switching equipment, this system puts no limit on the number of tapes which can be played. On the other hand, it must always be manned by a trained attendant and does not permit student control.

A variation of this system, used at a midwest university, consists of an audiotape source, a cable network to several campus buildings, and headsets plugged into wall-mounted terminals. A three-hour tape consisting of many programs is played on a time schedule. The student consults the schedule and "plugs in" at the time of his desired program. The system is simple and efficient, but access is limited to the contents of the tape, and a student may have to wait.

DIAL-ACCESS RETRIEVAL

"Dial-access" replaces the trained attendant with mechanical or electronic automatic switching equipment. It is more expensive, but almost maintenance-free. Instead of a voice request, a telephone dial or keyboard sends a series of pulses to a switching center which translates the pulses into addresses of sources, like your home telephone system.

An automatic playback deck is started and the program is sent to the student's headset. (If the source is a television program, the picture immediately appears on the student's screen and the sound comes through his headset.) If another student dials a program which is in progress, he joins in just as one enters a movie theater with a "continuous show." When the program ends, it rewinds automatically, and plays and rewinds as long as someone is listening. Then the tape is automatically rewound—from any point in the program. Local videotapes, films, or live programs must be played on a schedule or manually.

Dial-access individual student or classroom positions can be placed anywhere, as long as wire and amplifiers can be run to them. Long distances are only practical for sound, since television signals must be run on much more expensive cable and amplification equipment. Typical student positions are in individual study centers, school libraries, and dormitories.

The automatic control center should be monitored by an attendant whose responsibilities would be to issue headsets and keep records if desirable. Otherwise, headsets can be attached to the dials and the attendant can just make casual checks on the system, assign stations, etc. He might be a student or clerk whose regular work is near the control center.

Some optional added attractions are: Intercom, which is very useful for detecting human or mechanical problems; remote buffer recording, so that the student can utilize responsive language lessons or review parts of a program; and stereophonic programming for music programs.

Tape decks for dial-access systems may have one-, two-, or four-track formats on their audiotapes, retrievable by four different dial numbers. This increases the source capacity greatly, but can be a problem. If the tape has started, a student dialing any of its *four* numbers can't get the start of his program. It requires a special recorder and a four-programmed tape is difficult, if at all possible, to catalog. However, if the programs are short, changed rarely, and needed in great variety, multitracking is useful.

The prime drawback (other than cost) of dial access is the lack of student control of the program. Because every tape or track is available to every student, he can't stop or back up, as he could with his own tape or cassette.

The only way to solve this problem is with a remote buffer recorder in the switching center, to which the student can transfer the program, releasing it for others to use. The new recording can be started, stopped, rewound, and reviewed as long as desired and remains in the system for the next user to erase and re-record. The student can also add his responses or comments while recording.

An alternative is to transfer the program to a portable tape recorder through a "patch cord" connected between the recorder and a headphone jack at the student dial position.

RANDOM ACCESS RETRIEVAL

The most sophisticated electronics developed for the individual student is the random access retrieval system. It solves the main disadvantage of dial access, and adds some features. But the cost is high, and the system requires more trained personnel.

Master tapes are special loops with 32 tracks, containing 15-minute programs. Student position is connected to an individual two-speed "buffer" recorder-player, with a two-track 15-minute loop. When a student wants a program, he first erases his buffer tape, then "punches" his number and transfers the program from the master to buffer in 30 seconds. (Playback speed is 3" per second, transfer speed is 120" per second.) The student can then fully control the program by pressing buttons. Meanwhile the master program can be transferred to other buffers. (The second track on the buffer tape is for the student's voice.) Because loops are used, no rewinding is necessary.

Another innovation is a picture-sound synchronized program. By a slow-scan TV process, still pictures are put on the student's screen at pre-determined intervals. The state of the art does not yet permit action television in this system.

Because special loops are used, all programs must be transferred to the master tapes for retrieval. Students cannot request programs not on the schedule, and program schedules must be held for semesters, rather than days. ("Schedule" means a prepared, duplicated program stating the available lessons, or other programs, and the numbers to be dialed to gain access. On any other system, the audio tape sources are standard reels of tape or cassettes, and video sources are reels of videotape. These can be exchanged in a minute or two, so a "schedule" can be changed weekly, daily, or even hourly. If a number of tape decks are not loaded with lessons on the program, they could be used to gain access to the entire collection at any time. In order for the random access system to work, a desired lesson must be "scheduled" and recorded on a predetermined position on a 32-track, 15-minute master loop. If all master loops are filled, a new lesson cannot be entered into the system without erasing one already in, and removing a 32-lesson master from use temporarily.)

COMBINING SYSTEMS

There are hidden costs and staff time in all systems—advantages and disadvantages and again your individual needs and economic viability will have to be examined carefully. You might even find some combination of the two advantageous. Rather than make your school conform to a system, it is possible to have the systems conform to your school. For example, a dial system with a modest complement of 10 to 20 program sources may cover 75 percent of your needs. Instead of increasing these to 30 or 40 to cover 95 or 98 percent of your needs, one or two manual sources might suffice to cover all of them—if the attendant has a large collection of tapes.

An individual player with headsets may be desirable for dictation practice, but this need not preclude a media center dial-access system for review of classroom lectures.

My former central system, at Brevard Junior College in Florida, combined dial access monaural tape, stereo tape, TV and remote record, coupled with manual stereo request decks, cassette checkout, and an FM-stereo classroom network. Once the attendants and students become accustomed to the variety of services the system is very efficient.

My present system at Ocean County College uses cassettes and various projectors in a self-paced learning situation. Called the Multimedia Learning Facility (MLF), it is a row of ten modified carrels, called "modules," adjoining a sound conditioned storage and projection core. Each has a cassette player and headset, projector controls, and a rear projection screen which doubles as a service window. In a table, facing the back of the screens, are the slide, filmstrip, and film loop projectors which throw the image toward the student. Carrel-mounted tape decks, record players, and filmstrip viewers for browsing of non-programmed materials are also part of the MLF study, as well as a 50-position audio source dial-access system which is used for instruction materials best suited to that medium.

The media distribution clerk, or a trained student assistant, puts the appropriate projector in place, loads it, and hands out the cassette. (The student might also have classroom outlines or workbook materials if these are part of the learning package.) The key to the MLF is self-pacing. The student can start, stop, or review as desired, calling the attendant only for trouble or change of program. Cassettes and battery-operated cassette players may be checked out overnight as are reserve books. Non-book materials not on reserve may be checked out for a week.

But, whether you choose one system or a combination, none are worth the investment unless they are effectively used by the students and ardently supported and fed by the faculty. Your system must have enough relevant materials for the students to hear and see. As usual, success breeds success. When a few teachers record lectures or select commercially produced materials, suggest or assign students to listen, and receive favorable feedback, other teachers will want to do the same. When that time comes, your portable tape recorders, TV studios, and your materials catalogs should be ready.

TRANSPARENCIES: THE SIMPLEST TEACHING TOOL*

By Herbert Deutsch

The transparency, whose versatility in quickly training men of varied backgrounds, abilities, and skills was demonstrated by the Armed Forces in World
War II, has become one of the most popular teaching tools in the classroom.
Until 1960, the high cost of projectors forestalled their purchase in public schools,
but the introduction of lightweight, low-cost models encouraged science departments in high schools to use their NDEA grants-in-aid for this tool. Even today,
librarians trying to broaden and unify collections experience reluctance and
criticism or, worse yet, resistance on the part of some of these "pioneers" in
relinquishing supplementary materials housed in the department's office or in an
individual teacher's desk.

A major key to the success of transparencies is the ease and simplicity
involved in handling and projecting. Room lights may remain on, permitting
note-taking, since the projector itself throws tremendous light on the screen,
for it illuminates, without much enlargement, 7" x 9" acetate film rather than
16mm or 35mm. The teacher can face the class, observing student attention and
reaction, as materials are viewed and discussed. The pacing of the presentation
can be predetermined for slow as well as fast learners. The teacher may use an
entire set or a single transparency for a lesson. In other words, the teacher has
complete control of the medium. It is essentially a tool for classroom communication.

Transparencies are available from two sources. Specially prepared, curriculum-oriented visual aids are sold by commercial sources in the same manner as
filmstrips and 8mm single concept loops. Manufacturers have developed processes that allow for simulated motion and flow-action (polarization), making
them almost as life-like as movies but retaining the instant selectivity of individual transparencies. Book publishers frequently correlate transparencies with, or
geared to, a textbook series. Most sets come with teacher's guides containing
background information and, where applicable, further student activities. Full
value can be obtained from commercially produced transparencies when selection
is based upon the judgment of those who will use them. General criteria to be
applied include accuracy and up-to-dateness of subject matter, technical quality
(lettering must be large), contribution to learning, relevance to the curriculum,
vocabulary and interest level of the intended audience, and the cost justified.

Transparency masters, consisting of original art work on translucent or
opaque paper, with the choice dependent on the reproductive process (either
diazo or the quick heat-transfer method) are available from producers like
Ozalid, Keuffel and Esser, and 3M. These allow access to their use by more
than one teacher.

Another producer, Milliken Publishing Company in St. Louis, publishes
transparency-duplicating books. Each book, priced at $5.95, contains 40 per-
forated pages of transparencies and spirit duplicating masters. Included with

*Reprinted from *School Library Journal,* March 1970, published by R. R. Bowker (a Xerox
Company), copyright ᶜ1970, Xerox Corporation.

each set is a teacher's guide. The company describes each title as specifically designed to lend itself to a lecture and desk-work program. The catalog covers science, mathematics, social studies, map skills, map reading, and phonics.

Transparencies have proven themselves most conspicuously in the science disciplines, but are potentially far more versatile in any subject, depending on the teacher's ingenuity. In social studies, for example, the teacher uses his ideas to bring today's news into the classroom by reproducing editorial cartoons or newspaper headlines for lead-ins.

The arguments for commercial vs. locally produced transparencies depend on the kind of material being used. Materials with a great deal of detail, or many overlays, obviously cannot be prepared locally with anywhere near the professional quality of the commercial productions. Similarly, the color-lift process confines the user to paper with clay content and also involves destroying the original from which the transparency is made. Thus a transparency with original color, or with a high degree of photographic detail, is far superior in the commercial versions to the "home-made" products. The most obvious advantage of commercially produced transparencies is in showing movement or a process through polarization of light. Technamation, a fairly expensive process, lets the user create the illusion of motion himself. Milton Bradley has recently come out with a transparency series itself showing polarization. In both cases, an attachment, available from the projector manufacturers, is needed for the overhead projector to show polarization of light.

The lack of uniformity in packaging transparencies was not a very great problem when they were used just in the classroom, but today it creates severe problems for the librarian trying to store several sets together. Some manufacturers mount transparencies; others don't. Sizes are not all standard at 8½" x 11". And packaging varies—from Technifax' VisuBook to Milliken's excellent and inexpensive series, whose transparencies are packaged in a book but have perforations in the margins so that they can be removed. Jack Coffey and other companies provide vertical files for transparencies, but removing them from their original packaging often involves removing the teacher's guide—which is sometimes useful—and putting it in a separate area, with the appropriate references on a catalog card.

LOCALLY PRODUCED TRANSPARENCIES

Transparencies produced by teachers, students, and media specialists use one of the following methods: *handmade, diazo, heat-transfer,* or *color-lift.* Teachers like these products because they may choose the subject matter most suitable to their students' needs, which only they are aware of. Often, teacher-produced visuals are used in combination with commercially prepared ones.

Handmade. Materials needed for handmade transparencies include grease pencils in various colors, felt-tipped markers, artist's brushes and pens, technical pens, colored inks, india ink, dry-transfer letters and symbols, color-adhesive transparent tape, and any clear plastic or acetate sheet. Reprocessed X-ray film is available from dealers at five cents a sheet.

Diazo. These transparencies require specialized equipment and materials. Presses and supplies are distributed by Keuffel and Esser, Ozalid, Bruning, and

Viewlex. This somewhat sophisticated technique permits high-quality color tone on heavyweight plastic foil or sequences of transparencies called overlays. Diazo foil contains a base impregnated with a special chemical coating and comes in many colors. When pushed through the press with the master (image on either transparent or translucent material) on top, and the foil underneath, exposure to ultraviolet light, followed by exposure to the foil alone of ammonia vapors, produces a technically superior transparency.

Heat-transfer. The heat-transfer method copies any black-line original produced with a No. 2 pencil, carbon-base ink or type, on either opaque or translucent material. It also creates transparencies from printed pages. By placing the sheet of special transparency film, obtainable from many sources, over the original, setting the copy machine's exposure dial to the recommended speed, then inserting the film and original into the carrier slot, the transparency is ready for projection in a few seconds. Satisfactory results are obtainable by using 3M Company's Thermo-fax Secretary copy machine or their model 107 Book Copier.

If duplicated hand-out material is desired to accompany the transparency, ditto masters may be developed on the Thermo-fax Secretary.

Color-lift. Color-lift transparencies are developed from magazine pictures printed on coated paper to a sheet of transparent foil by first laminating the page by the above method (using specially prepared acetate) and then soaking both in a hot, soapy solution for 15 to 20 minutes.

Then the two are carefully peeled apart, the inks from the picture are transferred to the foil. After drying, the transparency may be projected in the original color to the screen.

A dry-mount press may also be used in place of the copy machine; the process is slightly more complicated.

Transparencies, whether commercially or locally produced, are often framed or mounted. These lightweight cardboard frames, priced as low as seven cents each, permit rigidity, making them easier to store and control in a vertical file. The outside of the mount should be about 12" x 10". The aperture of the mount is usually 7" x 9" since the stage area of most overhead projectors is 10" x 10".

The mounts help keep the transparency clean and provide an excellent place for attaching a call number, and writing notes.

Transparencies are mounted on the back side of the frame on all four sides with silver mylar or Scotch Magic Transparent tapes. Mounting in this fashion insures that they will lie flat on the projector's stage.

Overlays, combining images that are developed by superimposing one piece of foil on another, give the instructor a chance to emphasize complex ideas in any kind of progression desired.

Since the exact positioning of overlays over the transparent original is significant, they should be coded with reference marks such as a circle and cross, hinged with tape one at a time on all four sides of the mount so they may be aligned in any combination.

TRANSPARENCIES IN THE LIBRARY

The successful use of transparencies by classroom teachers, small groups in the library, or by one youngster, is heavily dependent on the attitude and services of school librarians. He must include in his budget funds to buy equipment and supplies, participate and assist in curriculum development to stimulate the use of this medium in the educational program, and offer guidance in the individual use of the materials.

Cataloging nonbook materials greatly facilitates their use. Since cataloging of most nonbook materials requires variations according to the kind or type of medium, transparencies no exception, certain essential items of identification are required on the catalog card:

1.   Classification or call number determined according to the Dewey Decimal system followed below by first letter of the title.

2.   Title entry followed by a description of the type of medium; e.g., *The moon, sun, and stars* (Transparency).

3.   Imprint signifying producer's name and copyright date.

4.   Collation to describe whether the set is in color, the number of visuals including overlays, and if any additional materials are included—e.g., teacher's guide.

5.   A brief annotation.

6.   Tracings should give a cross-section of categories used in *Sears' List of Subject Headings*. The headings should be used for several purposes, but they will be located primarily by the subject entries at the request of users; a title or series could be removed from its present assigned position and receive a new subject heading.

7.   The shelflist card should reflect the usual information including the source, price, and date of acquisition. Accessioning of transparencies should be in the same sequence of numbers as books.

Circulation procedures for transparencies should differ little from those for other a/v aids—or periodicals. Pretitled transaction cards, available in trays on the charging desk, facilitate borrowing quickly and accurately.

Other considerations like the use of color-banded catalog and transaction cards; storing transparencies in manila envelopes or folders; permitting the pasting of book pockets with cards; indexing nonbook media in separate catalogs; identifying transparencies through copy numbers or accession numbers or a combination of Dewey and the above, while worthy of attention and research, are not of paramount importance at this time. Each point requires an exchange of information among librarians and careful study of successful techniques.

What is of vital concern to librarians is that the profession has an unequaled opportunity to upgrade the collection and enrich the curriculum by helping to select, produce, catalog, house, and disseminate materials that are seeking an identity. The production characteristic is somewhat unique to libraries in this new and revolutionary trend, but the role and function of the school librarian has been traditionally to combine his efforts with the classroom teacher's to produce meaningful and effective learning experiences. As a means to this end, transparencies should not be overlooked.

THE CARTRIDGE LOOP . . . 8mm MADE EASY*

By Louis Forsdale

The question of whether libraries should house many media or only printed materials is hardly a major issue any longer. When it comes down to developing media collections, however, libraries seem often to favor one medium over another, largely, it seems to me, because of factors like cost and availability. In the school libraries I know, for example, it is increasingly common to find collections of audio recordings. I am certain that the acceptance of this medium in libraries has been enhanced by the fact that recordings are inexpensive and easy to use; they are, in a word, "accessible."

The motion picture, on the other hand, while obviously of great educational and cultural significance today, is just as obviously a troublesome commodity for traditional school libraries to deal with, although, of course, many do. Films in 16mm are expensive, they occupy a lot of shelf space, and they must be projected on machines which are not easy to use. Even the so-called "automatic threading" 16mm projector is often too difficult for the unmotivated and untrained, or anxious person to operate. As a result, where films have been incorporated in libraries, they are normally shown at scheduled times, in darkened rooms, with trained operators in charge. We treat them in something of the manner of the rare Shakespeare Folio in the Folger Library, which can be seen by appointment, a responsible person sitting by one's side to turn the pages. The comparison points up a rather amusing situation. The Shakespeare folio deserves such treatment, the average film in our school libraries ideally should be given about the same attention and care which we give to encyclopedias, novels, or children's picture books. That is, anybody—first-grader on—should be able to go to a school library and view or study a film when he wants to, alone if he prefers, and as many times as he wants to. He should also be able to take it home to use it.

Is it idle to think of a motion picture being used in a school library by a first-grader? It is, if we think of the film technology which you and I grew up with. It is not at all impossible if we think of the 8mm film revolution currently under way.

The facts are these. There are 8mm motion picture projectors now on the market which are loaded by cartridge, not by the tortuous threading methods—in, over, around, under, and through gears and wheels—which we grew up with. In the new cartridge projectors, the film is encased permanently in plastic containers which protect the film from handling and dust. But more important, the cartridges are simply plugged into the projector, an action which can be accomplished after a few seconds of instruction by anyone. "Anyone" means a four-year-old, or a "nonmechanical" adult. The action requires less manual dexterity than putting a phonograph needle down on a record, and the risk of damage is also less. The cartridge-loading projector is the most important technical advance since the invention of the motion picture projector, at least from an educational point of view. For the first time in the history of the medium, it makes film truly accessible to anyone on demand.

*Reprinted from *School Library Journal*, May 1967, published by R. R. Bowker Company, copyright ᶜ1967, R. R. Bowker Company.

The 8mm cartridge loop is a length of 8mm film encased in a plastic cassette with the beginning attached permanently to the end (the term "loop" designates this fact), so that, if left running, the film will go around endlessly. The great advantages of the loop are that no rewinding is required, and that the film can be viewed repeatedly with ease.

A disadvantage, particularly from the librarian's point of view, is that, if the film has a beginning and an end (and some 8mm cartridge loops with which we have experimented at Teachers College do *not* have beginnings and ends), then the learner must be taught to run the film to its beginning, or a library staff member must check this before storing the film. Mechanical means may also be devised to stop loops automatically at the end, for example, by notching the film and adapting the projector to stop when the notch is "felt."

There are also available a number of "reel to reel" 8mm projectors (standard threading projectors) but these, at the moment, require the same threading skills which, in my opinion, have hampered the growth of the 16mm film medium and which seem to me not to represent the solution librarians require.

MATERIALS IN 8

There are hundreds of educational and theatrical films which may now be purchased in 8mm form. The largest body of material now available is 8mm instructional film in silent cartridge loops. Such 8mm silent instructional loops accompanied by explanatory printed material are available in the sciences, the arts, health and nursing, and social studies, to note just a few fields. Loops are being prepared by dozens of firms in the U.S., Europe, and Canada. It is important to note that a silent film knows no language barriers except the barriers of *film illiteracy*, and let's not get into *that* discussion here! The Technicolor Corporation, which manufactures projectors for silent cartridge-loop films, has available a reasonably comprehensive listing of 8mm silent loops made for use on their machines. For further information on this catalog and others, see the source list below.

There are also 8mm *sound* motion pictures currently available in cartridge form, particularly in the areas of languages, social studies, the sciences, and mathematics. (See the source list below.)

THE FILM CLASSIC

It is particularly interesting to note that a large number of "classical" American and foreign theatrical films, particularly silent ones, may be purchased in 8mm from a number of sources. Cursory investigation at the Project in Educational Communication at Teachers College indicates that some 300 such films are available in all from a number of distributors. A school librarian can now buy such films as Edwin Porter's *The Great Train Robbery*; D. W. Griffith's classics, *Intolerance, Birth of a Nation, Way Down East, Orphans of the Storm*, and others; dozens of Charlie Chaplin two-reelers; Chaplin's *Gold Rush*; films by Valentino, Douglas Fairbanks, Sr., Mary Pickford, Laurel and Hardy, W. C. Fields, to name but a few. Several sources of these classic films are noted below. They do not come in cartridges, but the relatively simple encartridging job can be accomplished at many motion picture laboratories around the country.

A point should be made about the classic theatrical film in the school library. Little defense need be made of the purchase of films which are instructional in intent. Likewise, little defense *should* be necessary for school library holdings of films of the great cinema heritage of this and other countries. In fact, of all of the major arts of the day, the film is the one which receives least systematic attention in our schools. This has resulted partly from the failure of educators properly to realize the cultural importance of film, and therefore the necessity of studying it in the same sense that we study printed literature, art, and music. But another reason for our dereliction in not making important theatrical films available to our students is the expense of both prints and projectors and the previously great difficulty of operating projectors. The day is probably not yet near when the motion picture will take its place beside the book as an equally important resource—both in quantity and quality—in the school libraries of this country. Still, the use of 8mm films in cartridges in school libraries is by no means merely a dream today. Several school libraries have begun to experiment with the technique. Let me report only on those which are best known to me, with full awareness that others could be described as well.

We have at Teachers College begun in a modest way to establish 8mm cartridge film collections in two libraries, not to mention our reading center. One collection is in the college's library, where we have a cartridge library of some 30 classic silent film titles. A student who wants to see, say, *Birth of a Nation*, merely checks out from the central desk the ten cartridges which contain the D. W. Griffith masterpiece and retires to a desk to study them alone, with perhaps a minute of instruction by the attending librarian in use of the rear-screen projector. This 8mm small screen viewer is not intended to replace the larger screen 16mm showings in classes. But in this young library of 8mm classics there is already a far greater collection of such films than is available to the average college student. The films in this library of "classics" are used mainly by graduate students at the college, but they are also available to elementary school students in the college's Agnes Russell Center, a school which serves the children of teachers and students of the college.

The second cartridge-8 library at Teachers College is in the Agnes Russell Center itself. The self-help film library in this elementary school contains a collection of 8mm silent loop films designed mainly to be instructional. The films used in the Agnes Russell Center library have come from two sources. Some were purchased from commercial suppliers of films in the areas of social studies, the sciences, art, and the like. Others were made locally either by members of the Project in Educational Communication at Teachers College or, in a few instances, by teachers and students at the school.

PROJECTORS FOR CARTRIDGES

The sound and silent cartridge loops on the market today each require a different kind of projector. Technicolor puts out the only silent cartridge loop projector available today. The original producer of the 8mm cartridge-loading sound projector is the Fairchild Camera and Instrument Corporation.

Both companies provide a variety of models for their respective types of projector. Technicolor machines come in a wide variety. There are small machines which can be used by an individual, and which, in a well-darkened room, will project an image useful for a class. These small, silent projectors cost about $100, depending upon a number of factors, such as the kind of lens, and the presence of a stop-frame button which will "freeze" the picture when it is depressed.

By contrast with projectors which "throw" the image from the rear of the room onto a screen in front of the room, there are the more expensive rear-screen projectors, self-contained units which are placed in front of the room. When the cartridge is plugged in, the image appears on a translucent screen, looking something like a television image. Rear-screen projectors have certain advantages over the "front throw" models: they can be used in lighted rooms, with the instructor facing the class. The rear-screen models produced by Technicolor cost about $200 and up, depending on whether they have a stop-frame button.

Fairchild, producer of the projector for cartridge-loading *sound* film, has as its basic model the Mark IV, a rear-screen instrument. It is designed for small audiences or individual viewing and costs something under $500. Fairchild also has a front-throw model sound projector, which is suitable for class use and requires a darkened room.

Recently, Technicolor, M.P.O. Videotronics, and Jay Ark (a New York based form) have come out with 8mm cartridge-loading sound projectors.

No 8mm cartridge projector exists today which will accommodate both silent and sound cartridges—a fact that makes it important to determine the instructional purpose of the film purchase before deciding what equipment to buy. Sound and silent cartridge loops differ in length, too: silent cartridges accommodate a maximum of four minutes of 8mm film (although, of course, a shorter amount may also be held in the cartridge) and emphasizes teaching the single concept. The sound cartridges hold a maximum of about 20 minutes of film.

I have not tried in this brief article to examine fully the potential of 8mm film in education, or even in school libraries. I should emphasize, however, that we are undoubtedly in a major transitional period in the storage, retrieval, and use of the moving image in education. To date, the moving image, as compared with print, has barely played a role in education. Tomorrow it will play a far greater role, gravitating to a more central position. It will not replace print, of course, but it will supplement that medium in ways we have only been able to dream about before.

I would be remiss if I did not say quite pointedly that what I have talked about here is in an early stage of development. It is far beyond the dream stage, yet it has not "swept through" any school system that I know of. And it is probably better that way because with so much to be learned, the flexibility of the medium encourages the experimental work that librarians and other educators are beginning now. Among the problems facing the librarian are the very important and difficult housekeeping questions of how to deal with what will be, in the long run, thousands upon thousands of film titles in this new form, and how to relate them intelligently with corollary materials in other forms.

SOURCES OF INFORMATION

If you would like to get abreast of the growing 8mm field, may I recommend that you do these things in addition to reading the audiovisual and photographic journals:

Ask to be put on the mailing list to receive the occasionally published newsletter called 8: *Newsletter of 8mm Film in Education*, by writing to its editor, Louis Forsdale, Box 8, Teachers College, 525 West 120th Street, New York, N.Y. 10027. There is no subscription charge.

The Project in Educational Communication of the Horace Mann-Lincoln Institute of School Experimentation at Teachers College has, under a U.S. Office of Education contract, completed a 30-minute color documentary film titled *8mm Film: Its Emerging Uses in Education*. It is available to educational institutions for five-day preview if receiver pays postage, or for sale at $85.91 from Du-Art Film Laboratories, U.S. Government Film Services, 245 W. 55th Street, New York, N.Y. 10019.

Technicolor has a directory of cartridge-loading 8mm silent educational films as well as descriptions and prices of 8mm silent cartridge-loading equipment. Write to Mr. Robert Kreiman, Technicolor Corporation, Commercial and Educational Division, 1985 Placentia Avenue, Costa Mesa, Calif. 92627.

Fairchild has information about 8mm cartridge-loading sound projectors and sound films for use with them. Contact Mr. Nat Myers, Fairchild Camera and Instrument Corporation, Industrial Products Division, 221 Fairchild Avenue, Plainview, N.Y. 11803. Please state the level of education and the subjects in which you are interested.

No single, noncommercial catalog of all available 8mm films exists as yet. However, Emily Jones, administrative director of the Educational Film Library Association, advises that an 8mm film directory is now under active consideration.

Five representative firms which sell 8mm prints of film "classics" are noted below. All have catalogs available.

Blackhawk Films, 29 Eastin-Phelan Building, Davenport, Iowa 52808
Entertainment Films Company, 850 Seventh Ave., New York, N.Y. 10019
John Griggs' Moviedrome, 139 Maple St., Englewood, N.J. 07631
Movie Classics, P.O. Box 1463, Philadelphia, Pa. 19105
United Artists 8mm Films, 555 Madison Ave., New York, N.Y. 10022

LOCAL PRODUCTION WITH 35mm PHOTOGRAPHY*

By Otis McBride

There is a clear call for local production of materials to supplement what is available commercially. Local production may involve anything from a flat picture to a sound film. One of the simplest types, and yet most satisfying in result, is the process of 35mm photography. You may want one slide, several dozen slides forming sets, or a film strip from the camera.

Now hang on while we go into one or two technical aspects. Photography in the time of Matthew Brady, who took Civil War pictures that were surprisingly good, was not for those who gave up easily. It was a rugged and complicated business with a heavy percentage of trial and error. In contrast to all the heavy equipment that had to be lugged around, the *slow* emulsion, the necessity for immediate processing after the picture was taken, the chance for spoilage or for overdevelopment with crude equipment, the photographer of today "has a breeze." Nearly everything is done for you:

The camera. Small, light, easy to carry. Inexpensive (about $35 and up), unless you want to get into the mad whirl of the camera bugs.

The film. Choice of black and white or color. Results beautiful, unbelievable in both cases.

The rangefinder. Convenient but not essential. This device tells you how far you are from the subject, so your pictures will be in needle-sharp focus.

The exposure meter. Essential. This uses the magic of the photo-electric cell (referred to for years as the electric eye) to analyze the amount of light and indicate to you exactly how to set the camera.

The viewfinder. Essential. This is as necessary as sights on a rifle. In the viewfinder the picture appears exactly as it will show if photographed. In a regular camera, this is at the top or on one side. In the more convenient "single lens reflex," you look through the lens at the subject. No matter if it is only an inch away, you will have it centered in the picture.

Focus. Only the cheapest cameras have fixed focus. Don't get one of those. Nobody likes a picture out of focus, blurry, indistinct. By turning the lens, on practically all cameras from about $35 up, you can have a very sharp picture. You want that.

The shutter. Only a very cheap camera will lack a controlled shutter. Obviously if your camera is set to take a picture in bright sunshine, it will be wrong for a cloudy day. So part of your pictures will be bad, under- or over-exposed—or you will sit around and wait for just the right kind of day. Not much fun! You should be able to take a picture at a tenth of a second, a fifteenth, a thirtieth, a fiftieth, etc.

Stops. The "iris" diaphragm. An adequate camera will have a movable or controllable iris diaphragm—called that because it resembles the iris diaphragm in our own eyes. If you look into a mirror in a semi-dark room and turn on the light, the pupil will rapidly become smaller. That is the iris diaphragm working. In an adequate (not expensive) camera, the diaphragm works the same way. The

---

*Reprinted by permission from *School Libraries*, 20:25-27, Winter 1972.

settings are called stops. So we "stop" down or change the setting to f.2, f.3.5, f.4.5, f.5.6, f.8, f.11, f.16. Most 35mm cameras go down no farther than f.16, at which stop the lens has an opening behind it about the size of the head of a match. There is another good result: the iris diaphragm not only controls the amount of light but, at f.16, makes all the light go through the center or fat part of the lens. Refraction is not so great, the rays are bent less, and things are in focus from nearer the camera to much farther away. This characteristic is called "depth of field." I usually stop down as much as the amount of light will allow me to—and have great depth of field.

So, these are some of the main things about the camera. I trust it did not sound too complicated. Here is one more idea, very important to you if you put your camera to work at school.

The standard, regular 35mm camera uses film that has a width of 35 millimeters, or 35/1000's of a meter. On that film the camera, when the shutter is opened, will put a picture that is about 1" x 1½". The cardboard mount of your slide is 2" x 2"; but, count on it, the picture itself will be 1" x 1½". Now that size is fine for slides. You may want to prepare many slides and slide sets. And they will all be 2" x 2" slides (cardboard mount) with a picture area 1" x 1½".

What if some fine day you want to make a filmstrip? This may come as a surprise, but go measure the picture size of a commercial filmstrip. You will find it is 1" x ¾". It is only half as big as the picture area of a slide. Your roll of film has 36 exposures. The same length of filmstrip will have 72 exposures.

So how do we make a filmstrip with "single frame" pictures, size 1" x ¾"? Technically and actually, we can't. But we can fake it, very handily, to look as if we took single frame pictures. Suppose we prepare mounts or flats for a slide set on Chaucer's "Canterbury Tales." Let us pick a convenient size for our mounts, in proportion of 2:3. A convenient size, allowing space for captions, might be 8" x 12". We prepare forty mounts that size, with appropriate captions; and we could make forty slides. But we want a filmstrip. Put several of the pictures (flats, mounts) down, with about one inch between mounts. Then photograph two mounts at a time. To the camera, that makes up one picture; to you it will appear to be two, single frame pictures.

Caution: Stand over the pictures so as to take vertical shots, in relation to the whole row of mounts. And be sure the film, when you turn to the next shot, moves opposite to the way the mounts go. If the first mount is placed so you can read it as you face east, the second mount under it, etc., then be sure that the film, when you roll it for the next picture, moves west. If you don't care much for east and west, use opposite ends of the yard or the sidewalk.

What about light for all this? If you have had considerable experience, take care of lighting any way you choose. I've had some experience, but I still prefer the sun. If you put your work on the garage driveway, sidewalk, or shuffleboard court, you can use your light meter in the usual way—and lighting from the sun will do the job, without changing the color, getting reds too red, yellows a little sick, etc. The best time of day is from about 9:30 a.m. to 4 p.m. The sun is bright and at an angle so that when you shoot straight down your shadow will not fall on the material being photographed. When there isn't any sunshine, wait awhile. It will be worth it.

Working with 35mm photography is uncomplicated. After a few trials you will find it fast and easy. The guesswork has been taken out. Another important fact is that 35mm photography is comparatively inexpensive. You can produce a 72-frame filmstrip or a 36-exposure slide set for very little more than the cost of the film. And it will be yours—exactly the way you want it.

Bear in mind that it doesn't really matter who does the actual "shooting." Your worry is to set up exactly what you want: flat pictures in a series, live action, mounted material, etc. If you don't care for photography, you can easily find a neighbor, colleague, or student who is a "camera bug" and who will enjoy helping you out.

You will enjoy materials you have produced for yourself, in "living color," exactly as you want them. Reach up and get the "do it yourself" kit.

HOLOGRAPHY: A NEW DIMENSION FOR MEDIA*

By John Barson and Gerry B. Mendelson

The practical outcomes of research in laser beam technology are rapidly becoming evident with the advent of a radical new way to photograph and project a visual image—holography. Only recently a laboratory curiosity and research tool, laser technology improvements have advanced this revolutionary projection technique to the point where media specialists may seriously consider adding it to the pool of visual presentation devices used for classroom instruction.

The holograph was first developed as a laboratory technique or system for reducing the spherical aberration in high-magnification electron microscopes. However, through the work of a number of imaginative experiments, holography is now demonstrating a potential for creating spectacular aesthetic effects and projecting images in a way never before possible.

The hologram is in essence a picture in depth, a true three-dimensional representation of a given object, made by exposing a special photographic film plate to laser light that has been reflected from the real object. When this negative or slide is projected by the same laser beam that created it, it presents an image possessing almost all the physical qualities of the object and, perhaps most important, accurate perspective views of sides, top, and bottom.

In more specific terms, when a simple teacup is photographed using the holographic technique and then projected, the observer can actually view several sides of the cup using the single image, i.e., the same slide. In addition to this astonishing feat, he is also able to peer over the rim of the cup in the same projected image and examine some of its interior.

The word "hologram" comes from the Greek "holos" which means whole or complete, the entire record. For study purposes the holographic image is the next best thing to having the actual object present. Its ability to reproduce objects in 3D without the aid of any optical aids for the viewer makes holography a leading contender for creating a field of 3D photography.

While there is no attempt to discuss the physics of this remarkable medium here, it is worthwhile to speculate on the possible aplications of laser holography in the future to the media field and classroom education. One of the immediate applications that comes to mind is a possible solution to the limitation faced by schools in attempting to obtain and store the myriad of three-dimensional objects needed by imaginative teachers. Media specialists have dismissed the possibility of increasing the collection of models and other 3D materials because of the severe storage problems that now exist. Holography permits an approach to this problem by using some of the advantages inherent in the use of any of the newer media, namely, the simulation of the real world for learning purposes. For example, photographs, projected slides, and motion picture films become teaching aids when the real phenomena to be studied are too large, fragile, expensive, or hazardous to bring to the room, or inaccessible for learners to visit on a field trip. The hologram makes accessible to teacher and learner the whole universe of three-dimensional objects in a manner that permits study aspects never before thought possible with projected images. Equally important is the fact that the

*Reprinted by permission from *A V Instruction,* 14:40-42, October 1969.

holographic slide does not take much more room than the ordinary 35mm slide now widely used for reproducing two-dimensional images.

Various educational specialists might easily conjure the teaching possibilities holography holds for various subject areas. In the sciences the three-dimensional aspects of atomic structures may be better described and studied through this unique method of photographic projection. Most teachers of physics, chemistry, geology, astronomy, and other sciences lean heavily on visualization. Now pictorial presentation with almost complete dimension is available. In mathematics the relationship of the geometric figures such as planes and spheres might be made more concrete and explicit using the depth and space dimensions of holograms. Biology offers almost endless opportunities where the availability of non-deteriorating specimens in full perspective dimension would enhance teaching and individualized study.

The social sciences too employ physical models for describing concepts. The complexities of physical geography may become a little less complex and certainly less abstract through the use of visuals that permit unique spatial observations. The arts may especially benefit from the unique possibilities holography offers for studying sculpture, architecture, and other design forms. In short, wherever the use of three-dimensional representations of reality are needed, holography can eventually reproduce these images with fidelity.

The field of holography, and in particular laser holography, in some sense is still in its infancy. Yet present technical knowledge has reached a point where holography should no longer remain merely a nebulous area of conjecture. It is a reality and one that should be taken into account in the planning of innovative teaching developments by media people and other educators.

Even in its present technology the costs involved are reasonable. The basic components of a simple laser holography system can be set up and operational for an expenditure of less than $500. While this type and quality of equipment may not be entirely versatile, it could allow the purchaser to begin innovation of holography in teaching situations.

As has been the case with most evolving media projection devices, the software of holographic slides themselves are the scarce item. To this point in time holographed subjects consist mainly of materials under scientific study and some demonstration items as well. Selection of appropriate subjects for development of holographic slide series will require the attention of commercial media producers and educators. Because of the strict photographic demands involved in the holographic technique, it is unlikely that locally produced materials will be immediately feasible, but new engineering approaches may make even this possible.

The bibliography following this article may prove of value to those interested in further information on holography and its technical dimension. To date little has been written stressing educational implications.

The responsibility for employing holography to provide a literal and figurative new dimension to education belongs to the media specialist and educator. Hopefully, this discussion provides a beginning.

BIBLIOGRAPHY

1.   G. B. Brandt. *Hologram-moire interferometry for Transparent Objects,* Applied Optics Vol. 6, pp. 1535-40, 1967.

2.   R. E. Brooks. *Low Angle Holographic Interferometry Using Tri-X Pan Film,* Applied Optics Vol. 6, pp. 1418-19, 1967.

3.   R. E. Brooks. *New Dimension for Interferometry,* Electronics Vol. 40, pp. 88-93, May 1967.

4.   R. L. Carpenter and K. I. Clifford. *Simple Inexpensive Hologram Viewer,* Journal of the Optical Society of America Vol. 57, p. 276, 1967.

5.   R. J. Collier and K. S. Pennington. *Multicolor Imaging from Holograms Formes on Two-Dimensional Media,* Applied Optics Vol. 6, pp. 1091-95, 1967.

6.   R. J. Collier. *Up-to-Date Look at Holography,* Bell System Technical Journal, pp. 102-109, April 1967.

7.   *Holograms Produced in Ordinary Light,* Aviation World, pp. 86-87, January 1967.

8.   L. T. Long and J. A. Parks. *Inexpensive Holography,* American Journal of Physics Vol. 35, pp. 773-74, 1967.

9.   C. W. Stroke. *Hand-Held Holography,* Journal of the Optical Society of America Vol. 57, p. 110, 1967.

LIBRARY ORIENTATION IN A NEW MODE*

By Edward Peterman and Jim Holsclaw

"What impresses me is that somebody cared enough to try to help us." This opinion was voiced by one student participant in a project devised to help students find their way around a college library. The location is the Marshburn Memorial Library at Azusa Pacific College. The experiment was to find out how students would respond to a library orientation in a modern mode: No lectures, no examinations, no drag, just one and a half to three hours of time. And participation could be when the student had the time to spend even in 20 or 40 minute segments.

The inspiration for this program was the audio-tutorial method of learning: one person teaching one person by means of a programed tape. Four programs were planned. The first was an elementary introduction to the card catalog and its use. The second helped the student use the *Reader's Guide to Periodical Literature*. The third was an introduction to the reference area of the library. The fourth took each student to the *Education Index* and from that to the use of microfilm. A final program was a review which would begin at the card catalog and go through the programs rapidly. Each lesson was calculated to be progressively more difficult.

After initial planning, the programs were taped on cassette cartridges. The basic idea was that since the ideal method of teaching and learning is often a one-to-one relationship, that was the tactic to be used. One librarian would take one student, and through the cassette tape and a recorder (which the student carried around the library with him) would explain how to use the library. One important feature of the program was the behavioral response demanded by each tape. At the conclusion of each program the student, if he had completed all of the steps properly, would respond by bringing to the library's circulation desk some item— a magazine, a certain book, or a microfilm. It would be possible to tell if he had completed the tape properly by his response.

The next step was to solicit assistance. Chase Sawtell of the English department volunteered to use his classes in the experiment. He assigned 103 students, mostly freshmen, to participate in the experiment. Each student was given a one-week period to complete all five tapes. Next, a committee of the librarian, the director of Instructional Media, and the English professor met in conference with groups of 10 to 12 students and discussed the tapes and reactions to them. Interest ranged from aversion to deep appreciation. Two students did not like the tapes because they had already taken library orientation in junior high and high school. However, all said that if there had to be orientation, the audio-tutorial device was much better than a lecture, a guided tour, films, or manuals. Ninety-five percent believed that although the program on the card catalog was too elementary, it and some of the other tapes served as an information review and therefore had some value. Students were especially appreciative of the programs dealing with reference tools and microfilm.

Fifty students also completed an opinion questionnaire which was used to evaluate each program and the entire series.

*Reprinted by permission from *AV Instruction*, 16:46-47, February 1971.

The field-testing of the programs and subsequent interview conferences prompted the following conclusions:

- The technique is superior to any other method any student had used.

- The program is personal. It is one person talking to another.

- Students who dislike libraries and are afraid of them experience a noticeable attitude change toward libraries and library personnel.

- Students can do all of the programs at once or at their leisure. This time element is very important. Also, each tape can be completed in 20 to 40 minutes.

- The versatility of the cassette recorder is excellent for this type of operation. The cassette tapes are simple to use. The machines are easy to operate. Our recorder has versatility, quality sound and provides the adaptability for this specialized purpose. The tape may be rewound to any specific place if a student does not understand the directions, or if he wants to hear any portion of the program again. The recorders are portable. The headset or earplug individualizes the lesson. A change of pace may be programed into the lesson. At intervals, where pauses occur so the student can perform certain instructions, popular music is recorded onto the tape. Appreciation of this novelty was readily expressed by most students. The music seemed to break the instructional aspect and gave needed variety. The necessary performance of certain functions and the requirement of a behavioral response give support to the belief that the level of retention of information is high. Some students expressed the opinion that after experiencing the tapes they felt it would be difficult to forget the information. In addition, they were more inclined to use the library since they could appreciate its possibilities and potential, and therefore usage would reinforce what they had learned.

- It appears to be adaptable to most schools which have basic reference books, a nominal general collection, and the *Reader's Guide to Periodical Literature*. The system could easily be adapted to most high school and college situations; even many junior high schools could profit by it.

- It is possible to repeat the tapes at a future date if a student wishes. He may check out the particular program and recorder from the library and go through that program again.

- There are some disadvantages to note: If a student has taken library orientation previously, one or two of the tapes tend to be dull and repetitious. Unless special rechargeable batteries are used, the cost of replacements is expensive. The recorders should be of good quality and must have a rewind capacity. Most players have only a fast forward capacity and although they are less expensive to purchase, they will not adequately serve the purpose. The rewind capacity is necessary.

At Azusa Pacific this initial experiment has been so successful that the program will be required of all incoming students. Future planning calls for audio-tutorial bibliographic programs in specialized subject areas for majors in those

90

areas. Theoretically, each student will be required to take the particular bibliographic program developed for the area of his major field when he begins his junior year in college. He will then be exposed to a bibliographic background which will assist him in his study of subjects in his major field during the junior and senior years.

The object of this experiment is to assist the student in his understanding of and appreciation for the tools at his disposal in the college library. It is felt that this will aid him in his academic endeavors in college, and hopefully afterward. The initial experiment indicates that the use of the audio-tutorial method for library orientation may serve as an excellent method of training young people to use library facilities.

DEVELOPING TAPED NARRATIONS FOR SLIDE PRESENTATIONS*

By Joseph Gaunt

Many teachers have built a sizable file of slides taken during summer vacation trips or while visiting museums and historical sites, or know of such collections owned by students who have travelled or lived in foreign countries. In a few cases, the teachers or students have prepared slide presentations for limited groups, such as their own classes. Most will agree that classes for several years to come should have access to the slides, factual observations, and impressions now the property of students or teachers who will eventually be leaving the area. The project of developing a tape-recorded narration to accompany a slide presentation is not simple; yet the effort invested in polishing both the visual and the aural elements of the program will be repaid many times over by the enthusiasm of appreciative student and faculty viewers.

SLIDE SELECTION

Selection of slides to be included in the presentation and the order in which they will be revealed should precede any attempt to write narration. Teachers or students who have travelled extensively may own hundreds of slides, from which a selection of about eighty must be made. This number is suggested as a target quota for the finished presentation, because it allows the average slide to be projected for about thirty seconds during a program lasting approximately forty minutes.

After deciding upon a general theme around which the slide presentation is to be developed, every slide which may be useful should be projected on a full-size screen to be viewed by those involved in the culling process. This is the time to make notes on content and technical quality of slides, rejecting those which have little bearing upon the intended topic and those which are badly out of focus or poorly exposed.

Slides which have been composed vertically, rather than horizontally, should be subjected to criticism for that reason alone. Such pictures do not conform well to the dimensions of most projection screens, nor do they mix harmoniously in a presentation consisting of a majority of horizontal slides.

When the group of slides has been narrowed to 75 to 80, the most careful scrutiny is in order. The person in charge will want to use a viewing rack where at least 15 slides may be examined at one time. In this way, a smooth transition from one view to the next will be assured by painstaking arrangement and re-arrangement.

As a general rule, when showing several slides of the same building or object, the first one projected should be the widest shot which shows the entire view. Detail is best revealed by a progression of increasingly closer shots which will focus attention on a specific doorway, for example, or on one figure depicted in a painting. Each slide should be numbered in the proposed sequence, marking lightly with pencil.

*Reprinted by permission from *School Libraries*, 17:45-49, Winter 1968.

Teachers and students who have been involved in the process of slide selection will doubtless have several suggestions as the task of scriptwriting begins. If the fundamental outline shows a number of distinct segments emerging, consider incorporating several lettered slides in the presentation to simplify note taking, and to highlight the transition from one topic to the next.

Title slides, foreign names, and other detailed material can best be understood by visual portrayal as well as through the narration. Visually presenting words and names that are difficult to understand helps to prevent each student from recording a different spelling in his notes. The necessary printing may be hand-lettered on card stock by art students. The cards should then be tacked onto a bulletin board and photographed, with the resulting slides included in the presentation at the most effective intervals. Probably this is the least expensive and simplest method of including lettered slides.

Those striving for a more finished touch to the printed material should investigate the dry lettering products on the market. Simply by burnishing the pre-printed letters over a surface such as card stock, a very neat placard suitable for slide photography can be created. A little extra polish may be added by choosing a simple design from a discarded wallpaper sample book and burnishing the dry transfer letters onto the sample stock.

Have the slides which are included in the presentation duplicated by a camera shop to minimize the risk of loss or damage to the original slides, which will remain the property of the teacher or student who supplied them. As soon as the duplicates are delivered, pencil the sequence numbers on them to assist the projectionist in loading the slides and to form a basis for paragraph numbering as the narration is written.

SCRIPTWRITING

Now comes the task of writing a script which will heighten interest in the slides and complement each scene with information that is not apparent at first glance. The technique of writing for aural rather than visual understanding is most important. Remember that students will not have a second opportunity to listen to the facts included in the narration. Every concept of major importance should be clearly stated in brief, direct sentences, then restated shortly thereafter in similar language.

Experience in editing the first copies of scripts indicates that writers often overlook opportunities to use parallel structure for easier comprehension of co-ordinate ideas. Guard against the wandering pronoun or clause that lacks a clear reference in the main portion of the sentence. Think twice before writing forms of the verb "to be" and "to have"; the resourceful writer will frequently be able to choose a more colorful and specific verb to brighten the thought of the sentence. Occasional use of second-person pronouns ("you" form) assures the involvement of each member of the audience and provides relief from the monotony of third-person writing. Read your copy aloud as you finish each paragraph, to avoid combinations of sounds that are almost impossible to pronounce.

The best scripts are created by writers who are able to view the slides as they write. Each paragraph of the narration should be numbered to correspond with the slide it describes.

Experience indicates that most members of the audience will have adequate opportunity to examine a slide, correlating their observations with the narration they are hearing, yet will not become bored if the picture is projected for an average of 30 seconds. Some frames that require unusual concentration may remain on the screen as long as 45 seconds or even a full minute, while titles may be seen for only five or ten seconds.

How can the writer accurately judge the length of paragraphs of narration so that they average thirty seconds? If you read each paragraph aloud as you write it, you will get a true measurement of spoken length which cannot be obtained by darting the eyes swiftly over a page, and you will avoid grammatical constructions that are difficult to say.

TECHNIQUES OF RECORDING

At this point, the search for a capable announcer may begin. A resource center for schools located in medium-size and smaller towns is the local radio station. Not only will one of the announcers perhaps consider narrating the script, he may also have access to professional-quality recording equipment which allows the blending of voice with music and sound effects in a manner difficult to attain when using home devices and techniques.

Schools located in cities and suburbs would be well advised not to approach large radio stations seeking assistance. Their employees are generally busier and more carefully scheduled. Moreover, union regulations may prevent their announcers and engineers from working on your project, much as they might like to help.

If it is not possible to obtain the services of a professional announcer or other adult who reads well, or if the preparation of this program is to be handled strictly by students, auditions may be scheduled through the speech or drama club to screen pupils interested in recording the narration. Whenever it can be arranged, the audition copy should be extracted from the rough draft of the script itself and should include paragraphs containing some of the more difficult names and subtler shades of oral interpretation.

Revision of the first draft of the script should not be attempted until after the narrator has been chosen. If the announcer is a competent judge of grammar and the techniques of clear statement, he should be allowed to participate in revision of the script, suggesting changes which will adopt the narration to his manner of delivery. All changes desired by the announcer must be made in consultation with the writer of the script to ensure that the intended meaning or emphasis is not distorted.

Like the use of lettered slides, the addition of music and sound effects may be considered non-essential to a basic program but will surely impart lustre to the finished presentation. Usually the music chosen should be incidental to the narration. Music should seldom be heard at full volume for a period longer than ten seconds. Its greatest value will be found in setting a mood for the narration, never in calling attention to itself. For this reason, neutral compositions of a rather obscure nature should be chosen in preference to well known tunes, except when the popular melody has a distinct connection with the scene portrayed in the accompanying slide.

94

The same rule of moderation applies to sound effects. Just a few seconds at full volume, followed by a few more seconds in the background, is adequate exposure for most sound effects.

In addition to music and sound effects, another touch which may help to spell the difference between a merely acceptable recording and a truly polished program is the addition of a tone to cue a change of slides. Schools are gradually becoming equipped with projectors which automatically change slides at the command of a tone which is recorded at the same time as the taped narration. Some audiovisual specialists who find audible tones distracting recommend the purchase of sub-audible cueing sensors.

The tone cueing of a change of slides immediately follows the last sentence of each paragraph; then the announcer should pause before resuming the narration. This technique serves three purposes: it allows reaction time for the projectionist to change slides after hearing the tone, it permits students to view each new slide before the narration continues, and it creates an opportunity for easier editing of the tape recording.

When planning the taping session, the question of best recording speed will arise. Recommended is the use of 7½ inches per second, sometimes designated by the letter "F" or the word "Fast" on home tape recorders. Although twice as much tape stock is required to record at this speed as when using the slower setting, the quality of music will be enhanced and editing will be simplified if this suggestion is followed. Because the standard 1,200-foot reel of audio tape will accommodate only 30 minutes of recorded material at the 7½-inch speed, you may wish to purchase an "extended play" reel containing 1,800 feet of tape, preferably with a mylar backing if the presentation is to be given many times. Use of extra-length tape will allow recording at the faster speed without the necessity of changing reels halfway through the program.

Chances are good that all the participants will not be completely satisfied when they hear the playback of the first recording. You may decide to erase the tape and record the narration a second time, or perhaps you will consider editing the tape. This is accomplished by cutting out unsatisfactory portions with a scissors and rejoining the ends of the severed tape with splicing tape made especially for this purpose. Instructions for splicing are usually printed on containers of splicing tape.

EDITING THE PRESENTATION

Most persons will not wish to attempt a job of editing in such minute detail as would be necessary to remove minor slips of the tongue or momentary unintentional pauses in the program. If it is found that the narration has exceeded the time limit imposed by the school bell schedule, the most satisfactory remedy is to delete material at the rate of one full slide and paragraph of narration at a time.

Only the pauses between paragraphs should be considered suitable places for the amateur to attempt a splice. Cutting out a sentence or a few words within a longer passage usually requires professional equipment and some experience before satisfactory results may be expected. If a musical background has been used to join the unwanted paragraph to those preceding and following, the splice will probably cause an objectionable interruption in the flow of music.

Should it be absolutely necessary to eliminate such a paragraph, plan to record the entire passage from the beginning of the music until its conclusion and replace that section on the master tape.

The degree of success and professional polish surrounding the finished slide-tape narration will reflect the care exercised at each stage of production.

SIMPLE CASSETTE SYSTEM HELPS TEACH OPTOMETRY*

By Rollins Brook

In recent years many exotic audio systems for the library have been written up. Some are attendant operated, some are semiautomatic selectable channel, and the most expensive have been student selected dial access. Almost all these systems have three major characteristics in common: the student does not touch the tape, the systems are costly, and the programs are prepared especially for the teaching system.

At Southern College of Optometry, we have changed all these common points and have developed a workable, not very costly, system.

We began with two goals: to record every lecture in every class for the entire year on individual cassettes and store them in the library for student use and, secondly, to do so within a very limited budget. The task was accomplished at a total cost of less than $5,000 for 20 cassette machines and 2,500 C120 cassettes.

With typical classes of 125 or more students, we had already determined that the chalk boards in the lecture halls had to go. With the introduction of overhead projectors, it was a simple step to retrieve the acetates used daily and deposit them in the library for use with the cassette recordings. We now Xerox each transparency so the original acetate may be returned to the instructor. We also file paper blowups of slides used in each lecture.

The mechanics of the system are simple. Three recording machines are located in a drawer of the checkout desk in the library. They are readily available for the librarian to load and unload the cassettes each hour. The audio input for each machine is taken from a lecture hall PA system which is always left on. In fact, the system cannot be turned off by the instructors.

The cassette is started recording a few seconds before the hour, then rewound, removed and labeled at 50 minutes past the hour. The newly recorded cassette is filed in a cabinet arranged by course and date. The cabinet is in the open library so students may have direct access to the tapes. The recordings are held for one year before the cassettes are erased and reused.

So that the acetates may be easily identified, each instructor is provided with a supply of 8½ by 11 inch acetate with his name and course printed and with spaces for him to write in the date and sheet number. This printing is done on an offset press in the audiovisual department. The system precludes the use of acetate rolls, which are sometimes more convenient to use than single sheets. We use about 6,000 sheets of acetate per year at Southern College. When purchased in large quantities, the cost is not prohibitive—about $180 a year.

At first, opposition to the overhead projectors and the removal of the chalk boards was fairly strong from some of the faculty. No opposition developed toward the recording plan. After a few months, the opponents of the overhead projectors were won over and agreed they were better than a chalk board in large classrooms.

---

*Reprinted by permission from *A V Instruction*, 15:30-32, September 1970.

Surprising use has been made of the lecture recordings by the faculty. Some have listened to many hours of their own presentations for self-evaluation. Others have used the tapes to coordinate their teaching with other faculty members in overlapping subject areas.

Student use of the system has been much better than we had expected. We began two years ago with 10 machines, last year we added 10 more; this year we expect to add still more machines and a high-speed duplicator.

A library use survey of students was made after the recording system had been in use for several months. The lecture tapes were listed by the students as the single most important service of the library, out-ranking even reference works and reserve reading material.

When we began the system, there was some fear it might increase absenteeism. This has not happened. Certainly the system makes it possible to make up missed lectures, but the principal use of the tapes still seems to be review. The demand shortly before a major exam is often very great.

About 10 percent of the enrollment makes use of the recordings each day, with well over half the students making frequent use of the tapes. So popular has this program become among the students, that some who work at night and have very limited time to use the library, volunteered to install recording jacks in the classrooms so they might plug their own machines into the PA systems. This idea was approved and the students installed 12 jacks in each lecture hall. Frequent use is being made of this facility.

Because only one recording is made of each lecture, we expected to have problems with two or more students wanting the same tape. To our surprise, this has been only an occasional problem. When it does occur, it can almost always be resolved by using the built-in speaker instead of earphones in one of the library conference/study rooms. We do have some demand for tape copies for home use by students who were absent or lack a portable recorder. To answer these requests and to equip ourselves for the growing demand for tapes, we will be installing a high-speed duplicator soon.

Pilferage is an occasional problem. We have lost three machines from the study carrels in the past two years. From time to time tapes are taken. When tapes or Xeroxed visuals disappear, the librarian informs the affected class president. The missing material often reappears shortly afterward. The service is so important to so many students that they are able to police the system effectively themselves.

Once the initial investment in equipment and cassettes has been made, the cost of operating the program is negligible. There are occasional repairs to be made to machines, headphones, and broken tapes. All these are done by the audiovisual staff.

A large school with multisection classes and a variable program would probably have a hard time adopting our plan directly. At Southern College, however, the program has worked smoothly and has had more student support than we had expected when the program was begun.

MONSANTO INFORMATION CENTER'S AUDIO-VISUAL ORIENTATION PROGRAM*

By C. Warren Keller

In every organization, service-oriented groups are faced with problems of mass communication and orientation of those they serve. In the field of library science, these problems are compounded by the large number of services provided by a library with a small staff. As the number of people served increases, communication problems can reach a state of near crisis.

The Information Center at Monsanto's new Research Center found itself approaching just such a crisis. In 1961, scientists from Monsanto plants and laboratories all over the United States were relocated in new research facilities at the company's general offices site in St. Louis County. The Information Center was established as a central location for filing and indexing company technical reports as well as serving as a company-wide source of business and technical information published within and outside Monsanto. In its new location, the library directly served not only the technical and scientific personnel in the Research Center but also some 3,000 to 4,000 persons on the general offices site and at other Monsanto locations in the St. Louis area. In addition, it provided services requested by any other Monsanto library or organization throughout the world. Because the number of persons expected to visit and use the library was so large, the facilities were designed to provide ready "self-service" access to all library materials except for confidential company technical reports. This open access arrangement permitted the small staff to best serve users and to maintain the many library services.

The problem facing the library staff was, "How do we tell all these people what we have and how to find it?" Meetings were scheduled and conducted by the librarians every other week to discuss the library, its holdings, and services. These were only partially successful in that the discussion still left the potential user with no visual concept of the library and its physical facilities. A problem of semantics also existed in that the language used by librarians to describe a library and its services was not always fully understood by persons unfamiliar with library science terminology. Likewise, there was a distinct possibility that some material could be inadvertently omitted from any one presentation. It was obvious that an audio-visual presentation was needed.

CRITERIA FOR AND OBJECTIVES

Having decided upon an audio-visual approach, the next step was to determine what style of presentation would best fit the needs of the library. Some criteria used were: 1) the cost of preparation should be nominal; 2) the presentation should be easy to modify since it should be kept up to date when procedures in the library changed; and 3) where possible, the work should be done by Monsanto personnel.

The Engineering Services Section was asked to prepare such a film. Dis-

*Reprinted by permission from *Special Libraries*, 57:648-651, November 1966.

cussions with the librarians indicated that the most effective type of film to meet the criteria would be a sound-slide presentation. In this application, a projector would be integrally synchronized with a sound track to provide automatic slide changes at the proper time in the narration. Previously such a film had been prepared for use by the Safety Director in instructing new personnel, and photographic services in the Section were capable of handling the photographic and sound portions of a sound-slide presentation at a cost far below that of outside organizations.

In considering types of presentation for possible use, two often-used methods were discarded. They were film strips and movies. Film strips were considered difficult to modify and easily damaged in use. Movies were found to be impractical to revise and subject to an extremely high initial cost.

The overall purpose of Monsanto's programs of slide presentations was threefold: 1) to relieve personnel from routine orientation of new employees and give them more time to perform their other duties, being sure that new persons received all pertinent information on a subject; 2) to put this basic information in a form that would be easily understood by anyone desiring to use the services and facilities of the library; and 3) to establish the possibility of "open access" re-orientation when the user is most receptive, i.e., when he has a problem.

PREPARING THE SCRIPT

The first step in producing the film was preparing a script. Experience demonstrated that no pictures should be taken until a completed script was in hand. The outline of material presented in the group orientation meetings was used as a guideline to prepare the first draft. The introduction stated the purpose of the presentation. Then came a brief listing of the major subjects to be covered in the subsequent discussion, but no details were given at that time. Then details were presented in logical order. At the end of the film, the major subjects were reviewed to stress the most important points in the discussion.

After the script had been prepared along these lines, it was further divided into small sections—one section for each slide. At this point it was necessary to be highly critical of the material in the presentation. Each section could contain only *one* idea, and this idea had to be one that could be *exactly* illustrated by a slide. This is of utmost importance, as a slide being projected must be directly related to script material presented at that same time!

Every attempt was made to limit the amount of script material for each slide to no more than 15 or 20 seconds. After this time, with a single slide projected on the screen, the thoughts of the audience may begin to wander. Likewise, five seconds was considered to be a minimum for a slide to be retained. Within these limits, it was necessary to distill the information and present only specifics. This is precisely what was desired! Step-by-step instructional information had no place in an orientation film. It belonged to a separate "how to do it" film.

In dividing the script into sections, it was found most convenient to use a single 5 by 8 inch card for each slide. The script was typed at the bottom of the card. At the top, notations were made as to what picture or title was required to properly illustrate the text material. These cards were then arranged in proper order for a logical presentation.

PREPARING THE SLIDES

At this point, the script was ready for photography. The films were prepared on 35mm color slides. Photography was done "on location" in the library using all types of lighting from existing light to electronic flash. Experience in taking photographs for this purpose demonstrated the importance of moving in close to the subject and eliminating all extraneous material from the slide. Otherwise, the background of the picture would distract from the main subject.

In developing the techniques for preparing these films, one major problem was encountered. Not all ideas and thoughts could be properly and interestingly presented by a photograph of something or someone. It became necessary to utilize title slides to properly present succinctly a great deal of information. For example, in discussing a group of publications held by the library, a photograph of the documents meant nothing. A viewer would not remember the names, only how colorful the covers might have been. However, when a slide listed the names of publications and a viewer was given time to read the list, the slide not only held the viewer's attention but also transmitted information to him. One presentation in current use has a total of 68 slides. Only five of these are photographs; the other 63 are title slides. The presentation would have been impossible without using this technique, since photographs of forms and documents are unsatisfactory in programs of this nature—they are too difficult to read.

All the title slides for the presentations were prepared from black and white original drawings or typewritten material. In the process, white letters are superimposed on a colored background. Different colored backgrounds were used to delineate the outline or subdivisions within the discussion. The title slides were prepared using a Honeywell Repronar Slide Duplicator. Instructions for preparing the slides were found in the manual that accompanied the machine. Likewise, it was possible to employ a "split frame" technique in which two separate photographs were combined on a single slide. With these techniques, the complexity of the presentations could be expanded to maintain an integrated and cohesive show.

PREPARING THE SOUND TRACK

The first sound track recording for the presentation was then prepared. When the film was processed, the slides were sorted, and the best photograph selected for each portion of the presentation. They were then viewed along with the recorded script for analysis. At this point, the script and slides matched well in most cases. However, there were usually parts that would not fit together as they should. Here it was necessary to either modify the script to better describe the photograph, or take another photograph to better illustrate the descriptive material. This process continued until the best combination of slide and script was obtained.

The next step was to put the show into final form. The equipment used for Monsanto's presentations consisted of a Sony TC-211TS Tape Recorder and a Kodak Model 800 Carousel Projector. The tape recorder has a built-in synchronizer for use with almost any semi-automatic projector. This feature utilizes a synchronizer signal on a second channel of the tape to trigger the slide change.

101

Slides are retained on the screen for exactly the amount of time required. Another advantage of this system is that the tape may be completely erased and used again, or only a small portion may be corrected and the slide changing adjusted accordingly. This flexibility greatly reduces the labor involved in revising a film and making appropriate script changes.

MOUNTING AND VIEWING

The slides were mounted in aluminum-bound glass mounts to prevent "buckling" while in the projector. In this mount, every slide is in focus when it drops into the projector. One other treatment given to some slides was that of "masking." It is not always possible to exclude an extraneous area or objects from original photographs. In such cases, a mask was used which reduced the amount of the slide that was projected. Masks are available in many shapes and sizes to fit the subject of the slide.

Upon completion of the slide mounting, the presentation was ready for viewing. The system of Sony Recorder and Carousel Projector required only that the tape be placed on the recorder, the slide tray on the projector, and both units turned on. From this point until the end of the presentation, no further attention to the equipment was required.

RESPONSE AND COSTS

This type of sound-slide presentation has been of great use to the Monsanto Information Center. Orientation meetings are held for any number of persons, and a visual concept of the library and its services presented. The effectiveness of such presentations was graphically portrayed in one specific case. At considerable expense, Monsanto had embarked on a new method of indexing company technical reports. When the new index was issued, only 25 copies were requested. Most of these were in libraries throughout the company; a few went to personnel in the scientific laboratories. The overall response was quite disappointing. Though there were instructions with the index on its use, no one would take it upon himself to learn to use it. A 25-minute film was prepared on "How To Use the Monsanto Technical Reports Index." This film was exhibited to all interested personnel at the Research Center, general offices, Monsanto plants, plant and research libraries, and to any other interested groups within the company. The response to the show was gratifying in that requests for copies of the index rose from 25 the first year to almost 200 the next! This is just one example where films have more than returned their production costs.

Since each film is different, production costs have varied. In general, the overall cost has been in the range of $1,500 to $2,000 per film. All photographic and art work was done at the Monsanto Research Center. Costs would have increased considerably had we relied on outside studios for the photographic services.

The third goal of the films will soon be achieved when a special installation is completed in the Research Center. Copies of all Monsanto Research Center instructional films will be available on an "open access" basis for individual use in "re-indoctrination" on subjects of immediate interest. The system being installed uses the same Sony Recorder and Carousel Projector installed in a commercially produced unit sold under the name of Carousel Console. The console resembles a television set with the slides projected on the rear of a 21-inch screen. The unit is ideal for viewing by a group in a limited area, and it is not necessary to darken the room for projecting the slides. The overall user response will determine the value of this approach to personnel instruction.

Interest outside Monsanto in this type of slide-sound presentation has been widespread. The two library slide films were shown at the Midwinter Meeting and Annual Convention of Special Libraries Association, and many inquiries have been received from SLA members requesting loans of the films for exhibition at SLA Chapter meetings and management conferences. The demand was so great that Monsanto has donated a copy of each library film to the Special Libraries Association, which has assumed responsibility for scheduling and distributing them within the Association. "Monsanto's Information Center—Central Library" contains 74 slides, while "Monsanto's Information Center—Central Reports" contains 71 slides. Those interested in borrowing one or both presentations should write Association Headquarters, at 31 East 10th Street, New York 10003, giving three alternate presentation dates.

MICROFORM TECHNOLOGY

Microforms are frequently cited as a technology which will change library service patterns in the near future. The more common types are: roll microfilm in 16mm and 35mm format, microcards, and microfiche. Ultrafiche is a recent development and generally refers to a reduction ratio above 50x. The articles selected for this section provide a general overview of the field, present an analysis of user reactions to this technology, and explore some utilization practices in the field.

MICROFORMS, MICROFORM EQUIPMENT AND MICROFORM USE IN THE EDUCATIONAL ENVIRONMENT*

By Fritz Veit

The subject of microforms and microform equipment in the educational setting has many facets. In this paper I will first distinguish between the various kinds of microforms. In libraries microforms are chiefly used as carriers of micro-reproduced books, periodicals, documents, and similar materials, but, as will be noted, microforms may also contain lists of Library of Congress cards and related information and may serve as bibliographic search tools. I shall also note the criteria for evaluating microform equipment and review the large variety in both microforms and equipment needed for using the various forms. I shall then briefly mention what components are required to create a whole microform system, and next, indicate the importance of retrieval procedures. I shall stress the potential created by a close interrelationship between microforms and computers and note the reactions and comments of various microform user groups which were analyzed in several recent studies. I shall point to efforts toward standardization, and finally refer to Intrex, a computer-based project. While the discussion will refer to the impact of present copyright legislation upon microform publishing, I shall not discuss this form of publishing in detail. I shall also omit the topic of acquisitions of microforms and their bibliographic control.

MICROFORMS

Until recent years microforms have been used primarily for rarely needed items such as early periodical files which were usually no longer in print. In addition, libraries have maintained files of newspapers on microfilm because in their original form they were bulky, often turned brittle, and consumed much stack space. In nearly all instances these microreproductions were on 35mm roll film. Other film widths are 16mm, 70mm, and 105mm; the 16mm size is frequently used in industry, yet so far only infrequently in libraries, although an increase in 16mm film use may be expected. For instance, *Chemical Abstracts* and the journals issued by the American Chemical Society are on 16mm film.

*Reprinted by permission from *Library Trends*, 19:447-466, April 1971.

Several decades ago some librarians began to think that microforms should have a wider use and in particular that the use should not be limited only to items which are not in great demand. In his widely discussed book, *The Scholar and the Future of the Research Library*, Fremont Rider points out that academic libraries have been doubling their collections within sixteen-year spans.[1] To keep the expansion within manageable limits, Rider suggested the use of microcards. In appearance these cards would be similar to ordinary catalog cards and would have catalog information in front. The book or other library item would be microreproduced on the back side of the card and, if necessary, be continued on trailer cards. Microcards were used, but mainly by government agencies as media for recording research reports.

Microcards, on paper or other opaque material, appear in various sizes: 3 inches by 5 inches (the catalog card size), 4 inches by 6 inches, 5 inches by 8 inches, 6 inches by 9 inches, and others. The microcard image may be produced entirely by photographic process, or cards may be printed from plates made from negative microfilm. This latter procedure is used by the Readex Microprint firm. Readex Microprint cards (size 6 inches by 9 inches) are printed on only one side while most other microcards are printed on both sides. The Readex Microprint cards contain about 100 pages, while the smaller size microcards contain from one to ninety pages on one side. The generally favored reduction ratio is 1:18, the reduction ratio employed by Readex Microprint ranges from 12x to 20x.

While the microcards are sturdy and can withstand heavy use without being damaged, there are certain disadvantages connected with their use. Some kinds of microcards are more susceptible to message obliteration by scratches and erasures than microfiche. Reading machines require relatively powerful light sources. With film (fiche) one can obtain a sharper image and a higher reduction ratio than with micro-opaques, and since microfilm is now much more widely used than micro-opaques, manufacturers have devoted more attention to the development of film readers and printers than to readers for micro-opaques. Micro-opaques had been the favorite medium of the various United States government agencies for micro-reproducing reports until this form gave way to the film in sheet form.

Microfilm in sheet form was developed in France and in Germany before World War II. Intensive experimentation was also undertaken in Holland. It is interesting to learn that the word "card" was used both for microreproductions on film and for microreproductions on paper or other opaque material. The photographic expert of the British treasury, H. R. Verry, objected to this indiscriminate usage and urged that the French word "fiche" be employed for film in sheet form, and the word card for microreproductions on opaque material. Verry prevailed and after 1954 the literature distinguishes between microcard and microfiche. The Dutch founders of the "Microkaart Stichting" (Microcard Foundation) became largely involved in experiments with microfilm in sheet form. They found it therefore quite fitting that internationally their organization became known as the Microfiche Foundation.[2]

In the early 1960s the United States government agencies became convinced that microfiche is superior to the microcard as an information carrier. While in Europe 3 inch by 5 inch and 3½ inch by 4¾ inch are favorite fiche sizes, 4 inch

106

by 6 inch has been adopted as the standard size by the United States government for the reports issued by its various agencies. There was experimentation with other sizes. For instance, the National Aeronautics and Space Administration originally used the 5 inch by 8 inch size.

It should be noted that the same size fiche—4 inch by 6 inch, for instance—will contain various numbers of frames (images), depending on the manufacturers' preferences. For example, Bell and Howell microfiche provides for up to 72 images (6 rows of 12 images), and consequently can accommodate a document consisting of up to 72 pages. The same size COSATI (Committee on Scientific and Technical Information) microfiche provides for up to 60 images (5 rows of 12 images), and the COSATI trailer microfiche (intended for documents longer than 60 pages) provides for up to 72 frames (6 rows of 12 frames). The NMA (National Microfilm Association) microfiche may contain up to 98 frames (7 rows of 14 frames). Trailer microfiches are used when a document exceeds the number of pages that the main fiche can accommodate. Since microfiche unitizes information, it has become the favored medium for reproducing reports.

Microfiche may also appear in an aperture card. In standard form a single film frame is placed into a window-like opening of an IBM card. This frame can contain up to eight document pages. Aperture cards are mainly used for engineering drawings. It is easy to send drawings in this form and then to regenerate them at their destination.

Also used as information carriers are jackets made of very thin transparent material such as polyester, designed with chambers or pockets into which chips or strips of microfilm are placed. The microfilmed items can be unitized in the same fashion as if they were in a file folder. Transparent jackets are available in various sizes. They may be arranged in an alphabetic or other predetermined sequence or at random. The film in the jacket can be reproduced by contact methods without needing to be removed from the jacket. Microfilm jackets are especially useful when the information is subject to modification since the information in the jacket can be updated by adding or removing strips of film in the sleeves of the jacket.

At this point it may be noted that the several types of microforms have been described in various published sources. Especially helpful discussions regarding the characteristics of the several kinds of microforms may be found in the *Proceedings* of the National Microfilm Association.[3] Also releases by the microfilm producers often contain brief descriptions of their product. A few of these promotional publications, such as *The Microfilm Technology Primer on Scholarly Journals*[4] by Franklin D. Crawford, are broad in concept and stand out as clearly written general introductions to the field.

The documents—books, periodicals, reports, etc.—may be reproduced at varying reduction ratios of their original size: 1/14, 1/15, 1/18, 1/20, 1/25, 1/60, etc. The reduction ratio stipulated for government-sponsored (COSATI) microfiche is 18x. Up to this time the reduction ratio for materials used in libraries has generally, though not exclusively, been at 20 or below. While there is no generally accepted line of demarcation between regular and ultra-microminiaturization, ultra-microminiaturization generally means the reduction ratio exceeds 50x. However, some writers consider 60x as the lower limit, while still others consider reductions exceeding 40x as ultra-microminiaturization. If the miniaturization exceeds the stipulated reduction ratio–60x, 50x, or 40x–the form created is an ultra-microfiche (also called ultra-fiche). It is expected that normative agencies will ultimately establish the exact line of demarcation between regular and ultra-microfiche.

Ultra-microminiaturization would bring on one fiche not 60 to 100 images, but several hundred or even several thousand, depending on the reduction ratio. It is still necessary, as it was over a century ago, to produce ultra-microfiche in stages. Some of the problems of ultra-microminiaturization of library materials are discussed by the two firms which have embarked on such a venture: Library Resources, Inc., an Encyclopaedia Britannica Company,[5] and NCR.[6]

Library Resources, Inc., utilizes a 3 inch by 5 inch size fiche which has a capability of up to 1,000 pages. It employs a reduction ratio of 1:55 for book pages of approximately 5 inches by 7 inches and up to 1:90 for books with larger pages. The fiches are laminated on both sides for protection. As reading devices Library Resources, Inc., will have available an internal projection reader for use in the library and a portable lightweight reader, also called a lap reader. The portable lap reader has been designed to work at a fixed ratio of 75x, the desk top model at 90x.

A fundamental concern of Library Resources, Inc., has been a realization of the principle of bibliographic unity–to have one book or other bibliographic unit contained on one fiche, or, what may be necessary occasionally, a fiche followed by a trailer fiche. The fiche (or fiche and trailer fiche) could be placed in an envelope which has in front a reprint of the LC information pertinent to the fiche(s).

NCR uses a 4 inch by 6 inch fiche and a reduction ratio of about 1:150. One fiche can hold over 3,000 images, the equivalent of seven to ten volumes. NCR employs photo-chromic-micro-image recording. For protection, the NCR fiches are also laminated. NCR considers it an advantage that one fiche can hold the images of several volumes. For instance, one fiche may contain seven or eight volumes all dealing with one aspect of psychology. NCR uses the term ultra-fiche for its product while Library Resources, Inc., identifies its fiche as microbook fiche.

The pamphlets and descriptive folders issued by Library Resources, Inc., and NCR describe the selection policy used in assembling their respective ultra-microfiche collections. At this point it will merely be noted that these two firms differ not only in their technical approaches to microform production, but they also have very different bases for the selection of the materials to be microfilmed. The first library in the Library Resources microbook series will contain about 20,000 volumes, while the first group (consisting of five collections) of NCR will have a combined strength of about 3,500 volumes. Since at the time of this writing the exact composition of either collection is not known, it is not possible to attempt valid comparisons between the two.

When the uses to which the various microforms are put are examined, it is found that roll microfilm with or without cartridge is generally used for collections of items such as whole periodical files and series of books. Ultra-microfiche at the 1:150 reduction ratio also accommodates series since six to ten books may be placed on one fiche.

Bell and Howell, COSATI, and NMA microfiches are mainly intended for one to one relationships, one microfiche to one document, as are aperture cards with one engineering drawing on one card.

While a microfiche usually is large enough to contain the usual government research report, ordinary microfiche cannot accommodate the average library book of 300 to 400 pages. Arthur Teplitz therefore recommends a new size library fiche, a fiche with a reduction ratio of 1:50 or 1:60.[7] This fiche, which Teplitz calls the library fiche, would be either a 50x fiche which would contain about 390 pages (13 rows of 30 pages) or a 60x fiche which would contain about 475 pages (15 rows of 35 pages).

While the ultra-microfiche requires several stages for its preparation, the library fiche envisaged by Teplitz would be prepared in a single stage operation. He sees no difficulty in using present-day fiche equipment nor obstacles in manufacturing suitable readers and readerprinters. While ordinary COSATI or NMA fiche would be large enough to accommodate most periodical issues (average size 70 pages), he would nevertheless recommend the use of the library fiche for all library items in order that equipment for only one reduction ratio be needed.

One of the principal efforts of librarians has been to effect an increase in the use of microforms. A number of writers have long felt that only a change in the copyright law could bring about such an increase. According to the present law the copyright holder (usually, but not necessarily, the author or publisher) has the sole right over the copyrighted property. He retains this right also after graphic data have been converted into microform. Zurkowski, among others, feels that the person who converts printing or writing into a microform should be rewarded by being given copyright protection for the form he created, along with the owner of the original copyright.[8] Zurkowski further suggests that third or fourth persons who convert the information into still other microform formats should likewise obtain copyright protection for their respective formats. The original and the format copyrights need not be coterminus; the original could be for a longer period than the format copyrights. In another article the same author underlines how necessary it is to make it financially attractive for a publisher to convert graphic data into microforms, and he would therefore consider introducing a licensing system where those who use the microforms would pay a fee which would at least in part be turned over to the copyright holder or copyright holders.[9] Zurkowski further suggests that to forestall unauthorized copying it may be necessary to apply protective over-coating which would prevent contact duplication of the film sheet with ordinary equipment.

One of the strongest advocates of microform use in the library, Lawrence B. Heilprin, believes the aim of making the full range of the extant literature accessible to interested persons could be attained if copyright law were to be changed.[10] The currently prevailing form of making a book available is by circulating it through removal from the shelves. Instead of proceeding in this fashion, Heilprin urges that libraries maintain collections of materials in microform, leave them in their files and make copies of the units (books, articles) wanted. The library would no longer be a circulating (C) library but would become a distribution (D) library. A proposal by J. ver Hulst[11] would reduce the cost of acquiring microform collections by libraries and their dissemination to the user at the local library location. The system would be an integrated high/low density microform dissemination library. The library would receive ultra-microform printing masters for retention at anywhere from 60x to 200x reduction ratio. From these masters the library would reproduce low density dissemination microfiches at approximately a 20x reduction ratio. The dissemination microfiches would become part of the personal library of the user. The participating library would have a document indexing system, an integrated ultra-microform retrieval unit, and a microfiche printer.

In the library microforms are not only utilized as carriers of miniaturized books, periodicals, pamphlets and similar communication materials, but also for the listing of miniaturized catalog cards and related data. An example is the Micrographic Catalog Retrieval System (MCRS) of the Information Dynamics Corporation.[12] This system is designed for speedy searching and locating of cataloging data. The complete MCRS contains on microfiche the National Union Catalog from 1953 on, and the 1970 to present Union Catalog filmed in its entirety. Each title is listed under its LC card number; the titles are also noted in a main entry and title index. Printouts can be made with a reader-printer.

The Demco Educational Corporation furnishes the Microdata Cataloging System which is similar in nature and purpose.[13] It does not have as extensive a retrospective file as the MCRS. It differs also in scope of coverage for the current materials and the frequency in which cumulations appear. The fiche employed by Microdata is larger than that used for the MCRS. While Information Dynamics retains ownership of its MCRS service, Demco sells the Microdata system outright. Last but not least, there is a considerable price difference between the two, Demco's being the less expensive service.

To speed up library acquisitions, Bro-Dart, Inc., has devised a Direct Input Ordering System, "a computer microform interface."[14] On one 16mm roll of microfilm it lists all titles (in all editions) now in print of all (about 4,500) publishers as well as recent out-of-prints. The author and title files each number about 300,000 entries. This service is intended mainly as an aid in the acquisition of books through the Bro-Dart firm.

MICROFORM EQUIPMENT

The discussion concerning microforms has shown that there are many sizes and patterns. By the very nature of the microforms the communication carried by the form is reduced to such a degree that it cannot be read by the unaided eye. Readers are needed to make the message legible. The librarian is faced with the problem of selecting the reader which is proper for his collection (present and potential). He does not have a single set of performance standards against which he could measure the product. In the microforms and equipment section of the Library Technology Reports series, the ALA's Library Technology Project has been providing the kind of guidance librarians urgently need. In this section there are evaluative reports, each fully devoted to one individual piece of equipment, plus general articles. Until recently the reports in the microforms and equipment section were prepared by William R. Hawken Associates. The most recent reports were supplied by R. A. Morgan Company, Inc. The article entitled "Microform Readers for Libraries,"[15] like a similar earlier article,[16] should prove especially helpful in alerting the librarian to factors to be considered when acquiring microform equipment.

The Library Technology Project consultants selected readers which were designed to enlarge and project (to a size capable of being read) images in microfiche, micro-opaque cards, or 35 and 16mm reel or strip microfilm formats commonly found in libraries. The devices evaluated are manufactured and/or distributed on a nationwide basis in the United States.

The first part of the Morgan article is devoted to a discussion of the general factors considered in the selection of readers and readerprinters and to a description of the test procedures, tests, and their results. The second part of the article gives in tabular form an evaluation of individual microform readers and readerprinters. The Library Technology Project consultants as well as other experts stress the following considerations when equipment is selected:

When a reader is to be purchased, the librarian must first of all consider the kinds of microforms the library has or is likely to get. Does the reader need to accommodate only 35mm microfilm or also 16mm microfilm and microfiche? Some readers can accommodate several types of microforms, others can accommodate only one kind.

Another important consideration is the compatibility of the reduction ratio employed in the preparation of the micro-image with the magnification ratio of the reader. If the magnification ratio and the reduction ratio are identical, the image produced with the reader will be of the same size as the original. Ideally the screen should hold the full text. If a reader serves for instance to display a newspaper image, it should be 15½ inches wide, the original size of the average newspaper. For clarity of image the screen should be uniformly clear from edge to edge. The screen brightness likewise should be at a uniform level. Image rotation capability is necessary when maps and charts must be examined because they are often arranged in a different position from the text. Simplicity of operation is essential because often the user may not get expert help, as is ruggedness of construction because library equipment is exposed to hard wear.

This suggested list of criteria against which readers and reader-printers may be checked could of course be enlarged. For instance, it might be of significance to discover whether a microfilm reader features a multiple lens turret which at the "flick of a finger" offers a choice of one of several magnifications or has several different lenses which must be stored apart; or it might be of importance to know whether a microfilm printer can deliver dry positive prints from either positive or negative microfilm.

The promotional literature which is issued by practically all the manufacturers of equipment deserves special notice as an aid in evaluation. In this text there is occasion to refer to just a few of these publications. In practice it should often prove most rewarding to examine releases, folders, pamphlets and other publications which describe a manufacturer's product. Quite often the manufacturer's account is the most detailed one available and frequently it is illustrated.

Magazines (Cartridges)

In the use of microfilm it has long been considered a deficiency that film had to be threaded, sometimes awkwardly, and exposed to soiling and scratching.

Several manufacturers have developed containers variously called magazines (Kodak) or cartridges (3M, Bell and Howell). It is especially noteworthy that present reels (35mm or 16mm) can be converted to magazine format without much effort. Film in magazines such as the Eastman Kodak "Thread Easy" will thread itself through an "open-close" glass gate onto a take-up reel and will automatically rewind the film.[17]

DASA

The United States Office of Education, recognizing the need for a new, inexpensive, lightweight microfilm reader, awarded the development contract to the DASA Corporation.[18] The reader, DASA-PM R/50, weighs only 7½ pounds and the manufacturers say it can be held in the lap. Using the PM R/50 "is almost like reading a book." It has an 8½ inch by 11 inch viewing screen. It accepts 4 inch by 6 inch microfiche with interchangeable grid formats, including COSATI, DOD, and NMA. While it had been expected that the cost of the reader could be held below $50.00, the advertisement lists it at a unit price of $89.50, with quantity discounts beginning at fifty units.

ASPECTS OF MICROFILM SYSTEMS

In the discussion so far I have emphasized the microforms and the microform equipment useful in a typical library serving an educational institution. One should be aware of the fact that a complete microfilm system consists of more than microforms and microform readers and reader-printers. A complete system includes the equipment needed for the production of microfilms. L. A. Smitzer describes a complete typical microfilm system in detail.[19] He gives both the present state of the art and ventures predictions for the future.

The typical complete microfilm system consists of these elements: a document to be reproduced, either a paper document or a synthetic document (a document reproduced from a viewing screen); the cameras, planetary and rotary, the selection of the type depending on such factors as the document form, and the speed required for reproduction; and other equipment needed for the processing and duplicating of the film. All of these elements are part of the preparation stage. The use stage involves the storage of the film, its retrieval, its viewing and/ or copying by means of readers and reader-printers. The interdependence of the various components of the system is duly stressed by Smitzer. Along with many others he expects wide acceptance of the cartridges, for he thinks they will be used not only for film but also for fiche. He is also convinced that the computer-produced synthetic document will come into very wide use. The author gives special weight to the development of large-scale integrated electronics because it "will permit any requirement of logic, sensing or film manipulation to be packaged into the small space requirement of desk type units."[20]

Retrieval

Retrieval of microfilmed information is as important as its storage. Information is useful only if the searcher can find it conveniently and speedily. Producers of film and equipment are aware of this need and some have developed location devices. These devices may be crude or highly advanced; the degree of sophistication sought by the user will depend on the kind and amount of material to be retrieved and on the speed with which it should be located.

In the library field the retrieval procedures employed by the Chemical Abstracts Service deserve special mention. *Chemical Abstracts* employs four different coding systems to reach the desired portions of information. These are the binary code, the image code, line scale and odometer coding. Binary and image codes allow the use of keyboards in connection with reader-printer equipment, line and odometer coding are intended for non-keyboard assisted searching. To accommodate these different coding systems, *Chemical Abstracts* is issued in two forms, Edition I for the binary coding system and Edition II for the other systems.[21]

So far the more advanced automated systems have been used mostly in industry and special library situations, but with the expected increase in the use of microforms in libraries of educational institutions, advanced search methods will undoubtedly have to be more and more widely employed by them.

Sophisticated indexing and locating devices are well described by David R. Wolf.[22] He notes that automated microfilm files may generally be divided into two types: those requiring an external index and those that may incorporate the index information by recording it in coded form with the document itself. Wolf lists and evaluates representative examples for each type. Included among the examples of the second type is the MIRACODE System, a system which currently is being successfully utilized by Northwestern University's Medill School of Journalism for the retrieval of information contained in a miniaturized clipping file. Kenneth Janda and David Gordon describe in detail the operational problems encountered in preparing the index codes and in coding the clippings, and they outline the retrieval capabilities of the system.[23]

Computer Output Microfilm

One of the potentially most significant developments is the technology which establishes interconnections between microfilm and computer. In his excellent comprehensive survey of the field of reproduction of library materials and graphic communications for 1968, Robert C. Sullivan puts computer output microfilm (COM) at the head of the list.[24] In his equally comprehensive review for 1969, the same author can report that the COM field has been continuing in its rapid growth.[25] He estimates that by the end of 1969 there were about 300 COM recorders in use in the United States.

By joining the microfilm to the computer, it has become possible to take advantage of the tremendously increased speed and power potential of the newer computer models. Until recently the computer output was recorded on paper by means of mechanical printing devices. Even though an avalanche of paper records was created, the impact printer could not keep pace with the computer processing potential. The COM recorder has provided the long sought remedy with an output equivalent equal to about thirty impact printers working simultaneously. The computer output microfilmer converts the digital computer symbols into language understandable to humans and generates a microfilm copy directly without an intervening paper copy. There are two methods of recording directly on microfilm: the cathode ray tube (CRT) system and the electron beam recording (EBR) system. A concise explanation of these two systems may be found in Don M. Avedon's recent overview of the COM field.[26]

USER STUDIES

Librarians in educational institutions of all levels of education, as well as those serving special and public libraries, have been greatly interested in the extent of microform use. The increase in microform production was expected to be accompanied by a corresponding increase in microfilm utilization. As Norbert Stahl notes in a recent article, microfilm can no longer be relegated to a mere archival role; it must become action oriented.[27] But in general the increase in use did not keep pace with the increase in the quantity of microfilmed materials.

Various studies concerned with microfilm utilization in libraries have recently been undertaken or have been planned. Four of these will be briefly discussed here. On behalf of the Association of Research Libraries, Donald C. Holmes made an exploratory study designed to identify the needs of microform users.[28] He interviewed 89 persons at 25 institutions in all parts of the country. The findings offered no surprises. The reasons given by the interviewees for using microforms were conventional, such as: materials not otherwise available, to avoid keeping magazines and other serials in bound form, to preserve deteriorating material, to store bulky material, and to provide printout in hard copy form in lieu of use of rare or expensive originals. The comments on needs and shortcomings likewise were the expected ones and revealed why microforms so far have not been employed to their full potential. The lack of an optimum physical environment for microfilm use—suitable lighting, humidity control, suitable furniture, etc.—was deplored. It was also noted that there exists a large variety in types of readers and that there is no universal reader which would accept all kinds and sizes of microforms. It was further considered a deficiency that there are no inexpensive good readers which could be withdrawn for home use. The interviewees also indicated that users, when given a choice, preferred the hard copy. Users, however, did not show any preference for a particular kind of microform. Many of those questioned felt that bibliographic control must be greatly improved in order to facilitate access to the materials.

The suggestions made by the interviewees formed the basis for the nine recommendations of the study. These recommendations gave direction to research projects designed to overcome the difficulties which have hampered microform utilization. The Office of Education was willing to supply continued financial support to the Microform Technology Project of the Association of Research Libraries, and this association decided to concentrate on two of the several problem areas. Holmes was to concern himself with the impact of environmental conditions on the utilization of microforms. He presented his findings in a final report.[29] Felix Reichmann and Josephine M. Tharpe were charged with investigating effective systems of bibliographic control of microforms. Their findings appear as an interim report.[30] Reichmann and Tharpe, who are continuing their work for another year, are expected to present their final report by June 1971.

114

Holmes provides authoritative information on microform reading areas and work rooms, on microform carrels, and on storage and handling. He also includes a chapter on "Teaching the Use of Microforms and Related Equipment." In one appendix Holmes provides a glossary listing the most important technical terms, and in other appendixes he gives information on types of microforms, characteristics of films, as well as desirable characteristics of readers and reader-printers. Since bibliographic matters are outside the scope of this study I shall only briefly mention that in their broadly conceived investigation Reichmann and Tharpe deal with the various levels of bibliographic control—local, national and international.

Ralph W. Lewis undertook a study of users' reactions to microfiche in a research laboratory library.[31] He deemed such a study important since more and more research-oriented government agencies distribute their reports in microfiche only. It was surprising to discover that the majority of the researchers had a negative attitude toward the use of fiche, an attitude comparable to that held by early users of microfilm. This attitude prevailed even though the data were available in microform only. Lewis stresses that a considerable effort must be made to help scientists overcome this coolness, or at times even antipathy, toward microform use.

A study was conducted by James P. Kottenstette,[32] with the aid of a group of college students, to discover whether the reading skills of the students would be preserved if they used microforms rather than hard copy as the information carriers. Since ultra-microfiche is coming into its own, he used not only the conventional microfiche which he defined as reduced 40x or less but also ultra-microfiche which he defined as fiche at reduction ratios ranging from 40x to 150x. (Earlier I noted that the line of demarcation between conventional and ultra-microfiche is usually set at 60x.) The readers at the disposal of the students had magnification ratios corresponding to the reduction ratios of the microforms. For instance, an ultra-microfiche with a reduction ratio of 115x was read with a reader having a magnification ratio of 115x.

It should be mentioned that all materials which were in microform also were available in hard copy so that valid comparisons could be made by having the participants in the study use both hard copy and the corresponding microform. The study revealed that in the case of substantive reading materials (such as required reading) the reading ratio and comprehension level were not in any essential way affected by the kind of information carrier. Stated in a different way, in this experiment information transfer by means of microform, even ultra-microfiche, was essentially as effective as information transfer by means of a hard copy.

The American Association of Junior Colleges (AAJC) has set in motion a most ambitious project called the AAJC Microform Project.[33] It is divided into four phases and is expected to extend over a five-year period. Louise Giles was the principal investigator during Phase I (1969-70). Since July 1970 Dale Gaddy has been serving as the project director. The study is to determine under what conditions junior college students will select microforms and to assess the effectiveness of microforms in learning. The project provides, among other things, that bibliographies will be prepared for those courses which are nearly universally attended by junior college students; a research design will be developed; colleges for the pilot study will be chosen; materials used in courses will be filmed; colleges for a two-year field test will be selected; the necessary hardware will be procured; and finally, the data will be analyzed and reported.

While this study is projected against a junior college background, the breadth of its design assures that it will have at least partial applications to other levels of higher and even secondary education.

STANDARDIZATION

Many efforts have been made to bring about a higher degree of standardization than now prevails. As Peter Scott observed, it is not practical to have as many different formats of microforms as of books, because in the case of microforms a device—a reading machine—must be interposed between medium and user.[34]

The microfilm norms formulated by the ALA[35] are intended to bring about uniformity without stifling ingenuity. These norms are largely concerned with 35mm microfilm. They do not deal with 16mm microfilm, microfiche, nor readers and reader-printers. However limited the scope of these norms may be, they set a pattern for attaining a higher degree of uniformity than prevails now.

Of greater significance are the detailed technical standards which have been set by the USA Standards Institute, a voluntary organization of film users and manufacturers. The standards relating to films are in the institute's PH series.

Also pertinent are the federal microfiche standards by COSATI[36] and the specifications for Library of Congress filming by Stephen R. Salmon.[37] Scott's comment that all of these standards are voluntary and need not be followed would seem especially important.

So far no comprehensive guide for the evaluation of microfilm has been available. Though concise, Allen Veaner's series of articles that appeared in *Choice*[38] offer some guidance. Of considerable help should be a forthcoming publication by the same author. It was originally intended as a manual for microform reviewers for the magazine *Choice*. In its expanded form it is expected to serve generally persons who are responsible for the acquisition and evaluation of micro-publications.[39]

EXPERIMENTATION

The experimental computer-based technical library project which was established at the Massachusetts Institute of Technology in 1965 should have a great potential for effective and increased microform utilization. The project is known as Intrex, an acronym derived from information transfer experiments.

The prototype system which is now in operation contains a literature base composed of an "augmented" catalog and of approximately 12,000 complete microfilm texts. The augmented catalog, which is stored in the computer memory, contains not only the conventional catalog information for each article but also other data such as subject indexing terms, abstracts, tables of contents and reviews. In all, the augmented catalog gives information relating to each article in approximately fifty different field codes. The separate text base which contains about 12,000 complete articles on microfilm is being increased at the rate of 400 items per month.

From various locations within the library building the user may interrogate the computer and command the display of the desired data—catalog information or full text. The information is displayed on a cathode ray tube. It is also possible to obtain hard copies of the displayed item at a reproduction station.

The full range of the research and development activities and the status of the model library are well described and evaluated in the latest semi-annual report of Project Intrex. This report also lists the Project Intrex staff, and the current and past publications relating to the project.[40]

THE FUTURE

Microforms will have an ever brighter future if predictions made by G. B. Bernstein in the report entitled *A Fifteen-Year Forecast of Information Processing Technology*[41] come true. The section of this report which deals with microforms and related equipment has been reproduced in the magazine *Microdoc* under the title "Things Ahead?"[42] Forty-two categories which are expected to undergo changes are listed. It is predicted that some of the changes will occur very soon and others considerably later, but all within a fifteen-year period. Bernstein notes for each event the span of time within which he expects it to occur together with the likely year of occurrence.

Lack of space does not allow me to present this optimistic outlook in full, but I shall note here at least a few of the events with their "likely" year of happening.

Availability of a "universal" viewer for a wide variety of optical format microfilm (1972).

Increase in use of microforms and associated equipment by a factor of ten (1978).

Marriage of microforms with other information processing equipment; this will enhance the utility of microforms as dynamic elements in active current information systems (1975).

Conversion of one form into another (e.g., film to fiche) will be inexpensive and will increase; it will help to standardize film formats (1974).

Substantial improvement in quality of microfilm and microfilm equipment. Substantial improvement in light sources for making and using film (1980).

Capability of microfilm viewers for displaying images in color (1970), and of printers to print in color (1974).

Availability of compact, less expensive viewers as a result of breakthroughs in optic design (1973).

Radical change in policy and methods of publication, now hampered by present copyright laws (1974).

Decrease in use of conventional printed materials and corresponding increase in high density media and soft display (1980).

Availability of a microfilm reading device which will be as easy or easier to use than a book. This device will be so light and adaptable that in the author's words "you should be able to take it to bed with you if you like" (1975).

REFERENCES

1. Fremont Rider, *The Scholar and the Future of the Research Library, a Problem and its Solution.* New York, Hadham Press, 1944.

2. L. J. van der Wolk, "The Microfiche Foundation and the Availability of Information in Microfiche Form," *ASLIB Proceedings,* 20:525-26, Dec. 1968.

3. John Mill, Jr., *et al.* "Microform Selection /Application." *In* National Microfilm Association, *Proceedings,* Vol. 16, Annapolis, Md., 1967, pp. 205-12. See also footnote 29.

4. Franklin D. Crawford, *The Microfilm Technology Primer on Scholarly Journals.* Princeton, N.J., Princeton Microfilm Corporation, 1969.

5. William R. Hawken *et al. Microbook Publication: A New Approach for a Decade.* Chicago, Library Resources, Inc., 1970 (Processed); and Library Resources, Inc., *The Microbook Library Series.* Chicago, Library Resources, Inc., 1970.

6. NCR. *PCMI Library Collections: Here are the Books behind Bibliographies.* NCR, Educational Products Dept., 1970, pp. 1-4.

7. Arthur Teplitz, "Library Fiche: An Introduction and Explanation." *In* National Microfilm Association, *Proceedings,* Vol. 17, Annapolis, Md., 1968, pp. 125-32.

8. Paul G. Zurkowski, "Post-Gutenberg Copyright Concepts," *NMA Journal,* 2:70-73, Winter 1968/69.

9. _____. "Micropublishing–A Post-Gutenberg Medium." *In* National Microfilm Association, *Proceedings,* Vol. 18, Annapolis, Md., 1969, pp. 346-50.

10. Lawrence B. Heilprin, "Technology and the Future of the Copyright Principle," *Phi Delta Kappan,* 48:220-25, January 1967. Also in *American Documentation,* 19:6-11, January 1968.

11. J. ver Hulst, "An Approach to the Development of a Large Volume Microform Dissemination Library System," *NMA Journal,* 2:111-12, Spring 1969.

12. Information Dynamics Corporation, "Micrographic Catalog Retrieval Systems: MCRS-500; MCRS-800." Reading, Mass., Information Dynamics Corporation (Folder). Also folder entitled, "Title Index to MCRS."

13. Demco Educational Corporation, "The Demco LPS Microdata Cataloging System." Madison, Wis., Demco Educational Corporation (Folder).

14. Bro-Dart, Inc., "Direct Input Ordering System." Williamsport, Penn., Bro-Dart, Inc. (Folder).

15. R. A. Morgan Company, Inc., "Microform Readers for Libraries." *In* ALA Library Technology Project, *Library Technology Reports.* . . . Chicago, May 1970. See also footnote 29.

16. William R. Hawken Associates, "The Selection of a Microform Reader." *In* ALA Library Technology Project, *Library Technology Reports.* . . . Chicago, November 1968.

17. Loretta J. Kiersky, "New Developments in Photoreproduction," *Special Libraries,* 60:622, November 1969.

18. DASA Corporation, "Microfiche Users Asked for a Truly Low-Cost Portable Reader. DASA Delivered." (Prospectus.)

19. L. A. Smitzer, "Looking Ahead in Microfilm and Information Retrieval," *NMA Journal,* 2:77-82, Spring 1969.

20. *Ibid.*, p. 82.

21. Chemical Abstracts Service, "Answers to Questions about Abstracts on Microfilm." Columbus, Ohio, Chemical Abstracts Service, Marketing Dept., p. 4 (Folder).

22. David R. Wolf, "Automated Microimage Files and Other Advanced Techniques." *In* National Microfilm Association, *Proceedings,* Vol. 16, Annapolis, Md., 1967, pp. 87-89.

23. Kenneth Janda and David Gordon, "The Microfilm Information Retrieval System for Newspaper Libraries," *Special Libraries,* 61:33-47, January 1970.

24. Robert C. Sullivan, "Developments in Reproduction of Library Materials and Graphic Communication, 1968," *Library Resources & Technical Services,* 13:391-93, Summer 1969.

25. _____ . "Developments in Reproduction of Library Materials, 1969," *Library Resources & Technical Services,* 14:221, Spring 1970.

26. Don M. Avedon, *Computer Output Microfilm* (Informational Monograph No. 4). Annapolis, Md., National Microfilm Association, 1969, pp. 1-17. For a more detailed discussion of the CRT system, see: Donald F. Jackson, "Direct Microfilming of Computer Output in Dynamic Information Systems." *In* National Microfilm Association, *Proceedings,* Vol. 16, Annapolis, Md., 1967, pp. 34-43. (One of Avedon's principal sources.) For a more detailed discussion of the EBR system, see: Rolf E. Westgard, "Electron Beam Recording— Microfilm's New Method for Conversing with Computers." *In* National Microfilm Association, *Proceedings,* Vol. 16, Annapolis, Md., 1967, pp. viii, 124-30.

27. Norbert Stahl, "Problems and Opportunities with Microfilm," *Journal of Micrographics,* 3:66-67, Winter 1969-70.

28. Donald C. Holmes, *Determination of User Needs and Future Requirements for a Systems Approach to Microform Technology* (ERIC Document ED 029 168). Washington, D.C., Association of Research Libraries, 1969. See also (abbreviated report): Donald C. Holmes, "The Needs of Library Microfilm Users." *In* National Microfilm Association, *Proceedings,* Vol. 18, Annapolis, Md., 1969, pp. 256-64.

29. _____ . *Determination of Environmental Conditions Required in a Library for the Effective Utilization of Microforms* (Part I [final part] of Interim Report. Contract No. OEC-08-080786-4612 [095]). Washington, D.C., Association of Research Libraries, 1970, pp. 1-44. Appendixes B and C may be listed as additional sources in footnote 3, and Appendix D may be listed as an additional source in footnote 15.

30. Felix Reichmann and Josephine M. Tharpe, *Determination of an Effective System of Bibliographic Control of Microform Publications* (Part II [Interim Report] of Interim Report. Contract No. OEC-08-080786-4612 [095]). Washington, D.C., Association of Research Libraries, 1970, pp. 45-90.

31. Ralph W. Lewis, "Users' Reaction to Microfiche—A Preliminary Study," *College & Research Libraries,* 31:260-68, July 1970.

32. James P. Kottenstette, "Student Reading Characteristics: Comparing Skill Levels Demonstrated on Hardcopy and Microform Presentations." *In* American Society for Information Science, *Proceedings of the Annual Meeting,* Vol. 6, Westport, Conn., 1969, pp. 345-51.

33. American Association of Junior Colleges, "Microform Project: A Research Project to Determine the Student Acceptability and Learning Effectiveness of Microforms in Community Junior Colleges." Washington, D.C., 1970.

34. Peter Scott, "Scholars and Researchers and Their Use of Microforms," *NMA Journal,* 2:121-26, Summer 1969.

35. American Library Association, Copying Methods Section, Library Standards for Microfilm Committee, *Microfilm Norms; Recommended Standards for Libraries.* Chicago, ALA, Resources and Technical Services Division, 1966.

36. U.S. Federal Council for Science and Technology, Committee on Scientific and Technical Information, *Federal Microfiche Standards.* 2d ed. Springfield, Va., Clearinghouse for Federal Scientific and Technical Information, 1965.

37. Stephen R. Salmon, *Specifications for Library of Congress Microfilming.* Washington, D.C., Library of Congress, 1964.

38. Allen B. Veaner, "The Crisis in Micropublication," *Choice,* 5:448-53, June 1968; and Allen B. Veaner, "Microreproduction and Micropublication Technical Standards–What They Mean to You, the User," *Choice,* 5:739-44, September 1968.

39. _____ . *The Technical Evaluation of Micropublications: A Handbook for Librarians.* Chicago, ALA (In press). Announcement in *American Libraries,* 1:774-75, September 1970.

40. Massachusetts Institute of Technology, Project Intrex, *Semi-Annual Activity Report, 15 March 1970 to 15 September 1970.* Cambridge, Mass., 1970. See also Council on Library Resources, "Council on Library Resources Makes New Grant [of $400,000] toward Support of Experimental Computer-Based Technical Library System at M.I.T." (Release No. 298), Nov. 29, 1970.

41. G. B. Bernstein, *A Fifteen-Year Forecast of Information Processing Technology.* Washington, D.C., Research and Development Division, Naval Supply Systems Command, 1969. Obtainable from U.S. Clearinghouse for Federal Scientific and Technical Information (A.D. 681 752).

42. "Things Ahead?" *Microdoc,* 8:82-87, No. 4, 1969.

A REVIEW OF MICROPHOTOGRAPHIC TECHNIQUES AND GRAPHIC STORAGE AND RETRIEVAL SYSTEMS*

By Alfred Tauber

The microforms have a significant role to play in information transfer. It has been demonstrated that selective dissemination of documents (SDD) to the user's local work environment is of major importance in achieving user satisfaction within his energy limitations. Only the microforms possess a low enough cost per page (approximately $0.001 per page) to permit wide file dispersion, particularly for the class of information called strategic.

Let us examine the user and his information system setting. The user's behavior in his personal information system (what he does with the documents that flow across his desk) is governed by an energy equation that is intuitively recognized but rarely expressed:

$$I_d \times I_w = O_d \times O_w$$

That is, input documents x input work per document equals output documents x output work per document. This is a least cost systems equation. Normally, the number of documents input to the system is very large. Normally, the number of documents output from the system is very, very small. As a result, input work is minimized, and the user expends a significant amount of energy with each retrieval.

Psychologically, the user wants instant access with no energy expenditure on his part. Ideally, the user wants a staff assistant who gets him answers to his questions. Since he can't afford a staff assistant (unless he is a General), his psychological and energy needs are in conflict. Since he intuitively recognizes the energy equation and follows its dictates, he is always psychologically dissatisfied. The user's need to minimize his input energy results in a series of decisions about a document as follows:

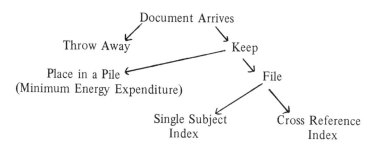

Document Arrives

Throw Away — Keep

Place in a Pile (Minimum Energy Expenditure) — File

Single Subject Index — Cross Reference Index

The initial decision to keep or throw away is easily made. The decision to place either in a pile or file is made within the viewpoint of the user, at that point in time, and is based on his estimate of the document's value to

*Reprinted from the *Drexel Library Quarterly*, 5:234-40, October 1969, by permission of the publisher. ^{c}1969.

him and its probable frequency of access. Similarly, the decision to place in a single subject file or to cross reference it is a function of its value and probable frequency of access. Therefore, a least cost system design for the individual has Piles, Single Subject Files, and Cross Reference Files. That popular pile of documents that we all have, and feel guilty about, deserves a respected place among the tools of the information user.

Now the role of an information center becomes clear. In recognition of the energy and psychological needs of the user, this information center assumes the burden of the input work. By provision of rapid access files in the user's office, by provision of frequently updated cumulative depth indexes to those files, by incorporation in those indexes of the individual's unique viewpoint and association trail descriptors, by becoming that staff assistant for every user, it is possible to achieve user satisfaction with minimum energy output on his part. Users have a tremendous latent need for information. In the past, their lack of energy has resulted in their not trying to secure information, even though they would be better for having it.

One criterion for evaluating alternative system designs is that the best system requires the minimum effort to reach user satisfaction. In fact, systems can be cost justified on difference in user efforts (a labor savings approach). Another reinforcing view of the user and his system setting is provided by a series of Department of Defense (DOD) user studies performed by Auerbach Corporation and North American Aviation. Auerbach performed a Phase I study of DOD personnel engaged in research and development and evaluation and test activities. North American Aviation (NAA) in its Phase II study covered 1,500 individuals in 83 organizations in the defense industry. The studies concentrated on the information wanted and used to perform specific tasks. They were not concerned with current awareness. Rather they tried to establish what the first source the individual with an information need turned to.

Users first searched for information in their local work environment 80% of the time. Libraries and information centers are used as the first source of information only 5% of the time. The local work environment is defined as the user's own mind, his own files, colleagues, departmental files, and internal company consultants. The local work environment does *not* extend as far as the company technical information center. The order of the first source of information was as follows:

1. Received with task assignment.
2. Recalled it.
3. Searched own collection.
4. Respondent's own action.
5. Assigned a subordinate to get it.
6. Asked a colleague.
7. Asked a supervisor.
8. Requested search of departmental files.
9. Asked an internal company consultant.
10. Searched company information center.
11. Requested a library search.
12. Requested data from a supplier.
13. Searched supplier records.

14. Searched an outside library.
15. Asked an external consultant.
16. Requested search of a DOD information center.
17. Searched DOD information center.
18. Asked a customer.

In the NAA study, the most frequent first source was the individual himself:

Recalled from memory	19.0%
Searched his own personal collection	13.0%
Produced information through his own action	2.5%
TOTAL	34.5%

Received with task assignment	10.5%

From the people immediately around him		29.5%
Colleagues	14.5%	
Subordinates	4.5%	
Supervisors	1.0%	
Internal Consultants	9.5%	

To people outside his immediate environment		7.5%
Suppliers	4.5%	
External Consultant	1.0%	
Customer	2.0%	

Non-personal document sources were utilized as the first contact		18.0%
Departmental Files	5.5%	
Company TIC	10.0%	
Supplier	1.5%	
External Libraries	0.5%	

The Auerbach study reported:

No answer	21%
Colleague	21%
Own collection	17%
Departmental files	13%
Received with task	11%
Library and information center	5%
Manufacturer or supplier	5%
Assigned to subordinate	4%
Supervisor	2%
Consultants	1%

The conclusions of these studies are:

1. Information policies should recognize and seek to strengthen the utility of local work environments.

2. The indexing, abstracting, organization, and analysis of information prior to its distribution should be tailored to the local work environment.

3. There should be a selective and automatic dissemination to the local work environment of these tailored indexes, abstracts, and organized and analyzed information.

4. The local work environment is the most important first source for information.

5. It takes longer to acquire information when the first source is more distant from the user.

6. The individual uses as the first source that which is readily available or easy to use.

7. The findings tend to confirm the existence and significance of an information system consisting of the user's personal files, his colleagues, and other local sources of information.

8. The features of this informal information system which the user apparently considers important are convenience, responsiveness, and the ability to conduct a dialogue, interplay, and feedback. The user apparently wants to deal with a system in which he can personally explain, modify, and clarify his requirements, and he can expect, in response, the right information in the right amount, in the right form, and in the time required.

9. What is required is a means of effectively integrating the formal and informal information systems so that the user actually becomes an integral part of the system. Until this is accomplished, it seems that even greatly improved formal information centers will receive less than a full measure of success.

Vannevar Bush's concept of the "Memex," in which a researcher had the entire collection in his area of interest in his desk, with an appropriate associative index tool, is a system concept that is hard to beat in terms of accomplishing our objective of maximizing the man-information interface. Let us examine an implementation of the Memex concept in terms of the tools, technologies, and cost restraints of today. A current first approximation to the Memex could easily exist within the framework of NASA's information activities. For a moment, let *STAR*, the NASA current announcement abstract bulletin, serve as the index tool. Second, let a NASA microfiche file, selected to suit each researcher's interest profile, to be delivered concurrently with each issue of *STAR*, serve as the file. Add a $100 microfiche viewer, and our Memex is ready for use. *STAR*'s subscription price is approximately $35 per year. One microfiche can disseminate information, a typical report, for example, at 10 cents per sixty pages. In time, as production is increased, the cost will be reduced.

The role of the information center becomes that of a manager. It gathers in material of interest to its mission, manages it, puts out announcement bulletins and critical reviews, handles exceptional requests and demand bibliographies, and is a republisher. The user gets complete information from which to determine relevance since, in the last analysis, only the document can be used to determine relevance. Serendipity is served by the fact that he gets the complete announcement bulletin for the entire field for browsing.

Another example of what can be done is a program under development at North American Aviation. They contemplate three types of document files: SDD microfiche to the individual; lower activity, general-use information, to departmental files in microfiche form; and microfiche master duplicating library at the technical information center. This is truly activity-oriented concept.

Library and information centers of tomorrow will become duplicating libraries instead of circulating libraries. Their files will be film masters, and the user will get either film duplicates or hard copy enlargements, depending on his ability to pay. Studies have shown that present university circulating libraries do not have items they own available 55% of the time. Obviously a duplicating library is a must. What about copyright in the framework of duplicating libraries? Encouraging progress is being made between publishers and republishers to create an accommodation that will permit widespread reduplication and still provide revenue to the copyright holder. It is reasonable to expect this problem to be resolved in the next three to five years.

Now that we have made the case for the microforms, let us examine the tools the librarian and system designer have to choose from. At the head of the list is microfiche. Microfiche are sheet microfilm. The most popular size and format in the information transfer field is the COSATI 105 x 148 mm (4" x 6") size, with human readable title and five rows of 12 images each for a total of 60 images. We are fortunate that the power of this microform was recognized at its inception, and that a major standardization effort took place. While there is room for improvement in the standards, they permit equipment manufacturers to focus their developments around a known element.

Microfiche should be considered a form of printing. As such, they offer the potential of a full range of equipment that we find in the printing industry, from gigantic high production presses to point-of-use copy machines. Because of the mass market they provide, viewing equipment is becoming lower in price and better in quality. Adequate viewers exist presently in the $100 to $200 range. The next generation of viewers will be in the $50 to $100 range. Automatic storage and retrieval devices have emerged. My company makes a desk top microfiche storage and retrieval device that can store 73,500 pages of information on 750 microfiche and get to any page in a maximum of five seconds. Future models will have readily interchangeable files and hard copy printers. This class of equipment was created with file decentralization in mind. Mosler Sale, focusing on file centralization, has an automatic retrieval device that sells for $40,000 and holds 100,000 to 200,000 microfiche. Semi-automatic retrieval equipment, such as elevator files, are widely used by many information centers.

There are a variety of ways to create microfiche to fit every pocketbook, and service centers which will make microfiche at reasonable prices are daily becoming more abundant ($0.05 per page for an original negative, and $0.001

to $0.002 per duplicate page, depending on volume). Microfiche, in a file dissemination application, are the least expensive microform.

The other major microform popularly available is 16mm roll microfilm in cartridges. A cartridge normally contains a 100 foot roll of film on which 2,500 document images are stored. At this point in time, cartridge roll film offers file integrity and machine access at lower prices for equipment than for comparative microfiche equipment. As such, it will continue to have a position in those applications involving public use (file integrity), where usage frequency is low and therefore, labor savings cannot justify more expensive equipment, and where purging and updating are infrequent.

The microforms provide the information system designer with powerful tools to aid the information transfer process. Freed at last from excessive concern over the cost of delivery of a document, new systems that provide tailored information collections at the point of use are now possible. The information center's role emerges as a manager who acquires, organizes, and republishes information and handles the exceptional question that cannot be answered by the decentralized files.

With all their current system power, the microforms are in their infancy. With a major marketplace emerging, equipment manufacturers are actively engaged in research and development for this field. The system designer can proceed today with the assurance that costs will go down, that new equipment will be compatible with his microform files, and that more building blocks for system improvement will be forthcoming.

USE OF MICROFILM IN AN INDUSTRIAL RESEARCH LIBRARY*

By Virginia Duncan and Frances Parsons

Lavoisier Library is one of 30 libraries in the du Pont Company, and is located at the Experimental Station, which is the major research center for the company. The library's collection reflects all fields of the company's interests but is particularly strong in chemistry, physics, engineering and biology. There are more than 65,000 bound volumes of periodicals and books, and extensive collections of pamphlets, technical trade literature, and government reports and documents. About 1,500 periodicals are received regularly. One copy of all important titles is retained in the library for reference while multiple copies of about 600 journals are available for automatic circulation throughout the Experimental Station area with assistance from the IBM 360/20 computer. Our periodical subscription program is also computer based.

Lavoisier Library has a staff of 28 people, including professionally trained librarians and catalogers, assistants, and clerical personnel.

The library serves primarily some 1,400 technical people at the Experimental Station and to a limited extent the laboratories and plants at other locations. The library is open 24 hours a day, seven days a week. The services offered are those common to many research libraries including preparation of bibliographies and literature searches, purchase of all literature (except patents), operation of a translation service, and interlibrary loan service. The library also maintains and operates a number of departmental reading rooms in the Experimental Station area. We issue two monthly bulletins, *Additions to the Library* and *Calendar of Scientific Meetings.*

Our 16mm microfilm program was begun when we acquired *Chemical Abstracts* on 16mm microfilm in September 1966. Because no other scientific journals were available in that form at the time, we enlisted the assistance of a commercial microfilm organization.

Test films were made of some basic titles in chemistry, physics, and biology. The results were very gratifying. As a result we added the following to our collection: *Annalen der Chemie* (Liebig's); *Chemische Berichte; Comptes rendus, Académie des sciences; Angewandte Chemie; Zeitschrift für anorganische und allgemeine Chemie; Biochemische Zeitschrift;* and *Zeitschrift für Physik.* These titles were filmed for the period open to public domain (through 1940); the remainder of our holdings are in hard copy. Though originally filmed for us, these titles are not commercially available from our supplier.

The American Chemical Society publications leased on 16mm film (through 1969) include *Analytical Chemistry, Chemical and Engineering News, Journal of the American Chemical Society,* and *Industrial and Engineering Chemistry.* The last five years of these titles are retained in hard copy also. The five-year period was chosen arbitrarily and will be adjusted as users' needs dictate.

Biological Abstracts was added in January 1969.

Four of our five reader-printers are in the Reading Room, and the fifth is on the third of our four stack levels. Having the reader-printers in the Reading

*Reprinted by permission from *Special Libraries,* 61:288-290, June-August 1970.

Room is not a satisfactory arrangement because the machines are very noisy, especially when all four are being used at once. In addition, two of the machines in the Reading Room were returned to the factory for a modification which has reduced the time required to make a print. An adapter kit—which increased the speed of the print cycle—was installed in each machine. As a result, there has been an increase in the frequency of noise generated by the printers. To minimize the noise problem in the Reading Room, which has high ceilings and metal shelving, we have both an acoustical ceiling and deep pile nylon carpeting as well as heavy draperies at all the windows. Nevertheless, the four reader-printers still generate enough noise to bring complaints from our patrons. We have no separate room where these machines can be located. We are looking into the possibility of noise reducers.

The reader-printers receive regular routine maintenance from a member of the library staff. All solutions are flushed out at least once a day and minor adjustments made as necessary. In addition, the equipment manufacturers provide very prompt and excellent service.

To give some idea of costs, here are estimates based on our 1968 statistics. The paper costs approximately $25/300 copies, or $0.08/copy. Developer solutions cost about $0.01/copy for a total of $0.09/copy. In addition, machine rentals average $100/month/machine.

With five reader-printers, the storage space for supplies of paper and developing solutions becomes appreciable.

The film cartridges are shelved in the stacks using a wooden strip approximately 5"D x 35½"W on the back of each shelf. The strip keeps the cartridges in a straight line at the front of the shelf. The bound volumes (1940+) of each title are shelved along with the microfilm.

Table 1. Storage Capacity: Bound Volumes vs. Microfilm

| | Bound Volumes | | Microfilm | |
Title	Number of Shelves	Linear Feet	Number of Shelves	Linear Feet
Biological Abstracts (without indexes), v. 1-49 (1926-68), 118 cartridges	11	33	3+	10½
Chemical Abstracts (including semi-annual indexes but not cumulatives) v. 1-69 (1907-68), 165 cartridges	30	90	4+	14
American Chemical Society Journal v. 1-90 (1879-1968), 123 cartridges	15+	46	3+	11

In general, microfilm has been well received by both library patrons and staff. When we acquired *Chemical Abstracts* on microfilm, we put the film and reader-printer in the Reading Room for maximum exposure. We did not remove any of our four bound sets of *Chemical Abstracts.* Nobody was forced to use the microfilm. The easy-to-use cartridge machine, quick access to individual abstracts, and high-quality photocopies helped make the selling job easier.

Some of the disadvantages are that all film is not always easy to read; and it can be tiring to the eyes, particularly if many references are to be checked at one time. Film increases the time needed to answer reference questions if no copy is needed. Reader-printers may be temporarily inoperative because of film jams or because the printer runs out of paper and/or developing solution. Checking in the cartridges on receipt takes more time than checking in bound volumes and is more tedious. Each reel needs to be run through the machine and rewound to adjust the tension on the film. Spot checking of each reel for coding (on film) and print-outs is needed. Labels and coding on cartridges should be spot checked. This is more of a problem at present when so many sets are being acquired than it will be later when only one or two reels/year/title will be added.

We were asked to place particular emphasis on *Biological Abstracts* on microfilm when we were invited to prepare this paper for presentation at the 1969 SLA Conference. The microfilm edition became available in November 1968, and—as indicated earlier—we added it to our collection in January 1969. Since this has been such a short time, we do not have as much user reaction to report as we would like. However, we can list the following observations.

Having an abstract journal such as *Biological Abstracts* on film presents certain advantages and adds something of a new dimension to preparation of bibliographies and literature searches. For example, a client requests a list of all papers by a given author or all references on a certain subject for the last ten years. The appropriate indexes are searched and references listed, possibly several hundred. The searcher can then locate the appropriate cartridges of film and make photocopies of each abstract, or request that the copies be made for him by a library clerk. For numerical sequencing, to expedite copying, we use a 360/20 program.

With regard to the film itself, reduction appears to be about 22x. Spot checks were made for density on a few frames. The density of one title page was 2.37 and the density of another was 2.49. Density on a page of abstracts was 1.96 (films can have a density from 0.0 to 3.0). The generally accepted range for microfilm is 0.9 to 1.1, and the higher the density the greater the loss in resolution; 1.96 is high, yet the resolution is very good. Reader-printer copies from *Biological Abstracts* have very good quality.

On further inspection of the film, one notes frames around each page and "blips" at the bottom of each page. Double "blips" appear at irregular intervals of three to ten or more pages. The "blips" are useless as coding devices because they cannot be seen when the film is run through the machine even at a reasonably low speed. Both the "blips" and the frames use up very valuable film space. On one specific frame in Abstract No. 71719 (v. 46) the name of the journal appears but the remainder of the reference is omitted. The margin was cut so close that the last line of print was lost. This is the only frame on which we have observed this defect, however.

It has been suggested that reduction ratio be recorded on the cartridges, so the user will know which of three lenses to use (18x, 20x, or 23x).

In summary, we feel that good quality, high resolution 16mm microfilm of the scientific literature is a very acceptable substitute for the bound sets. The film is certainly less expensive than adding a new wing to the library building! We expect that about 50% of our periodical collection will be converted to 16mm microfilm and we can continue to live in the present building for at least the next five years.

HIGH-REDUCTION MICROFICHE FOR LIBRARIES: AN EVALUATION OF COLLECTIONS FROM THE NATIONAL CASH REGISTER COMPANY AND LIBRARY RESOURCES, INC.*

By Charles W. Evans

Librarians should not reject the collections of high-reduction fiche being offered by either the National Cash Register Company or Library Resources, Inc., without considering seriously what this technology and the contents of the collections offer. The advantages and disadvantages of high-reduction microfiche are considered, as well as the reading machines required to view them. The content of the collections offered by these two major micropublishing firms is analyzed; the marketing strategies, cost, and bibliographical aids offered are compared; and some conclusions are presented based on the analysis and comparisons made.

Book collections reproduced on high-reduction microfiche are now being offered to librarians by two major micropublishers: Library Resources, Inc. (LRI), a subsidiary of Encyclopaedia Britannica, and the Educational Products Department of the National Cash Register Company (NCR).

Reduction ratios of conventional microfiche range from about 15:1 to about 40:1.[1] For example, the federal standard sets a maximum of 20:1; the NMA standard ratios are 20:1 and 24:1; and the standard ratios adopted by ALA for microfilm—including fiche—are 14:1 and 20:1.[2,3,4] Consequently, most of the fiche readers now used in libraries have magnification ratios that are too low to make high-reduction fiche legible. Indeed, few fiche readers currently on the market can be obtained with magnification ratios higher than 50:1. (Atlantic Microfilm Corporation's model F-66 and F-66A readers, with a magnification ratio of 70:1, are exceptions.[5]) Hence, any library that buys a collection of high-reduction fiche—from either of these two vendors—must also buy special readers. This, naturally, tends to discourage the purchase of high-reduction fiche collections. But no librarian should reject them without first considering seriously what high-reduction fiche—and the book collections recorded on them—offer to libraries.

DISADVANTAGES OF HIGH-REDUCTION MICROFICHE

Let us consider the disadvantages of high-reduction fiche first. High-reduction microfilming requires much more care and more technical skill than filming at low-reduction ratios. The technical problems involved in the production of high-reduction fiche are so great that only two years ago another writer was able to say: "Ultra or super microfiche systems at present are very interesting but not practical. It will be quite some time before substantial collections will be available in this form."[6] Obviously, both LRI and NCR have solved these technical problems, and

---

*Reprinted from *Library Resources and Technical Services*, 16:33-47, Winter 1972.

each has done so in a different way. NCR utilizes photochromic materials (which exist in either a colorless or a colored state, and can be changed from one state to the other by the action of light) in a process that has been described in some detail for librarians by Hawken.[7] As a name for this process, it has adopted the initials PCMI, from photo-chromic-micro-image.

LRI's process is quite different.

> . . . in the Library Resources program the volumes contained in the library are first filmed using the 35 millimeter planetary camera at reduction ratios of 5.5x to 9x depending on the original information area size. This work is done using a camera and lens having a 120 lines per millimeter minimum resolution. The output of this camera is then photographed again using a 10x step and repeat camera with resolution capability of over a 100 line[s] per millimeter. The resultant third and fourth generation copies have sufficient resolution to provide a sufficiently high quality image on a reader screen at a magnification of 90x to meet the system design requirements.[8]

The cost of each of these processes is higher than the cost of conventional microfilming—so much so that neither LRI nor NCR can use high-reduction fiche in the sort of "demand publishing" in which University Microfilms specializes, which requires low "front end" costs.[9] The economics of high-reduction microfilming limit its use to publishing—or republishing—in large volume, so that its heavy initial expense can be recovered through the economies of mass production. For this reason both NCR and LRI have chosen to market collections, rather than individual works, and have tried to assemble collections that are attractive to a wide range of libraries.

A serious problem in the use of high-reduction fiche is the susceptibility of small images to damage by scratches or dirt. Both firms have solved this problem by enclosing their fiche in a tough mylar outer layer which makes them practically indestructible. (The author did manage to inflict severe damage on a sample NCR fiche by stabbing it with scissors for ten minutes, but this is hardly normal library practice.) They are actually more wear resistant than conventional microfilm, and are—in this sense—much better suited to library use.

Another possible disadvantage associated with the use of high-reduction fiche was recognized by Verner Clapp some years ago: "The cost of the elaborate equipment needed for projecting them for use might, however, well nullify the savings obtained by the reduction."[10] Clapp also suggested that high-reduction fiche readers might prove to be exceptionally bulky.[11]

In fact, neither of these predictions has come true. The readers developed by both LRI and NCR compare favorably with lower magnification readers available from other firms, in ease of operation, maintenance, cost—they aren't the cheapest available, but neither are they the most expensive—and size. Both of LRI's two readers are exceptionally compact. In fact the smaller of the two—called the "lap reader" for an obvious reason—is one of the smallest readers that is suitable for library use. It weighs only four and one-half pounds, and, with a 7" x 10" screen, it is comparable in size and portability to a collegiate dictionary.

ADVANTAGES OF HIGH-REDUCTION MICROFICHE

The advantages of microforms to libraries are well known, and at least some of these benefits are increased by the use of high-reduction filming.

1. *Microform use conserves space.* It is said that "microfilm can achieve space savings of 95% plus as opposed to housing the original documents."[12] High reduction obviously can increase this space saving. It is true that Clapp has argued that space savings through use of high-reduction fiche would be unimportant, in practice:

> For example, at a 10-diameter reduction the reduced image occupies only 1 per cent of the area occupied by the original and the (area) space-saving is 99 per cent. At a 100-diameter reduction the area of images is reduced to one-tenth of 1 per cent of the original and the saving is 99.9 per cent. But to gain that additional nine-tenths of 1 per cent has required the transition from a comparatively easy technique to a very difficult one. Space-saving, then, is not the reason for using high-ratio reduction.[13]

In fact, however, the space saving obtainable through high reduction that concerns the librarian is not the saving in fiche area. It is the saving in library space. As Clapp himself shows (see p. 134), a fiche that would hold 100 images at 10:1 reduction would hold 10,000 images at 100:1 reduction. Hence, a single 100:1 fiche could replace one hundred 10:1 fiche, and the use of the former in place of the latter could result in a saving of 99 percent of the storage space allotted to microfiche—certainly not an inconsiderable saving in a collection of any great size.

2. *Microform use helps to preserve library collections.* Microforms are tough and durable. "Microfilm has a life expectancy equal to that of the finest rag paper, anywhere from 300 to 500 years"; i.e., it can outlast many of the original documents it might replace.[14] This characteristic is one that both the LRI and the NCR fiche share with other forms of microfilm.

Where microforms duplicate but do not replace original documents they can help to preserve such documents by rendering much of the service that otherwise would have to be obtained from the originals. Microform materials can take harder use and require less rigorous control than materials in other forms because they are easily replaced. Unlike conventional roll microfilm, high-reduction fiche can't be duplicated in the library, but can be kept "in print" indefinitely by their publishers.

3. *Full-size copies can be made easily from microforms.* All types of microforms can be copied easily by the appropriate reader-printers, and high-reduction microfiche are no exception. NCR already has a high-magnification reader-printer on the market which produces good, readable copies—described by a British librarian as "usable but not beautiful."[15] LRI's reader-printer is expected to be available early in 1972.

4. *Microforms are often easier to use than the original documents.* Any experienced librarian can attest that original documents are often heavy, bulky, and awkward to use. They may also be brittle or frail, and require very careful handling. In these cases, a microform copy often may be preferred over the original by the user. Something that many librarians fail to realize, however, is

that the microcopy actually may be more readable than the original. Modern microforms, with good resolution and a modern viewer, may produce an image that very nearly equals the quality of the original. At the same time the reader image may be larger, and hence easier to read, than the original. The image is larger whenever the enlargement ratio of the reader is greater than the original reduction ratio of the microform. This enlarged blow-back is especially desirable where the original documents are printed in small, closely set type, as are many of the books included in the LRI collection and in NCR's *Library Collections*. LRI deliberately planned to provide this enlargement, which it points out as one of the desirable features of its system.

> Statistical studies of book page sizes show that with a substantial percentage of the volumes which will make up the *Library of American Civilization*, the size of the page will be larger on the screen of the portable reader than the original page, with a consequent gain in legibility and ease of reading. With the desk-top reader all but a small percentage of all pages will have a screen image substantially enhanced in size over that of the original, but not so large as to cause needlessly tiring eye-movements in the course of sustained reading.[16]

NCR's promotional material does not stress the advantage of an enlarged blow-back, but its system also provides it.

5. *High-reduction microfiche can be lower in cost than conventional microforms.* Microfilming at high-reduction ratios is more costly than conventional microfilming. Even so, perhaps the greatest advantage over low-reduction filming that it offers to micropublishers is a cost advantage. As Clapp put it:

> The real advantages should derive not from space-saving but from inexpensiveness of dissemination. Let us suppose, for example, that an 8" x 10" photographic print costs $1. At a 10-diameter reduction, this print could hold the images of 100 8" x 10" original pages, and the per-page cost would be $0.01. At a 100-diameter reduction, the print would hold 10,000 images, and even if the cost of the print were doubled (because of the extra care required in processing), the per-page cost would still be only $0.02. At a 200-diameter reduction the print would hold 40,000 images, and if the cost of the print were now tripled over its original price, the per-page cost would still be only $0.0075.[17]

Of course, such cost reductions can be achieved only through mass production, but they are possible. NCR's PCMI process puts more than 3,000 frames on a single 4" x 6" fiche; and, as an illustration of the low costs possible through high-reduction microfilming, NCR says, "On a mass production basis, where a great number of distribution transparencies are needed, the cost per copy drops close to one dollar . . . about 1/30 of a cent per page."[18]

6. *High-reduction filming can lessen some of the drawbacks that librarians find in the use of microfiche.* One of the complaints from librarians about microfiche is that they are easily smudged or damaged while being handled.

> Fingerprints of users . . . often smudge the film. Fingerprints cause the accumulation of "goo" on optical flats, which, in turn, accelerates the gathering of dirt and resultant film damage. Microfiche, microcards and

microprint cards all must be individually handled while being positioned in the readers and when they are removed from the machines. Since the average microform sheet contains many fewer pages of [sic] frames than an average microfilm roll, microform sheets are generally handled more frequently during machine viewing. Added handling increases the hazard of contamination of the microforms and increases the danger of damage both to the sheets and to the machines used in viewing them.[19]

Since high-reduction fiche contain far more frames than ordinary fiche, their use does not involve so much handling of individual fiche by the user, hence they are less liable to fingerprint smudges. Moreover, the plastic laminate with which both NCR and LRI coat their fiche renders them practically immune to any damage from ordinary use. They can get dirty, of course, but they are easily cleaned. (The author has rinsed PCMI fiche under a hot water tap without any apparent ill effects.)

Filming problems are a second cause of dissatisfaction with fiche among librarians. A study of microforms in libraries showed that:

> The most repetitive complaint about the use of microform sheets for library materials was the inordinate amount of time required to replace the sheets in proper order after each use; loss or improper filing of the microform sheets often resulted.[20]

The recording of an average book-length document in conventional microfiche (e.g., fiche meeting the COSATI or NMA standards) requires the use of trailer fiche, as there are too many pages to be recorded on a single fiche. Where several fiche are used together to record a single document, they are usually kept together, in order, in an envelope. This envelope, in turn, is then stored in a file with similar envelopes. Under these conditions, it is relatively easy to misfile a single fiche by putting it into the wrong envelope—and it might be very difficult to locate the missing fiche. Then, too, it would be easy to lose a single fiche from an envelope without being aware of the loss.

The obvious method for minimizing this problem is to use a higher reduction ratio so that a single fiche could contain all of any document likely to be recorded. Consequently, for library use, a "library fiche" has been proposed, with a "reduction ratio of 50 or 60 to 1."[21] Use of this fiche, which LRI calls a "Microbook," would practically eliminate the need for trailer fiche and, with them, most of the serious problems involved in keeping a file of microfiche in order.

LRI uses what it terms "bookrange reduction" ranging from 55:1 to 90:1 to create just such a library fiche: 1,000 frames on a 3" x 5" (75mm x 125mm) piece of film. This allows LRI to adhere closely to the principle of "bibliographic unity"—putting only one title on a fiche except for special material—and to minimize the number of trailers utilized.[22, 23]

NCR has gone to the opposite extreme in order to take full advantage of the high reductions possible with the PCMI process. It uses ultimate reduction ratios of about 120:1 in filming its library collections and so can record over 3,000 pages on its 4" x 6" (actually 105mm x 148.75mm) "Ultrafiche." It puts several books—the average is about seven—on each fiche. Hence its collections are somewhat less flexible in use than LRI's. On the other hand, it goes even further than LRI in simplifying file maintenance.

Because of their small size, fiche pose another problem for librarians. They are especially vulnerable to unauthorized removal from the library. High-reduction microfilming does not help to solve this problem, but it does help to make replacements less costly. Both LRI and NCR plan to keep the material in their collections permanently "in print," and will sell duplicates of individual fiche that may be lost—LRI for $1.50 per Microbook, and NCR for $6.00 per Ultrafiche.

THE READERS

The greatest single drawback to the use of microforms, when compared with the use of books, is the need to employ a reading device with them. Readers are even more necessary—if that is possible—with high-reduction fiche than with other microforms, but these readers are neither more costly nor more difficult to use than those employed with other microforms. In fact, users may consider LRI's lap reader less of a drawback than most other readers. It is being manufactured for LRI by Technicolor, and will sell for less than $450. Because of its portability, its simplicity in operation and maintenance, and its low cost, LRI calls it "the key that will free Microbook materials for circulation."[24] Since it is suitable for use outside the library, in homes, dormitories, or offices, LRI hopes that it will be bought by libraries and circulated like a book, just as some libraries now circulate cassette tape players and film projectors.

LRI's larger reader, for table-top use, is manufactured by the DuKane Corporation. Its price is under $400. It has an enlargement ratio of 90:1 and an 8½" x 12" screen.

The NCR 455 PCMI Ultrafiche reader produces images at a 150:1 magnification on an 11" x 11" screen. A simple X-Y indexing system enables the operator to locate a specific work quickly on the fiche. Like Ultrafiche, this reader already is in worldwide use in nonlibrary applications. Among its users are the Ford Motor Company and Sears Roebuck; both publish parts catalogs on Ultrafiche. (You probably could see an NCR 455 in use at the customer service desk of your local Sears store.) The price of this reader is $650, but educational and cash discounts can reduce it to $552.50.*

The Ultrafiche reader-printer is the NCR 455-21, an adaptation of the Ultrafiche reader. It produces copies by an electrostatic process in about seven seconds at a cost of about 2½ cents. It can be adapted to coin operation (using either nickels or dimes). It has a list price of $650 but, like the price of the reader, it may be reduced by discounts. Then too, NCR has extended payment plans for both the reader and the reader-printer.

Today there is no reader that can be used with both Microbooks and Ultrafiche. One of LRI's two readers must be used with the former, and the NCR 455 with the latter. Soon, however, there will be at least one reader available that can be used with both of these fiche and with fiche of lower reduction ratios as well. NCR is expected to have a new machine on the market late in 1971, which with three interchangeable lens systems will enable its users to read fiche that range in reduction ratio from 18:1 to 225:1. The author has seen a prototype of this

*All prices mentioned in this article were obtained by the author from NCR or LRI representatives. They are subject to change, and some may vary from one purchaser to another, depending on the terms of the purchase contract, the nature of the material purchased, and the volume of material purchased.

136

reader, which in appearance is much like the NCR 456-300 (not an Ultrafiche reader). The latter machine is a portable reader designed originally for office rather than library use. It weighs fifteen pounds and has a 10½" x 9½" screen. The selling price of the new reader has not been announced yet, but it is expected to be lower than the price of the NCR 455.

NCR'S COLLECTIONS

NCR's PCMI *Library Collections Program* includes five series: American Civilization; Literature-Humanities; Social Sciences; Science and Technology; and Government Documents. NCR plans to publish in Ultrafiche a collection of works in each of these series each year. Its first five collections were published in 1970, and the second five in 1971. All ten of these collections are available for purchase, either individually or in any combination.

The materials in these five series are classified according to the Library of Congress classification scheme. Together, their scope is universal, but the subject range of the collections published in any one year may be much less than universal. For example, the literature sections of the 1970 and 1971 collections are composed chiefly of works on English literature. Works on American literature and on other European literatures are included, to a lesser extent, but there is nothing in either collection on literature in non-European languages. Of course, any gap in subject coverage like this may be eliminated by the collections published in succeeding years.

The collections already published in the *American Civilization* series deal with the history and description of the United States, and include biographies of prominent Americans. Those in the *Literature-Humanities* series include works on philosophy and religion, music and the fine arts, philology, and literature. The contents of the music and literature sections are primarily works about these subjects—histories, criticisms, and commentaries—rather than examples of music or literature. Some examples of literary writing are included, however. For example, in the 1970 collection, there are the complete works of several writers, including Rousseau, Voltaire (in 70 volumes), Carlyle, De Quincy, Walter Pater, Oliver Wendell Holmes, and Harriet Beecher Stowe.

The *Social Sciences* collections include works on history—other than U.S. history—geography, anthropology, folklore, economics, sociology, political science, law, education, and psychology. The *Science and Technology* collections include a number of works on medicine, as well as on the pure sciences and technology. The *Government Documents* collections—at least, the 1970 and 1971 collections—include only publications of the United States government. Government publications are included in other collections as well, when their subject matter is appropriate; e.g., *Public Papers of the Presidents of the United States: Truman, Eisenhower, Kennedy, Johnson* (27v., Washington, G.P.O.) is in the political science section of the 1970 *American Civilization* collection.

Each of the works in these collections has been found in at least two "recognized standard subject bibliographies" like these used for the *American Civilization* series:[25]

Bartlett, John Russell. *The Literature of the Rebellion.* Boston: Draper & Haliday, 1866.

137

Carty, James, ed. *Bibliography of Irish History, 1912-1921.* Dublin:
Govt. Stationery Office, 1936;
Handlin, Oscar, et al., eds. *Harvard Guide to American History.*
Cambridge, Mass.: Harvard University Press, 1962.
Sonnenschein, William S., ed. *The Best Books.* 3rd ed. 6v. London:
Routledge, 1910-35.

All but four of the bibliographies used in making up the 1970 collections were
published either in the United States or in England. Even so, over 13 percent of
the titles included in these collections are in western European languages other
than English.

Nearly all of the material in the *Library Collections* so far was published
originally before 1940. However, about 85 percent was published after 1900
and less than 10 percent before 1850. A very few works were published before
1800.

Each individual collection in these series consists of 100 Ultrafiche, and
they average about 700 volumes per collection. The number of titles and volumes
does vary considerably from one collection to another, however. For example, in
the 1970 *Science and Technology* collection there are 294 titles in 561 volumes,
while there are 836 titles and 1,382 volumes in the 1970 *Literature-Humanities*
collection.[26, 27]

Each Ultrafiche in the *Library Collections* series contains several works on
a single subject, which is identified by a Library of Congress class number in the
upper-left corner, followed by the corresponding subject heading. In the upper-
right corner is an Ultrafiche call number assigned by NCR. These Ultrafiche
are intended to be kept in call number order and retrieved through LC catalog
cards filed in the library's main catalog. A complete set of cards for each work—
ready for filing—is supplied by NCR with every collection.

The basic price of each collection is $1,200, which includes the cost of the
accompanying catalog cards. It may be reduced by discounts, and NCR has an
extended payment plan for this, too.

The *Library Collections Program* was developed by NCR for sale primarily
to academic libraries, and especially to those that are new or are expanding
rapidly. NCR has also developed two other series, which make up its *College-
Bound Program.* These series were intended for sale to school libraries, but they
might be equally valuable in some public or academic libraries.

The *Essential Books* series in the *College-Bound Program* is like the *Library
Collections* series. It consists of a series of annual collections, which are expected to average about 500 volumes each. (The 1971 collection is the first to be
published; it contains 422 titles in 547 volumes.[28]) The price of the collections
in this series is $550. The works included in the 1971 collection are of the same
type as those in the *Library Collections* and were selected in the same manner;
each is listed in two or more standard bibliographic sources. The scope of this
series is probably intended to be as broad as that of the *Library Collections,* but
the first collection consists mainly of works on U.S. history, description, and
biography (96 titles); English literature (115 titles); and science (92 titles).

Unfortunately, the contents of the first collection in the *Essential Books*
series are duplicated in *Library Collections* to some extent—though it is obvious

that *Essential Books* is not simply an abridgment of the larger program. For example, of the nine titles listed under *U.S.—Description and Travel* in the *Essential Books* catalog, five are also listed in the 1971 *Library Collections* catalog; nine titles are listed under *Arthurian Legends* and five under *Astronomy*, and while none of these is duplicated in the *Library Collections* for 1971, two of the former and three of the latter are in the *Library Collections* catalog for 1970.[29, 30, 31, 32, 33] This duplication is regrettable because any library that buys the *Library Collections* might also elect to buy collections in the *Essential Books* series. Indeed, some prospective purchasers of the *Library Collections* might prefer to begin by buying the *Essential Books*.

The second part of the *College-Bound Program* is the *College Catalogs* series. The first collection in this series, published in 1971, contains catalogs from "about five hundred colleges," ranging from junior colleges to major universities.[34] In 1972 a second collection of catalogs, from another 500 schools, is to be published. Thereafter, these two collections will be updated in alternate years. Current catalogs for the first group of schools will be published in odd-numbered years and for the second group, in even-numbered years.

The price of the first *College Catalogs* collection is $250 (both of the 1971 *College-Bound* collections can be purchased for $700) and its value is obvious to anyone who has ever maintained a collection of catalogs in a library, whether it be a school, public, or academic library.

NCR is developing another Ultrafiche publication that should be of interest to librarians. Although it is not now available for purchase, it is being tested in British libraries. This is a current bibliography of books in English, compiled from MARC data generated by the Library of Congress and the British National Bibliography. The main sequence of entries in this bibliography is arranged in Decimal Classification order. It is planned as a throwaway bibliography, with new entries interfiled among those that went before, on new Ultrafiche. During the British experiment the Ultrafiche are being discarded and replaced at six-week intervals.[35]

LRI'S COLLECTION

NCR and LRI have much in common. They share the same basic problems in their efforts to fill library needs with high-reduction microfiche reproductions. But LRI's marketing strategy is quite different from NCR's; consequently, their products, which seem very much alike, are really quite different.

Where NCR has defined a group of subject areas and planned to publish a series of relatively small collections in each area, LRI plans to publish a series of larger collections, each on a different subject, and each one independent of the others. So far, LRI has produced only one of these collections, the *Library of American Civilization*, though two others are in preparation, and others are being planned. The two collections in preparation are *Medieval Civilization* and *English Literature*.[36] Presumably, these collections and those that follow them will be similar to the *Library of American Civilization*.

The *Library* is limited to works about the United States and American life, and works by Americans—as evidence of American thought—before 1914. Within these limitations, its scope is quite broad, as this list of its subject subdivisions shows.

Politics and Government	The Frontier
Constitutional History	The South
Foreign Affairs	Agriculture
Military History	Business
Reform	Labor
Intellectual History	Literature
Science and Technology	Music
Education	Visual Arts
Religion	Architecture
Afro-Americans	The City
American Indians	Manners and Customs
Immigration and Minorities	Local History
Early Exploration	

In addition to the works listed in its catalog under these subject headings, the *Library* includes runs of 62 periodicals like the following.[37]

> *The American Magazine and Historical Chronicle.* Boston, 1743-46.
> *Godey's Magazine.* Title varies, 1830-1860. 60v.
> *Overland Monthly and Out West Magazine.* San Francisco, Overland Publishing Company: etc., etc., 1883-1905.
> *Scientific American* . . . New York, Munn & Co., 1845-1905. 120v.

It also includes an added documents collection. In contrast to NCR's *Government Documents* series, this collection is composed chiefly of documents other than federal publications, e.g.:

> *Calendar of (N.Y.) Council Minutes,* 1668-1783. N.Y. State Library, Albany, 1902.
> *The Jesuit Relations and Allied Documents: Travels and Explorations of the Jesuit Missionaries in New France,* 1610-1791. Cleveland, The Burrows Brothers Company, 1896-1901. 73v.
> *Proceedings of the Sessions of the General Assembly of the Knights of Labor,* 1878-1897.
> *South Carolina (colony) Assembly, Journal of Commons House of Assembly of South Carolina,* 1692-1727. 19v. Columbia. 1907-1946.

All of the government publications in the *Library* aren't listed in this collection. The majority of them are scattered throughout its various subject areas.

The *Library* contains approximately 20,000 volumes, recorded on the same number of Microbooks. Its more than 15,000 titles were selected by a team of fifty scholars. Its contents are, on an average, older than the works in the *Library Collections.* Only about 2 percent of its titles were published after 1920, though a few of the editions included were published in the 1940s and 1950s. Eighty-five percent were published before 1900, and nearly ten percent before 1800. A few of the works included date from the sixteenth century. Most are American in origin, and less than 1 percent of them are in other languages than English.

Some parts of the *Library Collections* cover subject areas also covered in the *Library of American Civilization.* In these areas, many of the titles in the

140

Library Collections are also included in the *Library of American Civilization*. For example, of a sample of sixty titles in NCR's 1970 *American Civilization* collection, 37 are also in the catalog of the LRI collection. On the other hand, in other areas there is much less duplication. For example, in NCR's 1970 *Science and Technology* collection there are 294 titles; of these, only one is listed in the Science and Technology section of the *Library of American Civilization*— and that one in a different edition.

In its collections, NCR is seeking to provide "monographs, source materials, and treatises in every major discipline."[38] Its emphasis, however, is on major works that are frequently cited—works of the sort that every serious student needs to know within his own discipline. The *Library of American Civilization* contains works of the same type; but, in addition, it contains a great mass of contemporary writing—directories, tracts, sermons, pamphlets, and propaganda. For example:

> *The American Alarm, or the Bostonian Plea, for the Rights and Liberties, of the People. Humbly Addressed to the King and Council; and to the Constitutional Sons of.* . . . Boston, Printed by D. Keeneland, and N. Davis, 1773.
>
> *A Sketch of the Origin and Progress of the Causes Which Have Led to the Overthrow of Our Union* . . . Washington, D.C., 1861.
>
> *Serious Facts, Opposed to "Serious Considerations," or, The Voice of Warning to Religious Republicans* . . . 1800. New York, 1800.
>
> Livermore, Abiel Abbot, *Lectures to Young Men on Their Moral Dangers and Duties.* Boston, J. Munroe and Company, 1847.
>
> Ragan, John, *The Emigrant's Guide to the Western States of America.* 2d ed. Edinburgh, Oliver & Boyd; etc., etc., 1852.
>
> Duer, William Alexander. *A Reply to Mr. Colden's Vindication of the Steam-Boat Monopoly.* Albany, Printed and pub. by E. and E. Hosford, 1819.

The *Library*'s literature section contains a wide range of American writing— poetry, drama, and prose by authors ranging from Henry Adams to Constance Fenimore Woolson. Both well-known and little-known writers are included. The *Bay Psalm Book* and Samuel Willard's *A Compleat Body of Divinity* are here, too. The section on music is also larded with examples, e.g.:

> *Beadle's Dime Songs for the War.* New York, Beadle and Company, 1861.
>
> Christy, Byron. *New Songster and Black Joker.* New York, 1863.
>
> Hopkinson, Francis. *Seven Songs for the Harpsichord or Forte Piano* . . . Philadelphia, 1788.

Each Microbook in this collection is identified by a shortened form of the author's name and the title, printed at the top of the fiche. They are intended to be filed in alphabetical order. Each Microbook is stored in an envelope with a complete Library of Congress catalog entry printed on its face. As aids to retrieval, five sets of book-form catalogs—in which each work is listed by author, title, and subject—are supplied with the *Library of American Civilization*. Ten sets on fiche of the same catalogs and a "Biblioguide" topical index to the collection are also included. The price of the *Library*, with these catalogs, is $21,500. Catalog cards aren't included in this price, but a complete set of cards for the entire collection can be purchased.

141

CONCLUSION

LRI and NCR are offering competing products. Which of the two is the better? The individual library must answer this question for itself. Both firms are reputable, and both groups of products—readers and fiche collections—are good. Each has some advantages relative to the other, or might suit an individual librarian and library better than the other.

The cost of LRI's *Library of American Civilization* and NCR's *Library Collections* is about the same, slightly more than a third of a cent per page. And that's cheap, in comparison with print or conventional microforms.

Neither of these collections is a library in itself. Both are intended only to support or to enrich existing libraries and are expected to be used with books and other record forms. The *Library Collections*, especially, are destined to be incomplete in themselves. NCR generally excludes from them any works, however useful, that can be purchased from other reprint sources for $15.00 or less: it expects such works to be obtained elsewhere by libraries.

Both collections have value—if properly used—for any library that supports or prepares people for higher education, including public libraries. But one might describe NCR's collections as resources for students, and LRI's collection—which contains more source material—as a resource for scholars. The *Library Collections*, then, might be more attractive to junior colleges and other undergraduate schools, and the *Library of American Civilization* (and the collections that will follow it) to schools that support graduate study.

Both collections should be welcome additions to the new library. They would add works that are practically unobtainable from any other source. Paradoxically, however, these collections should be even more valuable additions to well-established libraries with strong collections. Books gain in utility by being associated with other similar books, and the individual works in these collections would be much more useful if added to a library that is already rich than if added to a library that is relatively poor. And it is unlikely that any library has all of the works in these collections. For example, the University of Kentucky's library, which boasts of more than a million volumes and is especially strong in history, has only about 60 percent of the titles in the 1970 *Library Collections*, and about 50 percent of the titles in the *Library of American Civilization.*

Finally, these collections really should not be regarded as alternatives. They do overlap to a degree, but they are also complementary. So the library that decides to buy either should give serious consideration to the acquisition of the other as well.

REFERENCES

1. National Archives and Records Service, *Managing Information Retrieval: Microform Retrieval Equipment Guide.* Washington, 1970. p. 6.

2. Committee on Scientific and Technical Information, *Federal Microfiche Standards.* 3rd ed. Springfield, Va., Clearinghouse for Federal Scientific and Technical Information, 1968. p. 1.

3. National Archives and Record Service, *Managing Information Retrieval,* p. 5.

4. *Microfilm Norms Recommended for Libraries.* Chicago, ALA Resources and Technical Services Division, 1966. p. 33.

5. National Archives and Records Service, *Managing Information Retrieval,* p. 36.

6. Franklin D. Crawford, *The Microfilm Technology Primer on Scholarly Journals.* Princeton, N.J., Princeton Microfilm Corp., 1969. p. 16.

7. William R. Hawken, *Copying Methods Manual.* Chicago, Library Technology Program, American Library Association, 1966. pp. 192-93.

8. Karl K. Klessig, *The Technical Considerations of Micropublishing,* prepared for Electro-Optical System Design Conference, New York, September 1970. Chicago, Library Resources, Inc. pp. 9-10.

9. Robert F. Asleson, "Microforms: Where Do They Fit?," *LRTS,* 15:58 (Winter 1971).

10. Verner W. Clapp, *The Future of the Research Library.* Urbana, University of Illinois Press, 1964. p. 20.

11. *Ibid.,* p. 19.

12. Crawford, *The Microfilm Technology Primer,* p. 11.

13. Clapp, *The Future of the Research Library,* p. 19.

14. *Microfilm: the White Rabbit.* Wooster, Ohio, Bell & Howell, Micro-Photo Division, 1970. p. 5.

15. "Books in English: a Microform Bibliography Goes on Trial," *Bookseller,* 3384:2226 (31 October 1970).

16. William R. Hawken, Karl K. Klessig, and Carl E. Nelson, *Microbook Publication, a New Approach for a New Decade.* Chicago, Library Resources, Inc., 1970. pp. 8-9.

17. Clapp, *The Future of the Research Library,* p. 19.

18. *NCR's Answer to the Problems of Printing and Distributing Vast Amounts of Information.* Dayton, NCR Microform Systems, 1970. p. [1].

19. Donald C. Holmes, "The Needs of Library Microform Users," in National Microfilm Association, *Proceedings of the Seventeenth Annual Meeting and Convention,* ed. by Vernon D. Tate. Annapolis, 1968. p. 258.

20. Holmes, "The Needs of Library Microform Users," p. 258.

21. Arthur Treplitz, "Library Fiche: an Introduction and Explanation," in National Microfilm Association, *Proceedings of the Seventeenth Annual Meeting and Convention,* ed. by Vernon D. Tate. Annapolis, 1968. p. 129.

22. Hawken, *Microbook Publication,* p. 9.

23. *Unique Features of the Microbook Library Series.* Chicago, Library Resources, Inc., n.d. p. 3.

24. " 'Microbooks,' a New Library Medium?," *Publishers' Weekly,* 198:50 (9 November 1970).

25. *Here Are the Books Behind the Bibliographies . . .* Dayton, NCR Educational Products Dept., 1970. p. 1.

26. *Ibid.,* pp. 67-78.

27. *Ibid.,* pp. 29-59.

28. *College-Bound Collections—1971.* Dayton, NCR Educational Products Dept., 1971. pp. 3-10.

29. *Ibid.,* p. 3.

30. *1971 Edition, PCMI Collection, American Civilization.* Dayton, NCR Educational Products Dept., 1971. pp. 3-8.

31. *College-Bound Collections—1971,* p. 5.

32. *Ibid.,* p. 9.

33. *Here Are the Books Behind the Bibliographies,* pp. 40, 71.

34. *College-Bound Collections—1971,* p. 11.

35. "Books in English," pp. 2222-28.

36. Robert C. Sullivan, "Developments in Photo Reproduction of Library Materials, 1970," *LRTS* 15:164 (Spring 1971).

37. *The Microbook Library of American Civilization.* Chicago, Library Resources, Inc., 1970. 351p.

38. *Here Are the Books,* p. 1.

UNDERTAKING A SUBJECT CATALOG IN MICROFICHE*

By Katherine Gaines

In June 1970 Ramapo Catskill Library System initiated a subject catalog in microfiche form. This consists of 178 (4 x 6) microfiche including approximately 60,000 subject entries for books available throughout the Ramapo System. Each microfiche has at the top in eye-readable text the first and last subject heading included on that microfiche. The complete set of this subject guide takes up four inches of filing space. One set has been given to each of the 45 libraries in the system free of charge.

The headquarters staff felt that a subject listing to Ramapo Catskill Library System (RCLS) area library books would provide not only quicker access to what patrons wanted but also would spur interest in other referred subjects. *Books in Print, Cumulative Book Index*, and other standard bibliographies with their thousands of entries can be self-defeating to many patrons. If the subject is all that is needed (not a particular book or author) and cannot be found in the local library, Interlibrary Loan Department time can be saved for more specialized tasks, since three vital conditions are met to expedite the filling of the request satisfactorily.

1. Item has been selected by the patron himself.
2. Automatic verification (copied from reproduction of Union Catalog record).
3. Availability in the area.

Hopefully, an increasing percentage of TWX (teletype) items will no longer have to be diverted to the state or other institutions outside RCLS. This will result in future costs savings to the taxpayer, albeit proof of this claim would be improbable.

Throughout library literature of the 60s were found statements such as: "Initially microfilming was thought of as a technique for space reduction in some special libraries or in connection with the need for preservation of materials in scholarly libraries. This was true both for files that were going to be stored away for safekeeping and for the preservation of much more fragile documents, such as newspapers. However, microforms are now beginning to be used as a medium of communication, much as books and report literature are used."[1]

We at Ramapo are enthusiastic about microfiche applied to a subject catalog because:

1. It is a microform system designed and tailored for user requirements.
2. Our pattern of learning and knowledge from earliest childhood is divided into units or categories or subjects. This concept is easiest for us to handle. A unit microform merely adds a new technical dimension to aid us in switching, copying, or redistributing information.
3. A unit microform is a simple economical means of preparing and distributing technical documents where the unit is generally 5 to several hundred pages long.

*Reprinted from *Library Resources and Technical Services*, 15:297-308, Summer 1971.

4. Within the last year, major federal government technical information service and others, here and overseas, have standardized on microfiche to distribute technical report literature. They use a standard format recommended by the National Microfilm Association, and the COSATI group of the Federal Council for Science and Technology. The outputs of these agencies represent the greater percentage of technical report literature being distributed today. Continuity and compatibility will bring a greater availability of pertinent information, a wider range of good low cost using equipment.
5. Unit microforms are easily filed, easily found, and easily retrieved. They can be interfiled, regrouped for user convenience, used one at a time as a unit, and stored in a minimum of space. The user has a choice of copying the documents in a miniaturized form or full size. He can select and copy pages at will. Convenient equipment, including readers, reader-printers, hard copy printers of many manufacturers are available to make full use of the unit microform.[2]

National Cash Register (NCR) has put it this way: "One 60-page report on one microfiche. No need to wind through 100 feet of film to find the report you want. No need to tie up 100 feet of film while you look at one report."[3]

In other words, once the machinery was available for the use of the micro-fiche catalog, the machine could be put to other uses in reading actual books and articles, and only limited by what the mushrooming micropublishers will be issuing and, of course, the capabilities of the machine itself.

It was felt, therefore, that the new catalog would be put to the most effective use if each library purchased a machine, which is called a reader, to be used exclusively for microfiche. The Atlantic F66 Microfiche reader, which we chose, had several definite advantages.
1. It is sturdy and simple to operate.
2. It enables the user to adjust the focal point in such a manner that it moves over the entire surface of the fiche vertically and horizontally at will, both backwards and forwards. Subjects could thus be easily searched, compared, and identified.

Some of the larger libraries wanted expensive machines which operate both microfilm and microfiche. The use of time-consuming attachments, i.e., a micro-fiche attachment to a microfilm machine, etc., was discouraged. Immediate access to a dependable microfiche reader was essential if proper use of the catalog was to be rewarding. Also, it was strongly felt that our libraries would particularly benefit from the economy of the low prices of materials on microfiche. Constant and ready accessibility to microfiche through a machine was of utmost importance.[4]

Throughout the project, which truly began in the middle of December 1969, many decisions had to be made under pressure. We set a deadline of April 15, 1970. We undertook the project with no extra filing or typing staff, but our staff did a magnificent job of filing 58,500 cards in the five and a half months while keeping other essential duties going. We logged 659 hours of filing including the revision of each card according to the second edition of *ALA Rules for Filing*.

CATALOG CARDS

After considering the advantages and disadvantages of using negative or positive film, we decided on recommending negative film for the following reasons.

1. Articles definitely are easier to read on negative film because less light reaches the reader's eye and we felt that librarians should train patrons to feel comfortable with negative.
2. Presumably card catalogs seldom will be used for reading, instead they will be used for locating subjects quickly.
3. Scratches are distracting on positive fiche, particularly in the case of catalog card reproduction.
4. Negative replacements are quicker and cheaper to reproduce.
5. Most reader-printers are designed to work best with negative microfiche because black and white is reversed in printout.
6. Used by government agencies for distributing reports.[5]

Although it is true that positive film renders photographs easier to interpret and many people find positive easier to adjust to, we felt that the advantages outweighed the disadvantages of the negative.

Therefore, fifty sets of negative were contracted for. Five positive sets were ordered at a greater cost and the first five libraries requesting these received them. We felt that through system-wide discussion and debate we will have learned much in this area when we update the catalog in 1971.

This subject guide on microfiche is referred to when the patron of the library cannot find subject access in the library's own card catalog. (However, it should be borne in mind that this edition of the catalog is restricted to the selection of Central Book Aid (CBA) materials and 68-69 RCLS pool collection books plus three hundred selected holdings from member libraries which are not duplicated in the pool collection. Therefore, representation of many *popular* subject areas is excluded.) Depending on each library's decision, especially during the first months of getting acquainted with the actual physical use of this form of a catalog and the machine, the patron may or may not look for subjects on his own. In particular regard to this question (and other related matters), please refer to the results of a survey conducted among the member libraries and given in Appendix 1.

In making a search for subjects requested, the librarian goes to the microfiche file holder and simply selects the correct microfiche (i.e., by looking at the index guide at the top) and inserts the sheet of film into a microfiche reader. The image of the original catalog card with its subject heading at the top of the card appears clear and enlarged on the screen (actually several cards are seen at once on the screen). Since microfiche is the fastest way of retrieving *so long as the filing is free of error*, an important step has been made economically in enabling the people in our communities to know immediately if any of these subjects can direct them to the material they need. If the catalog is heavily used, a cumulation will be planned in 1971; the goal is at least an additional 40,000 entries. The usefulness and value will be tripled because of the experience we have gained in producing this first catalog.

Filing integrity is not a serious problem with the short four inches of 178 subject guide fiche, each one of which is marked clearly: "1 of 178," "2 of 178," etc. However, when the library's files are increased to more than fifteen inches, a simple system of color coding will be introduced to assure with ease the accurate replacement of fiche in their holder cabinets.

By October it is hoped that library patrons can benefit from using the guide for themselves at certain times. The user is asked to fill out a brief charge slip. Upon return of the fiche to the desk, the slip is torn up and the fiche is immediately refiled by the librarian. However, if time is required to teach a patron how to use a reader during busy hours, it should be understood that he can use the card catalog and subject bibliographies in book form and be invited to come back when time can be devoted to introducing him to the use of microfiche. Also, during the busier hours, written requests for subjects could, of course, be put aside for the librarian to search at some more convenient time.

For easier and more direct subject access we are experimenting with truncated subject headings. The Library of Congress advocates abbreviated 17th edition Dewey classification numbers for certain libraries. To help libraries determine a shorter number without having to take time to think out the structure of the classification scheme of that number, the number is truncated by prime marks (i.e., 021'0095) on the Library of Congress card. A local library can then use the truncation mark as the cutoff point. The computers of processing centers in reproducing catalog cards, as we understand it, can be economically instructed to stop at such a symbol and do one of the following:

1. Ignore what follows the mark in the printout (providing there is consistency in always wanting this to be done).
2. Overlook what follows the mark in the filing scheme.

We indicated our truncation of certain redundant subdivisions by utilizing a tiny dividing black bar inked on the card in front of the dash before an undesired subdivision. Thus we could consolidate subject areas for public library use. It was agreed that this consolidation is more essential than separating materials merely by the fact that it is a "popular work," an "introduction," or an "essay." Such subdivisions especially become lost among essential subdivisions such as "–AFRICA"; "–BOSTON"; "–BIBLIOGRAPHY"; and "–HISTORY."

Knowledge and experience in the handling of materials, however, is essential to ascertain what subjects might *need* to keep selected subdivisions, which in most cases should be truncated for average public library use. For instance, literature works might best be kept separated by "–ADDRESSES, ESSAYS, LECTURES" when this subdivision applies to the work being cataloged (i.e., AMERICAN LITERATURE–ADDRESSES, ESSAYS, LECTURES, but there is little significance in using *GEOLOGY–ADDRESSES, ESSAYS, LECTURES*).

Following are examples of subject headings which include truncated subdivisions with the tiny black bar. Please note that these subdivisions are ignored in the filing order of the microfiche subject catalog.

1. –ADDRESSES, ESSAYS, LECTURES (as is illustrated in figure 1)
2. –POPULAR WORKS

Of what practical use is this differentiation to the public library catalog? This subdivision should be interfiled among the main headings GEOLOGY and not "lost" on another fiche among *fifty* necessary subdivisions of *GEOLOGY*.

The truncation sign before "Collections" has consolidated the filing of these two works by Bartlett on the same subject.

This entry would have filed 200 cards afterwards if the truncation sign had been omitted.

U.S.–FOREIGN RELATIONS
327. Bartlett, Ruhl Jacob, 1897–
73   Policy and power; two centuries
Ba   of American foreign relations. [1st
        ed.] New York, Hill and Wang
        [1963]

UNITED STATES–FOREIGN
RELATIONS ▌–COLLECTIONS
327. Bartlett, Ruhl Jacob, 1897– ed.
73   The record of American diplo-
Ba   macy; documents and readings in
        the history of American foreign
        relations, edited by Ruhl J. Bart-
        lett. 4th ed. enl.

U.S.–FOREIGN RELATIONS ▌–
ADDRESSES, ESSAYS, LEC-
TURES
327. Bemis, Samuel Flagg, 1891–
73   American foreign policy and the
        blessings of liberty, and other essays.
        New Haven, Yale Univ. Press, 1962.

U.S.–FOREIGN RELATIONS
327. Bemis, Samuel Flagg, 1891.– ed.
73   The American Secretaries of
Be   State and their diplomacy. New
        York, Cooper Square Publishers,
        1963–   [v. 1-10. c1928]

Figure 1

149

"Necessary" subdivisions are:
GEOLOGY–BIBLIOGRAPHY
GEOLOGY–CANADA
GEOLOGY–HISTORY
3. –COLLECTIONS
Many people looking in a public library catalog can see no advantage in particularizing most subjects as "COLLECTIONS" or as "COLLECTED WORKS." Anthologies of poems or essays–yes! *AMERICAN POETRY–COLLECTIONS* is necessary to lead patrons to anthologies.
4. –INTRODUCTIONS
Similar to the subject heading POPULAR WORKS, the above subdivision can serve to separate in the catalog an author's works (see in figure 2 the three cards having Karl Barth as the author). A sensible policy would be to rely on subtitles, annotations, etc., in browsing among catalog cards to find this aspect of a subject. In most cases this would not take long. (See illustration in figure2.)

THEOLOGY, DOCTRINAL
238. Barth, Karl, 1886–
11   Dogmatics in outline. With a
Ba   new foreword by the author. [Trans-
        lation by G. T. Thompson] New
        York, Harper [1959]

This card
would have
been filed
50 cards after-
wards if the
truncation sign
had been
omitted.

THEOLOGY, DOCTRINAL –
INTRODUCTIONS

230. Barth, Karl, 1886
081   Evangelical theology; an intro-
Ba   duction. Translated by Grover
        Foley. [1st ed.] New York, Holt,
        Rinehart and Winston [1963]

THEOLOGY, DOCTRINAL
238.5 Barth, Karl, 1886–
Ba   The knowledge of God and the
        service of God according to the
        teaching of the reformation, re-
        calling the Scottish confession of
        1560.

Figure 2

Furthermore, it is too much to expect cataloging consistency in these particulars. The Library of Congress itself omits the subdivision "–Introductions" in the tracing for several titles even though there are clues to this fact on the card, such as the subtitle reading "an introduction," etc. For example, perhaps there is an obscure technical reason for omitting "Introductions" in the subject tracing "1. Insects" for the work entitled *Entomology for Introductory Courses*, 1951, by Robert Matheson. Nevertheless, public library cataloging should not have to involve itself in trying to be consistent with Library of Congress practice in tracing comparatively useless subdivisions.

Moreover, for the patron who is looking for "an introduction" or for the scholar who wants "collections" on a subject, the information is still there on the microfiche reader screen. The subdivision is simply not used in the filing order. However, as has been implied, we hope the Library of Congress offers the service of truncated subject tracings. The cards which are commercially produced will no longer show certain subdivisions in the heading at the top although the tracing at the bottom of the card would still be printed in and could therefore be used for its information value. For example, the subject at the top of the card might read as "POVERTY" but the tracing would still show as "1. Poverty ▮–Addresses, essays, lectures."

On the microfiche project there were two subdivisions which were marked out (there was no time for either retyping or erasing) as being confusing and misleading. "Translations into English" was deleted, since this catalog is one of English works and is therefore completely redundant. The second one is "Selections: Extracts, etc."; and "Collections" instead was preferred and added.

"Selections: extracts, etc." separates collections of works too particularly for most tastes, assumes too much knowledge of subdivision on the part of both patron and librarian, does not apply to many books, and is often too time-consuming to verify for catalogers. What practical advantage can there be, therefore, in such a distinction?

We just did not foresee certain unfortunate results from filming the catalog cards in this manner. And although the usefulness of the catalog is not diminished, its critics can find the points described below irritating and time-consuming. Now that we have gained hindsight in the traditional trial-and-error way, we can promise far more effectiveness in the next edition by instructing the company on how to avoid these flaws.

First, the most serious time-consumer is finding the continuation of the same subject on a second fiche without any indication of its being continued; that is, it should have had on the label: ARTHUR, KING (Continued on fiche 12). Since it is undesirable to have headings split in this manner, however, the next edition of the catalog will not have this drawback at all. It is true that often a main heading would have to be split, but one subdivision of that main heading (or subject) would be completely listed on one fiche before beginning on the next with another subdivision of the same subject headings.

Included in the index labels were see references. On fiche no. 19, the label has: *BOOKS–HISTORY to BRIGHT CHILDREN see GIFTED CHILDREN*. The word "see" was fortunately typed in lower case but see references should never have been included in the labels at the top of the fiche (the part of each fiche that is in eye-readable print). However, once the confusion is explained "away," time can be saved since fiche no. 19, for example, does not have to be placed in the reader at all; that is, if one wants material on BRIGHT CHILDREN, one should extract fiche no. 64 which includes material about *GIFTED CHILDREN*. If this catalog is updated, see references will be omitted from the labels, notwithstanding the advantage just mentioned.

Naturally, inaccuracies in filing resulted but the error incidence is surprisingly low considering the rate of speed at which the filing was implemented in changing over to the new ALA rules. "AFL-CIO" is found mistakenly after "Afghanistan" instead of where it should be: the first card ahead of *AACHEN–HISTORY*. It is a peculiar rule to understand at first since periods are not used with the initials; i.e., AFL instead of A.F.L.

The print on the cards themselves was uneven. In some cases, it was very light; this resulted in uneven exposure because camera registration was set in such a way to keep labor costs down. Some of the fiche are thus difficult to read. Many are being turned in because they are blurred. However, the master copy renders legible copies and replacements are sent immediately to the member libraries.

Regrettably, there was not enough time on this edition to treat cancelled subject headings properly or give enough explanatory references. For example, do people know the distinctions Library of Congress makes between *MARRIAGE, MIXED* and *MISCEGENATION*? In a new edition of this catalog, we will treat cancelled subjects as illustrated in Figure 3.

The present
microfiche
catalog has
only the
suggestion:
"*See also.*"

FACTORIES–MAINTENANCE AND REPAIR For works cataloged since 1966 see PLANT MAINTENANCE
PLANT MAINTENANCE For works cataloged before 1967 see FACTORIES–MAINTENANCE AND REPAIR

Figure 3

One side effect that has not been mentioned is that small libraries will be able to catalog some of their holdings just as if it were a "cataloging-in-publication" (formerly "cataloging-in-source") service.

Since cross-referencing will be tailor-made for RCLS, all personnel in our libraries will probably begin to see the advantages of knowing about true subject access. One of our librarians wanted material on "Language Arts." Library of Congress does not recognize this as a "bonafide" subject heading but guidance is given in the following: "LANGUAGE ARTS, *see* COMMUNICATION, ENGLISH LANGUAGE, LITERATURE, LITERATURE–STUDY AND TEACHING, READING, SPEECH." The referred subjects are now listed in a column, but we receive most cross-references from commercial firms with each one separately printed, and we have to revise and edit them. Since hundreds of revisions are made by the Library of Congress each year in both subject and name headings, each New York State Library System headquarters should aid the member libraries in basic updating. All public libraries in a given area cannot be expected to keep up with the supplements to *Subject Headings Used in the Dictionary Catalogs of the Library of Congress,* 7th edition, and *Sears* does not keep up with language changes.

Introducing microfiche to libraries required further education and aid in gathering the right kind of materials. Effective implementation of the project necessitates many hours on the phone, and a personal visit to each member library was made by the cataloging and reference headquarters staff to demonstrate microfiche readers.

In order to insure the all-important integrity of filing of the fiche, a simple means of color-coding, using a permanent felt-tip marker, will be introduced to each member library when it requests it. One member library is acquiring a sizable microfiche collection and we have already suggested a simple method of drawing straight lines diagonally on the bottom of a group of fiche. If a fiche is not found in its regular place or two or three places either way (and, of course, if it is not a numbered group as, for example, our subject catalog on microfiche), the group of usually three to seven inches is gripped together, turned upside-down, and the missing item shows up easily by the markings being out of line.

The opinions about the project from the directors of the member libraries are variable, but on the whole, this catalog is a successful and economical means of getting better subject access in the hands of our readers (cf. Appendix 2). Meanwhile, at the system headquarters we are busy working on a bigger and better edition!

In closing, I wish to quote some choice statements from an article entitled "Little Fiche Eat Big Librarians—One Whale of a Story," by Edward C. Jestes.

Librarians are now drowning in the flood of paper produced by the polluting pulp mills. Our weakness is our meticulous record keeping. In the process of record keeping something rubs off—we have memories, and human librarians are the best information retrieval system in existence. Lack of information and its dissemination could be blamed for the very possible destruction of the delicately balanced life system of earth and atmosphere which took millions of years to evolve. Lack of information on how people might learn to be gentle and loving could make life miserable for our children. The world's information is channeled across the desks of librarians, and if some of this information can be put into machines and compacted to save space and time and permit more efficient retrieval, then librarians should be the most efficient candidates for the job.

Librarians must flow over, under, around, and into the black boxes, put them to good use, and not let technology dehumanize anybody— librarians or patrons.

It might help if librarians were given an hour each day to read about microfiche, systems analysis, programming, critical path analysis, use and control of media centers, and one's own subject specialty. How about it, administrators? Industry has been supporting continuing education of its employees for years.[6]

APPENDIX 1

This questionnaire was sent to RCLS Member Libraries. The answers which were returned are summarized on the right-hand side below.

Affirmative answers
(Approximate figures)

I. Subject catalog on microfiche
  1. Do you find this catalog useful?   84%
  2. Have you allowed the public to use this
     catalog by themselves?
     Comment *"They love it"–"We are still in*
     the process of educating"–"As setup permits"–
     etc.   52%
  3. If you had an extra set, would you like to see
     the public use it in the same way a book or card
     catalog is used?   68%
  4. The new edition of the subject catalog will
     have at least twice as many entries. Are
     you looking forward to the ENLARGED
     edition of subjects?   94%

II. Use of the microfiche reader in your library
  1. Do your patrons use the reader for
     ERIC articles?   42%
  2. Have you ordered periodicals or other
     materials on microfiche?   36%
  3. How often is your subject catalog used each
     week?   ?:4; never:1; 1-5:6; 6-10:6;
                         more than 10:2.
  4. Do you have any plans to purchase other
     materials on fiche?   52%
  5. Has any attempt been made to help older
     people overcome objection to reading
     material in this manner?   21%

The latest complete tabulated system report (1969) was used as the basis for eliminating certain small libraries from being included in the percentages on the preceding page. These "small" libraries serve less than 5,000 populations and/or are locally funded less than $15,000 a year. Eight of the fifteen libraries

154

in this group sent in answers and only two of those eight answered I. (1) and I. (4) negatively. More bibliographic selection aid and personal visits will be required before the smaller libraries derive the most benefit from the microfiche project. In the aforementioned group of better funded libraries, 79 percent of these 24 libraries selected to be included in the table answered the questionnaire.

The following three libraries were also excluded in the report: Newburgh, the RCLS central library (a complete CBA subject card catalog is housed there); Monroe (only recently received their microfiche reader); and Spring Valley (now withdrawn from the system).

APPENDIX 2

Cost comparison with the book catalog.
CBA book catalog (printed by Data-Matic Systems Corp.)

			Entries	
1967	100 copies:	Author and Subject entries for each work	51,000	$11,264.00
1968	100 copies:	Author and Subject entries for each work	4,153	922.00
				$12,186.00

(Approximately 55,000 entries)

Subject Microfiche Catalog (1970)

Ordered		Quantity	Unit	Price
178	Masters 105 x 148 per 1,000 images	178	25.00	$1,467.97
8,900	Diazo Duplicates backed each 105 x 148	8,900	.13	1,157.00
890	Silver positives duplicates each	890	.15	133.00
		(58,720 entries)		$2,757.97

(Approximately 60,000 entries)

Another way to put it:

	50 sets (negative) $23.14 each	$1,157.00
	5 sets (positive) $26.75 each	133.00
	Basic costs of master set	1,467.97
		$2,757.97

Microfiche holder cabinets	
46 (Demco) with discount	$ 497.06
Money set aside for readers to each	
member library (110.07 plus delivery)	$5,535.00
approx.	
Total for catalog sets, readers, and holders	$8,790.53
approx.	

REFERENCES

1. Douglas M. Knight, ed., *Libraries at Large.* New York, Bowker, 1969. p. 622.

2. A. I. Baptie, ed., *Microfiche Planning Guide for Technical Document Distribution Systems.* West Salem, Wis., Microcard Corp., c1965. p. 2.

3. NCR Microcard Editions, *Catalog 10. 1969-70.* Washington, D.C., Industrial Products Division, National Cash Register Co. p. 1.

4. The author wishes to express special appreciation to the following: Mrs. Joseph Gobolos, RCLS Reference Coordinator; Mr. Sumner White, former RCLS Assistant Director; and Mr. Joseph Kelley, Production Manager for the Atlantic Microfilm Corp. Also, Mr. James Connolly, Program Manager, Arcata Corp.

5. NCR Microcard Editions, *Catalog 10, 1969-70*, p. 2.

6. Edward C. Jestes, "Little Fiche Eat Big Librarians—One Whale of a Story," *Wilson Library Bulletin,* 44:650-52 (February 1970).

COMPUTER TECHNOLOGY

It is generally agreed that the computer is destined to significantly change library operations in the future. The quantity of literature generated on this subject is enormous. One cannot, in a work of this type, do justice to the field. The articles selected do provide an overview of the field, some utilization practices today, and will perhaps lead the reader to further explore implications for the future.

HISTORY OF LIBRARY COMPUTERIZATION*

By Frederick Kilgour

This historical scrutiny seeks the origins of library computerization and traces its development through innovative applications. The principal evolutionary steps following upon a major application are also depicted. The investigation is not confined to library-oriented computerization, for it examines mechanization of the use of library tools as well; indeed, the first half-dozen years of library computerization were devoted only to user applications.

The study reveals two major trends in library computerization. First, there are those applications designed primarily to benefit the user, although few, if any, applications have but one goal. The earliest such applications were machine searches of subject indexes employing post-coordination of Uniterms. Nearly a decade later, the first of the bookform catalogs appeared that made catalog information far more widely available to users than do card catalogs. Finally, networks are under development that have as their objective availability of regional resources to individual users.

The second trend is employment of computers to perform repetitive, routine library tasks, such as catalog production, order and accounting procedures, serials control, and circulation control. This type of mechanization is extremely important as a first step toward an increasingly productive library technology, which must be an ultimate goal if libraries are to be economically viable in the future (1, 2).

Historical studies of library computerization have not yet appeared, although some reports beginning with that of L. R. Bunnow (3) in 1960 contain valuable literature reviews. Both editions of *Literature on Information Retrieval and Machine Translation* by C. F. Balz and R. H. Stanwood (4, 5) are extremely useful. In addition, J. A. Speer's *Libraries and Automation* (6) is a valuable, retrospective bibliography of over three thousand entries.

ORIGINS

The origins of library computerization were in engineering libraries newly established in the 1950s and employing the Uniterm coordinate indexing tech-

*Reprinted by permission from *Journal of Library Automation*, 3:218-29, September 1970.

niques of Mortimer Taube on collections of report literature. The technique of post-coordination of simple index terms proved most suitable for computerization, particularly when the size of a file caused manual manipulation to become cumbersome.

Harley E. Tillitt presented the first report, albeit unpublished at the time, on library computerization at the U.S. Naval Ordnance Test Station (NOTS), now the Naval Weapons Center at China Lake, California. The report, entitled "An Experiment in Information Searching with the 701 Calculator" (7), was given at an IBM Computation Seminar at Endicott, New York, in May 1954. The system was extended and improved in 1956, and a published report appeared in 1957 (8). Tillitt subsequently published an evaluation (9).

The NOTS system mimicked manual use of a Uniterm card file. This noteworthy system could add new information, delete information related to discarded documents, match search requests against the master file, and produce a printout of document numbers selected. Search requests were run in batches, thereby producing inevitable delays that caused user dissatisfaction. When the user did receive results of his search, he had a host of document numbers that he had to take to a shelf list file to obtain titles. Subsequent system designers also found that a computerized system could cause user dissatisfaction if it did not speed up and make more thorough practically all tasks. Because use of the system dwindled, it was not reprogrammed for an IBM 704 that replaced the 701 in 1957. However, a couple of years later, when an IBM 709 became available, the system was reprogrammed and improved so that the user received a list of document titles (10).

Tillitt, Bracken, and their colleagues deserve much credit for their pioneer computerization of a subject information retrieval system. The application required considerable ingenuity, for the IBM 701 did not have built-in character representation. Therefore it was necessary to develop subroutines that simulated character representation (11). Moreover, the 701 had an unreliable electrostatic core memory. On some machines the mean time between failures was less than twenty minutes (12).

In September 1958, General Electric's Aircraft Gas Turbine Division at Evendale, Ohio, initiated a system on an IBM 704 computer (13) that was similar to the NOTS application. Mortimer Taube and C. D. Gull had installed a Uniterm index system at Evendale in 1953 (14, 15). The GE system was an improvement over the then-existing NOTS system because it printed out author and title information for a report selected, as well as an abstract of the report. Like the NOTS system, however, the GE application provided only for Boolean "and" search logic.

The celebrated Medlars system (16) encompassed the first major departure in machine citation searching. The original Medlars had two principal products: 1) composition of *Index Medicus*; and 2) machine searching of a huge file of journal article citations for production of recurrent or on-demand bibliographies. The system became operational in 1964.

The NOTS and GE systems coordinated document numbers as listed under descriptors. Medlars departed from this technique by searching a compressed citation file in which each citation had its descriptors or subject headings associated with it. The Medlars system also provides for Boolean "and," "or," and "not" search logic.

The next major development was DIALOG (17), an on-line system for machine subject searching of the NASA report file. Queries were entered from remote terminals. The SUNY Biomedical Communication Network constitutes an important development in operation of machine subject searching and production of subject bibliographies of traditional library materials. The SUNY network went into operation in the autumn of 1968 with nine participating libraries (18). Its principal innovation is on-line searches from remote terminals of the Medlars journal article file to which book references have been added. The SUNY network eliminates the two major dissatisfactions with the NOTS system and all subsequent batch systems, in that it provides the user with an immediate reply to his search query.

CATALOG PRODUCTION

In 1960, L. R. Bunnow prepared a report for the Douglas Aircraft Company (3) in which he recommended a computerized retrieval system like the NOTS and GE systems that would also include catalog card production. Bunnow's proposal was perhaps the first to contain the concept of production of a single machine readable record from which multiple products could be obtained, such as printed catalog cards and subject bibliographies produced by machine searching. Catalog card production began in May 1961 (19), the cards having a somewhat unconventional format and being printed all in upper-case characters as shown in Figure 1. Cards were mechanically arranged in packs for individual catalogs, and alphabetized within packs—an early sophistication. Accompanying the production of catalog cards was production of accession lists from the same machine readable data.

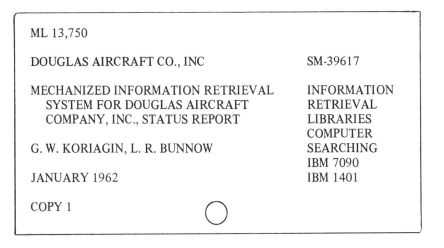

Figure 1. Sample Catalog Card

The next development in catalog card production occurred at the Air Force Cambridge Research Laboratory Library, which began to produce cards mechanically in upper- and lower-case in 1963 (20). A special computer-like device called a Crossfiler manipulated a single machine readable cataloging record on paper tape to produce a complete set of card images punched on paper tape. This paper-tape product drove a Friden Flexo-writer that mechanically typed the cards in upper- and lower-case. Two years later, Yale began to produce catalog cards in upper- and lower-case directly on a high-speed computer printer (21). The Yale cards were also arranged in packs, as had been those at Douglas, but were not alphabetized within packs.

The New England Library Information Network, NELINET, demonstrated in a pilot operation in 1968 a batch processing technique servicing requests from New England state university libraries, via teletype terminals, for production of catalog card sets; book labels, and book pockets from a MARC I catalog data file (22). The NELINET system became operational in the spring of 1970 employing the MARC II data base. Also in 1968 the University of Chicago Library brought into operation catalog card production with data being input remotely on terminals in the Library, and cards being printed in batches on a high-speed computer printer centrally (23).

Bookform catalogs began to appear in the early 1960s, and it appears that the Information Center of the Monsanto Company in St. Louis, Missouri, published the earliest report on a bookform catalog that it had produced by computer in 1962 (24, 25). The Center discontinued its card catalog in the same year. Book catalogs can increase availability of cataloging information to users while reducing library work, and the Monsanto book catalog is an example of such an achievement, for it provides a union catalog of the holdings of seven Monsanto libraries, and is produced in over one hundred copies. As would be expected, the catalog appeared all in upper-case. However, in September 1964 the Library at Florida Atlantic University produced a bookform catalog in upper- and lower-case (26) and the University of Toronto Library put out the first edition of its upper- and lower-case ONULP catalog on 15 February 1965 (27, 28).

The Monsanto catalog format called for author and call number on one line, with title and imprint on a second, or second and third, line. Both Florida Atlantic and Toronto catalogs were essentially catalogs of catalog cards. Under the leadership of Mortimer Taube, Documentation, Inc., was first to produce a bookform catalog in upper- and lower-case, with a format like that of bookform catalogs in the nineteenth century(29); Documentation, Inc., prepared the catalog for the Baltimore County Public Library. Entries were made once, with titles listed under an entry if there were more than one. The Stanford bookform catalog appeared late in 1966, introducing a new type of unit record, whose first element is the title paragraph.

H. P. Luhn proposed selective dissemination of information (SDI) in 1958 (30), and perhaps the first library application of SDI was in the spring of 1962 at the IBM library at Owego (31), where special processing was given to new acquisitions for input into the SDI system. At about the same time, the library of the Douglas Missile & Space Systems Division instituted an SDI system that employed as input a single machine readable record from which catalog cards and accessions lists were also produced (32).

160

The introduction of SDI into library operation is a major, historic innovation, for SDI is a routine but personalized service in contradistinction to the depersonalized library service characteristic of all but the smallest libraries. Selective dissemination of information is one of the few examples of library computerization that takes full advantage of the computer's ability to treat an individual as a person and not as one of a horde of users.

CIRCULATION

The Picatinny Arsenal reported the first computerized circulation system (33). The Picatinny application produced a computer printed loan record, lists of reserves, overdues, lists of books on loan to borrowers, and statistical analysis, in a system that began operation in April 1962. The charge card at Picatinny was an IBM punch card into which was punched the bibliographic data and data concerning the borrower each time the book was charged. In the fall of 1962, the Thomas J. Watson Research Center (34) activated a circulation system much like the Picatinny system, except that bibliographic data were punched into a book card by machine, but information about the borrower was manually punched.

The next step forward occurred at Southern Illinois University (35), where a circulation system like the two just described began limited operation in the spring of 1964 employing an IBM 357 data collection system. By using the 357, it was possible to have a machine punched book card and a machine readable borrower's identification card that could be read by the 357, thereby eliminating manual punching. The Southern Illinois system became fully operational at the beginning of the fall term of 1964, as did a similar 357 system at Florida Atlantic University (26).

Batch processed circulation systems periodically producing a listing of books on loan have a built-in source of dissatisfaction, particularly in academic libraries, for current records are unavailable on the average for half the period of the frequency of the printout. Such delay can be eliminated in an on-line system, wherein information about the loan is available immediately after recording the loan. However, not all circulation systems with remote terminals operate interactively.

In an on-line system introduced at the Illinois State Library in December 1966 (36) the transactions were recorded on an IBM 1031 terminal located at the circulation desk, data transmitted from the terminal being accumulated daily and processed into the file nightly. As first activated, the system did not permit querying the file to determine books charged out, but this capability was added in 1969. Also in December 1966, the Redstone Scientific Information Center brought into operation a pilot on-line book circulation system based on a converted machine readable catalog consisting of brief catalog entries. This pilot system remained in operation until October 1967, and was capable of recording loans, discharging loans, putting out overdues, maintaining reserves, and locating the record in the file (37).

The BELLREL real time loan system went into operation at Bell Laboratories Library in March 1968 (38). BELLREL has a data base consisting of converted catalog records, so that in effect it also is a remote catalog access system.

161

BELLREL serves three libraries remotely from two IBM 1050 terminals in each library. BELLREL is a sophisticated on-line, real time circulation system that not only records and discharges books, but also replies to inquiries as to the status of a title, and the status of a copy, and will display the full record for a title, as would be required for remote catalog access.

SERIALS

The Library of the University of California, San Diego, activated the first computerized serials control system (39). This system has as its objective production of a complete holdings list, lists of current receipts, binding lists, claims, nonreceipt lists, and expiration of subscription lists. Checking in was accomplished by manual removal from a file of a prepunched card for a specific title and issue. The check-in clerk sent this card to the computer center for processing and the journal issue to the shelves. This technique of prepunching receipt cards has generated new problems in some libraries, for professional advice is often needed as to action to be taken when the issue received does not match the prepunched card. Nevertheless, the San Diego system still operates, albeit with modifications.

The Washington University School of Medicine Library activated a serials control system in 1963 (40) that was essentially like that at San Diego. A series of symposia held at Washington University, with the first in the autumn of 1963, widely publicized the system and led to its adoption elsewhere. The University of Minnesota Biomedical Library introduced a technique of writing in receipts of individual journal issues on preprinted check-in lists (41). Check-in data were then keypunched from the lists. This system obviated the problem generated by prepunched cards that did not match received issues, but, of course, reintroduced manual procedures.

Difficulties with check-in procedures, and delays in receipt of printed lists of holdings made it clear that an on-line real time circulation control system would be superior to the batch systems described in the previous paragraph. Laval University in Quebec introduced the first on-line, real time system in 1969 (42). In September 1969 the Laval on-line file held 16,335 titles. Access to the file from cathode ray tube terminals is by accession number and the file, or sections thereof, can be listed. The system also produces operating statistics and contains the potential for automatic claiming.

The *Kansas Union List of Serials* (43), which appeared in 1965, was the first computerized union list to contain holdings of several institutions. The *Kansas Union List* recorded holdings for nearly 22,000 titles in eight colleges and universities. Reproduced photographically from computer printout and printed three columns on a page, this legible and easy-to-use list set the style for many subsequent union lists.

ACQUISITIONS

The National Reactor Testing Station Library was first to use a computer in ordering processes (44). A multiple-part form was produced for library records and for dealers. The Library of the Thomas J. Watson Research Center activated a more sophisticated system in 1964 that produced a processing information list containing titles of all items in process, a shelf list card, a book card, and a book pocket label (45).

The Pennsylvania State University Library put a computerized acquisition system into operation in 1964 (46). This system produced a compact, line-a-title listing of each item in process, together with an indication of the status of the item in processing. A small decklet of punch cards was produced for each item on a keypunch, and one of these cards was sent to the computer center for processing each time its associated item changed status. The Pennsylvania system also produced purchase orders.

In June 1964, the University of Michigan Library (47) introduced a computerized acquisitions procedure more sophisticated than its predecessors. The Michigan system produced a ten-part purchase order fanfold, an in-process listing, and computer produced transaction cards to update status of items in process; and carried out accounting for encumbrance and expenditure of book funds. In addition, the system produced periodic listings of "do-not-claim" orders, listings of requests for quotation, and of "third claims" for decision as to future action on such orders.

In 1966, the Yale Machine Aided Technical Processing System began operation (48). It produced daily and weekly in-process lists arranged by author, a weekly order number listing, weekly fund commitment registers, and notices to requesters of status of request. Subsequently, claims to dealers were added, as well as management information reports on activities within the system. Like the Pennsylvania and Michigan systems, its in-process list recorded the status of the item in processing.

The Washington State University Library brought the first on-line acquisition system into operation in April 1968 (49). Access to the system was by purchase order number, with records arranged in a random access file under addresses computed by a random number generator (50). The Stanford University Libraries on-line acquisition system began operation in 1969 (51), and employed a sequential file of entries having an index of words in author and title elements of the entry. The Stanford system calculated addresses of index words by employing a division hashing technique on the first three letters of the word.

STANDARDIZATION

By 1965, a dozen or more libraries had a dozen or more formats for machine readable bibliographic records, and an impenetrable thicket of such records was evolving. Fortunately, the Library of Congress, with the help of the Council on Library Resources, took the initiative in standardization of format of bibliographic records and produced the now familiar MARC format (52). Just as standardization of catalog card sizes enabled interchange of catalog records, so has MARC made possible interchange of machine readable catalog records.

This standardization has encouraged developments of networks, such as the SUNY Biomedical Network, NELINET, the Washington State Libraries network, and that of the Ohio College Library Center. With each of these regional networks employing the MARC bibliographic record, it will be possible to integrate these regional nodes into a future national network.

SUBSTANCE AND SUM

The first half of the first decade and a half of library computerization was confined almost entirely to two major mechanizations of Mortimer Taube's Uniterm coordinate indexing. The computerization of single descriptors with attendant document numbers was a relatively easy task.

The first breakaway from computerized subject searching came at the Douglas Aircraft Corporation, where the technique of producing one machine readable record from which multiple products could be obtained was introduced in 1961. The last half of library automation's decade and a half has been largely consumed with efforts to automate existing library procedures.

Although notable departures have occurred that take advantage of the computer's powerful qualities, on-line, real time techniques introduced at the very end of the historical period under review began again to use individual words as words, not unlike the logic in which the first applications employed Uniterms; and it seems likely that the immediate future will witness increasing degrees of computerization based on individual words in bibliographic descriptions rather than on the record as a whole.

ACKNOWLEDGMENTS

The author is grateful to Sheila Bertram for identifying, searching out, and gathering most of the references used in this paper. Cloyd Dake Gull furnished in correspondence invaluable information about events of the fifties and early sixties, and various librarians supplied photocopies of early documents.

REFERENCES

1. Frederick C. Kilgour, "The Economic Goal of Library Automation," *College & Research Libraries*, 30 (July 1969), 307-311.

2. William J. Baumol, "The Costs of Library and Informational Services." In *Libraries at Large*. New York, R. R. Bowker, 1969, pp. 168-227.

3. L. R. Bunnow, *Study of and Proposal for a Mechanized Information Retrieval System for the Missiles and Space Systems Engineering Library*. Santa Monica, Calif., Douglas Aircraft Co., 1960.

4. Charles F. Balz and Richard H. Stanwood, *Literature on Information Retrieval and Machine Translation*. International Business Machines Corp., November 1962.

5. *Ibid.*, 2nd ed., January 1966.

6. Jack A. Speer, *Libraries and Automation; a Bibliography with Index*. Emporia, Kansas, Teachers College Press, 1967.

7. Harley E. Tillitt, "An Experiment in Information Searching with the 701 Calculator," *Journal of Library Automation*, 3 (Sept. 1970), 202-206.

8. R. H. Bracken and H. E. Tillitt, "Information Searching with the 701 Calculator," *Journal of the Association for Computing Machinery*, 4 (April 1957), 131-136.

9. Harley E. Tillitt, "An Application of an Electronic Computer to Information Retrieval." In Martha Boaz's *Modern Trends in Documentation.* New York, Pergamon Press, 1959. pp. 67-69.

10. Jerome L. Zaharias, *LIZARDS; Library Information Search and Retrieval Data System.* China Lake, Calif., U.S. Naval Ordnance Test Station, 1963.

11. Robert H. Bracken and Bruce G. Oldfield, "A General System for Handling Alphameric Information on the IBM 701 Computer," *Journal of the Association for Computing Machinery,* 3 (July 1956), 175-180.

12. Saul Rosen, "Electronic Computers: A Historical Survey," *Computing Surveys,* 1 (March 1969), 7-36.

13. A. R. Barton, V. L. Schatz, and L. N. Caplan, *Information Retrieval on a High Speed Computer.* Evendale, Ohio, General Electric Co., 1959. p. 8.

14. C. D. Gull, Personal communication (22 August 1969).

15. B. K. Dennis, J. J. Brady, and J. A. Dovel, Jr., "Five Operational Years of Inverted Index Manipulation and Abstract Retrieval by an Electronic Computer," *Journal of Chemical Documentation,* 2 (October 1962), 234-242.

16. Charles J. Austin, *MEDLARS; 1963-1967.* Bethesda, Md., National Library of Medicine, 1968.

17. Roger K. Summit, "DIALOG: an Operational On-Line Reference Retrieval System." In Association for Computing Machinery, *Proceedings of 22nd National Conference.* Washington, D.C., Thomson, 1967. pp. 51-56.

18. Irwin Pizer, "Regional Medical Library Network," *Bulletin of the Medical Library Association,* 57 (April 1969), 101-115.

19. Gretchen W. Koriagin, "Library Information Retrieval Program," *Journal of Chemical Documentation,* 2 (October 1962), 242-248.

20. Paul J. Fasana, "Automating Cataloging Functions in Conventional Libraries," *Library Resources and Technical Services,* 7(Fall 1963), 350-365.

21. Frederick G. Kilgour, "Library Catalogue Production on Small Computers," *American Documentation,* 17 (July 1966), 124-131.

22. Nugent, William R., "NELINET–The New England Information Network." In Congress of the International Federation for Information Processing, 4th, Edinburgh, 5-10 August, 1968, *Proceedings.* Amsterdam, North-Holland Publishing Co., 1968. pp. G 28-G 32.

23. Charles T. Payne, "The University of Chicago's Book Processing System." In *Proceedings of a Conference Held at Stanford University Libraries,* October 4-5, 1968. Stanford, Calif., Stanford University Libraries, 1969.

24. W. A. Wilkinson, Personal communication (November 1969).

25. W. A. Wilkinson, "The Computer-Produced Book Catalog: An Application of Data Processing at Monsanto's Information Center." In University of Illinois Graduate School of Library Science, *Proceedings of the 1964 Clinic on Library Applications of Data Processing.* Champaign, Ill., Illini Union Bookstore, 1965. pp. 7-20.

26. Edward Heiliger, "Florida Atlantic University Library." In University of Illinois Graduate School of Library Science, *Proceedings of the 1965 Clinic on Library Applications of Data Processing.* Champaign, Ill., Illini Union Bookstore, 1966. pp. 92-111.

27. Ritvars Bregzis, Personal communication (November 1969).

28. Ritvars Bregzis, "The Ontario Universities Library Project–An Automated Bibliographic Data Control System," *College & Research Libraries,* 26 (November 1965), 495-508.

29. Charles W. Robinson, "The Book Catalog: Diving In," *Wilson Library Bulletin,* 40 (November, 1965), 262-268.

30. H. P. Luhn, "A Business Intelligence System," *IBM Journal of Research and Development,* 2 (October 1958), 315-319.

31. Richard H. Stanwood, "The Merge System of Information Dissemination, Retrieval and Indexing Using the IBM 7090 DPS." In Association for Computing Machinery, *Digest of Technical Papers* (1962). pp. 38-39.

32. E. J. Young and A. S. Williams, *Historical Development and Present Status–Douglas Aircraft Company Computerized Library Program.* Santa Monica, Calif., Douglas Aircraft Co., 1965.

33. I. Haznadari and H. Voos, "Automated Circulation at a Government R & D Installation," *Special Libraries,* 55 (February 1964), 77-81.

34. R. W. Gibson, Jr., and G. E. Randall, "Circulation Control by Computer," *Special Libraries,* 54 (July-August 1963), 333-338.

35. Ralph E. McCoy, "Computerized Circulation Work: A Case Study of the 357 Data Collection System," *Library Resources & Technical Services,* 9 (Winter 1965), 59-65.

36. Robert E. Hamilton, "The Illinois State Library 'On-Line' Circulation Control System." In University of Illinois Graduate School of Library Science, *Proceedings of the 1968 Clinic on Library Applications of Data Processing.* Urbana, Ill., Graduate School of Library Science, 1969. pp. 11-28.

37. "Redstone Center Shows On-line Library Subsystems," *Datamation,* 14 (February 1968), 79, 81.

38. R. A. Kennedy, "Bell Laboratories' Library Real-Time Loan System (BELLREL)," *Journal of Library Automation,* 1 (June 1968), 128-146.

39. University of California, San Diego, University Library, *Report on Serials Computer Project; University Library and UCSD Computer Center.* La Jolla, Calif., University Library, July 1962.

40. Irwin H. Pizer, Donald R. Franz, and Estelle Brodman, "Mechanization of Library Procedures in the Medium-Sized Medical Library: I. The Serial Record," *Bulletin of the Medical Library Association,* 51 (July 1963), 313-338.

41. Karen C. Strom, "Software Design for Bio-medical Library Serials Control System." In American Society for Information Science, Annual Meeting, Columbus, Ohio, 20-24 Oct. 1968, *Proceedings,* 5 (1968), 267-275.

42. Rosario de Varennes, "On-line Serials System at Laval University Library," *Journal of Library Automation,* 3 (June 1970).

43. *Kansas Union List of Serials* (Lawrence, Kansas, University of Kansas Libraries, 1965), 357p.

44. Hillis L. Griffin, "Electronic Data Processing Applications to Technical Processing and Circulation Activities in a Technical Library." In University of Illinois Graduate School of Library Science, *Proceedings of the 1963 Clinic on Library Applications of Data Processing.* Champaign, Ill., Illini Union Bookstore, 1964. pp. 96-108.

45. G. E. Randall and Roger P. Bristol, "PIL (Processing Information List) or a Computer-Controlled Processing Record," *Special Libraries*, 55 (February 1964), 82-86.

46. Thomas L. Minder, "Automation—the Acquisitions Program at the Pennsylvania State University Library." In International Business Machines Corporation, *IBM Library Mechanization Symposium, Endicott, New York*, May 25, 1964, pp. 145-156.

47. Connie Dunlap, "Automated Acquisitions Procedures at the University of Michigan Library," *Library Resources & Technical Services*, 11 (Spring 1967), 192-206.

48. Sally Alanen, David E. Sparks, and Frederick G. Kilgour, "A Computer-Monitored Library Technical Processing System." In American Documentation Institute, 1966 Annual Meeting, October 3-7, 1966, Santa Monica, Calif., *Proceedings*, pp. 419-426.

49. T. Burgess and L. Ames, *LOLA; Library On-Line Acquisitions Sub-System.* Pullman, Wash., Washington State University Library, July 1968.

50. Patrick C. Mitchell and Thomas K. Burgess, "Methods of Randomization of Large Files with High Volatility," *Journal of Library Automation*, 3 (March 1970).

51. Edwin B. Parker, "Developing a Campus Information Retrieval System." In *Proceedings of a Conference Held at Stanford University Libraries, October 4-5, 1968.* Stanford, Calif., Stanford University Libraries, 1969. pp. 213-230.

52. "Preliminary Guidelines for the Library of Congress, National Library of Medicine, and National Agricultural Library Implementation of the Proposed American Standard for a Format for Bibliographic Information Interchange on Magnetic Tape as Applied to Records Representing Monographic Materials in Textual Printed Form (Books)," *Journal of Library Automation*, 2 (June 1969), 68-83.

COMPUTER IN THE SCHOOL LIBRARY*

By Mary Ann Swanson

Since I am familiar with only one computer-supported library program, I shall use that experience as the basis for my paper. At Evanston Township High School, Evanston, Illinois, data processing, and especially the computer, play an important role in the life of the school. (Students in their annual show a couple of years ago did a skit about who or what runs the school, and in it they pointed out that it was "mostly IBM.") Since ETHS is a multi-school arrangement of four schools within a school, the computer helps tie together the various areas of this large secondary school and, from the librarians' point of view, especially the library and the resource centers.

The library's involvement in the data processing program of the school began with circulation. It is now three and a half years since the data collecting system was installed. I can safely say that it was not until the computer was installed in the data processing center that the system worked to the satisfaction of the staff.

A look at the circulation system from the patron's viewpoint begins with an identification card used as a borrower's card and a punched card as a book card in each book in the library. The borrower takes the book to the desk where the student assistant puts the book card and the ID card into the 357 IBM input station. A key-punch machine which is located in the computer center is wired to the input station and is activated by the transaction in the library to produce a punched transaction card. The assistant returns the book card to the book pocket and stamps the due date in the book, and, from the patron's point of view, the book is now charged to him.

Several years ago each student at ETHS was given an ID card containing the usual information: name, ID number, school, year of graduation, photograph and signature. When the IBM charging system was installed, the ID number, school code, and year of graduation were punched into the card. Thus, the transition was not difficult. Incidentally, teachers' cards are kept on file in the library, so that it is not necessary for teachers to give ID cards to student messengers if they wish to send for books from the central library.

An auxiliary attachment which is yet to be installed will give the circulation greater flexibility. The 374 cartridge reader will make it possible for us to expand the number of loan periods. Currently, the system is programmed for a two-week loan period; but when the cartridge reader is used, three-day, one-month, and even semester loans will be possible.

Each day the machine operator in the computer center takes the punched cards from the keypunch, sorts the return transactions from the new charges, and updates the circulation disc. Returns are cleared from the disc, new charges are added, and a print-out of all the charges currently stored on the disc is produced.

Each Friday an additional set of reports is produced. These are the overdue notices, which are four-color forms containing the name of the student, ID

*Reprinted from the *Drexel Library Quarterly*, 5:101-103, April 1969, by permission of the publisher. ^c1969.

number, the school to which he is assigned, and a list of overdue books. Since the notices arrive at the library arranged by school and in alphabetical order, hours of clerical and student assistant time are saved. A usual print-out of overdue notices takes less than 30 minutes for all four schools.

The computer in the library is not limited, however, to the circulation function. It is a very important part of order and acquisition procedure. The first step in this procedure is the production of a preliminary order slip. Some librarians do not believe that this slip is necessary, but in a school operation where the key punch operator works on payroll, scheduling, attendance, and report cards, it seems unreasonable to assume that she should be responsible for looking up or memorizing the publishers' code used by the librarian. The preliminary order slips are sent to the keypunch operator who punches the order cards. After the cards have been revised, they are sent to the computer center where a six-copy list is printed. (At ETHS lists are used by the business office to be attached to order forms and sent to jobbers.) This list of several hundred titles formerly was hand-typed, taking the clerical assistant several hours, even more than a day, to produce. The computer does the job in a matter or minutes.

The punched card is filed in the library technical processing department in the "orders out" file. When the book arrives, the card is pulled (manually) and is mark-sensed by the cataloging assistant at the direction of a cataloger. The assistant adds the classification number, the accession number, and the number of the library or resource center to which the book is to be assigned. Although the card includes space for the mark-sensing of a copy number, this information is no longer added. The circulation system makes this information unnecessary. After the mark-sensing has been completed, the card is returned to the key punch where the new information is added. The completed card becomes the shelf-list card, and from it the book card is produced. The book is now ready for circulation.

The shelf list record on punched cards has been a real asset as the new resource centers were completed. In recent years, many titles which department supervisors had requested for the resource centers had been added to the library. The punched cards could be divided by library number, and student help could go to the shelves, pull the books, stamp them with the new location stamp, and send them to the new location. The deck of cards was then fed into the computer to produce a spirit master list, and each resource center had its own classed catalog of its holdings. Librarians and teachers recognize that this is only a stopgap measure to serve until the book catalog of the entire holdings can be produced.

When the bindery man arrives early, it is possible to take the deck of book cards from those books ready to be sent to the bindery to the data processing center and have a list in a matter of only a few minutes. The bindery man does not have to wait, and the busy library clerk is delighted not to have to type another list.

Plans for future expansion of the library's use of the computer include the production of a book catalog. Before I dream with you, let me describe the school in which this library operation takes place. The school, as I indicated earlier, is four schools within a school organization, with each school having a principal, counseling staff, school nurse, its own cafeteria and student lounge, faculty, and resource center. The central library which serves all four schools has a collection of 40,000 volumes, 200 periodicals, 4,000 filmstrips, 3,000 long-play records, and a film library, transparency collection, and a collection of some 35 periodicals on microfilm. Each resource center has a book collection of four to five thousand volumes, 35 periodicals, and a limited filmstrip and record collection. The music, art, and industrial arts departments which serve all four schools have the beginnings of subject resource centers which are supplied with materials processed in the central library.

Now back to the dreaming. A book catalog seems to be the only logical solution to the need for information on what the school owns in the way of instructional materials and where they are located. The production of more than 100 copies will permit a variety of uses. Members of the seminar group can each have a catalog rather than the usual two or three students of the group using the two or three catalog trays containing information on the subjects on which the group is working. The students will be permitted to take the catalog home on overnight loan so that library hours can really be extended in this way. Department supervisors can be assigned copies so that when curriculum committees meet in their offices, the library catalog will be available for consultation without a long walk to the other side of the campus.

When I really start dreaming, I see the day of the larger computer when the computer memory will be able to supply the library patron at a terminal in the library or resource center with a bibliography of the library's holdings—book and non-book—on any subject. If he is working at home in the evening, he can get this information on equipment he has there, and he probably will not be limited to information in the ETHS library.

In the intervening period, we are aware that these possibilities exist and we have the obligation as professional librarians to prepare for the day when we have all of these and many more aids to library service at our fingertips.

THE COMPUTER-MICROFILM RELATIONSHIP*

By George Harmon

Two individual tools of graphics which will have an enormous impact on the information field and influence the operation of libraries during the 70's are microfilm and the computer. Each will have its own effect. Where they operate together the changes in information handling will be dramatic.

Before examining the various ways in which the computer and microfilm interrelate, let us look at each individually. First the computer, specifically the digital computer.

THE COMPUTER

Computers, in the minds of many, are large devices—expensive, mysterious, and capable of doing many wonderful things. However, they do not have to be large or expensive but, like any machine such as an automobile or an airplane, one must learn how to operate the particular device. One should look at a computer as a unit which converts signals or manipulates information.

A computer is composed of five parts. There is an input, a memory, a processor or arithmetic unit, a control unit, and an output.

Input devices convert signals to electrical pulses that can be used by the computing portion while the output devices convert the final signals to a form which can be used by other machines or to a human readable form. Input can be from punched paper tape, magnetic tape, analog to digital converters, teletypewriters, or display scopes with a light pen.

The *memory unit* holds information in a computer usable form for future use or while arithmetic operations are being performed on other data. There is information in memory that is immediately accessible, while other memory units may hold information only occasionally required and less easily removed for computing operations.

The *arithmetic unit* is capable of receiving numbers in a binary form and performing various operations. This is the unit which actually produces the new data as a result of combining the various input information.

The *control unit* coordinates all the parts of the computer so that events happen in a logical sequence and at the right time. The input is controlled, the data is placed in memory or removed when needed, the proper arithmetic functions are performed and the output device is controlled.

Output devices convert the electrical pulses back to an information form usable by human beings or other machines. Output can be punched paper tape, magnetic tape, printed information or images on a display scope.

MICROFILM

Microfilm is a completely different type of tool for handling information. It is basically a storage device which allows a great amount of information to be

*Reprinted by permission from *Special Libraries,* 62:279-282, July-August 1971.

placed in a small area and retrieved with relatively inexpensive equipment. There are various forms and sizes. Roll film is normally 16mm or 35mm in width, but some is 70mm and 105mm. Containers designed for automatically handling roll images and called cassettes, cartridges or magazines handle primarily 16mm film, but some handle 8mm or 35mm film.

A specialized format for microfilm is the *aperture card*. An image on 35mm film is placed within a cutout portion of an EAM card. The other part of the card is punched with data processing equipment for sorting or machine marking. This format may not seem familiar to many librarians but the possibility of placing the equivalent of twenty pages of data on one 35mm frame makes this form a future way of representing reports which average from 4 to 40 pages.

Jackets are another unitized form in which strips of either 16mm or 35mm film are inserted into a carrier. Headings are man-readable to define what images are on the jacket. Many varied images can be accommodated. Microfiche is the name given to the unitized form which has many images exposed by step and repeat cameras or by "stripping up" sections of 8mm or 16mm film. There are various standard sizes such as 4" x 6" or EAM card size with various standards for number of images such as 60 or 98 and various specified reduction ratios such as 24x and 42x.

New developments, particularly those intended for the micro-publishing field, are establishing higher reduction types of fiche. Some systems are 90x, 150x, or 210x. These new systems point out one of the biggest problems that will be faced by all types of librarians. There will be less standardization before true standards are established in the microfilm field. Each new form needs new retrieval equipment. Special systems will continue until users such as librarians and their customers complain and refuse to accept the great variety.

INFORMATION RETRIEVAL

These two information handling devices—the computer and microfilm— have been combined in four ways:
1. A computer controls a microfilm system
2. The computer output is microfilm
3. The computer input is microfilm
4. The computer memory is microfilm

1) Control of the retrieval process of a particular image from a large store of microfilm has become necessary with the increasing proliferation of information placed on microfilm. Units have been designed which store any of the forms of microfilm and automatically retrieve the desired image or page. The Miracode®system of Eastman Kodak handles roll film in containers. Mossler developed a unit to handle both aperture cards and microfiche. Image Systems' product is known as CARD (Compact Automatic Retrieval Device), and utilizes microfiche. The Sanders-Diebold units also handle the information in the microfiche form.

2) It has been stated that the computer is the greatest generator of information while microfilm can store information best. It was only natural that eventually the output from the computer would be placed on film. The amount

of paper output from the impact printers caused difficult storage problems and practically impossible retrieval problems. Devices were built which would microfilm the unburst paper, thus solving most of these problems. It was shown that a more economical method would be to record directly on microfilm rather than first on paper. Units which perform this function are called COM (Computer Output Microfilm) devices.

The basic COM unit converts digital information from a computer either directly or from magnetic tape to an image on a cathode ray tube (similar to a television tube). This image is photographed producing the microfilm. The film usually must then be developed. Technological developments have made it possible to record up to 90,000 characters per second on film. Output is normally 16mm or 35mm roll film although new units produce microfiche as 105mm roll film. Many companies produce units, and in order to accommodate all users, have created many new output frame sizes. Since the normal paper output from computers is 11" x 14", there has been an attempt to match that form on microfilm. Effective reduction sizes of from 16x to 48x have been produced. In addition, there is production of formats similar to 8½" x 11" and 8½" x 14" at various effective reductions, creating a plethora of image sizes. It is impossible to enlarge on a microfilm reader or blowback to paper all of these various images on a single unit. Computer Output Microfilm has thus accentuated an already difficult problem for librarians—how to use all the various forms of microfilm.

New developments in the COM field will create new output forms and thus create more problems. Multiple images on the same frame make compact information storage but require special reading equipment. Four images per frame, eight images per frame and twenty images per frame have been generated for 35mm film. Two 8mm images upon 16mm film is also being produced. Higher quality graphic output requires high quality readers to retrieve all the recorded information. Inexpensive COM devices produce a poorer quality output which requires high quality readers to maintain readability. Color microfilm from COM devices requires that readers have non-colored viewing screens for true reproducibility.

3) A third way in which there is a relationship is where microfilm is the input to the computer. In most units now marketed, a beam of light passes through the film and is measured. With a known location and known value of density of the film the computer is in a position to evelute the information on the film. Recent developments in computer software have made possible the rapid reading of characters. This is known as OCR (Optical Character Recognition). This technique will aid extensively in maintaining index card files. The cards can be microfilmed and then read by an OCR device. The computer can then reformat cards for mass distribution.

4) Since computer information can be recorded on microfilm and then read back, microfilm can act as the memory of a computer. The device that is nearest to a complete memory is a unit made by Synergistics. A laser beam is split and the 36 channels are placed on film as signal or no signal duplicating the type of information normally on magnetic tape. The same unit can read back the information for the computer. This process will make possible the conversion of large files of magnetic tape to microfilm. Storage and retrieval may then change from a data processing operation to a library operation.

There are various relationships which exist between microfilm and computers. The mating has created new problems for librarians. It is now necessary for all concerned—manufacturers, data processing personnel, microfilm specialists, and library science specialists—to work together to take advantage of the specialized characteristics of the tools to make better information-handling systems.

COMPUTERS IN LIBRARIES*

By Ellsworth Mason

In the recent past very powerful forces have emerged in our society whose effect has been to weaken greatly our ability to distinguish between alternatives which are useful and alternatives which are useless. It is argued here that library automation emerged right in the middle of these mental disabilities, was spurred on for personal and institutional ego reasons; its acceptance reflecting a total lack of the critical evaluation that its expense would seem to require.

If there is any honor in this country equivalent in stature to the British Order of the Garter, it certainly is that of having been called twice to speak to this group of remarkable technical service librarians, and I thank you for this honor. It reminds me once again of three most rewarding years spent as serials librarian at the University of Wyoming in the days when the Serials Round Table (which has never really been replaced since the reorganization) was making signal contributions to the profession.

I am taking the prerogative of the speaker, which always places programs in jeopardy, of departing from the topic on which I was asked to speak, to wit, "Library Automation: A State of the Art Review" for the simple reason that I am not a specialist in library automation. Instead, I will talk about "Brainlessness: A State of the Art Review." I have become a considerable expert in detecting brainlessness, and since, as will become obvious, I consider library automation to be to an overwhelming degree the backside of brainlessness, my remarks may add something to your concern with the stated topic.

I first want to summon as witness what you already know about major tendencies of mind that have dominated our entire culture in recent times. On the one hand, we have dug up the considerably decayed bodies of Romanticism and Rousseau, and on the other the dear departed myths about the industrial system of the boom 1920s. At a time when as never before we need hard-headed thinking about realities that seem always to hover in the crisis range, we have had a massive retreat from reality.

To a very great extent, we know increasingly better how to do things, but we seem to have lost our grip on the reason for doing them. As we accumulate more exact knowledge, we seem to have less wisdom. Some time ago, in an interview with Herman Kahn, a very perceptive British journalist asked him whether the United States had really produced the most foolish educated class in history. I regret to say that Kahn's response, "Not quite," is thoroughly defensible in the light of the recent past.

Reasons for this phenomenon are not hard to find. The long-term strains of an uncertain international situation have combined with conditions of daily life, increasingly riddled with frustrations. My wife produces impressive evidence weekly to the effect that we really do no more than our ancestors, but everything we do takes more time and is filled with more frustrations, and therefore

*Reprinted from *Library Resources and Technical Services,* 16:5-10, Winter 1972.

seems more. Consequently, two main drives for a remarkably large number of people are for certainty and for easy solutions. In the bulk of my library building consulting situations, now more than 75, the hardest problem is to bring the people in the operation to think with precision about why they are doing what they are doing, what are their real aims, and how best to achieve them. It is impossible to exaggerate how strong is the tendency to want answers that are so obvious you don't have to think about them and so true that they make you feel good. This tendency is found not only in the young and foolish, but in responsible people in high places. As I will indicate, it is a bread-and-butter condition in library automation.

The second major factor in the intellectual quicksand I am trying to describe is the reemergence of the myths of the beneficence of the commercial world and the infallibility of industrial procedures. My college years were during the heady thirties, in which it was obvious to the whole country that industry didn't know its ear from a hole in the ground about what it was doing. The shambles were still spread out around us. We understood that a system based on personal greed (known as economic motivation) involved ruthlessness and deception, and was rife with meretricious motives. Anything connected with the commercial world was automatically, for this reason, suspect, likely to be invalid, and probably dishonest.

A miracle as great as the recovery of the German and Japanese economies is this recovery of the American commercial world from its ultimate, and rightly deserved, disgrace. After the Second World War, from which we are still suffering morally, we discovered that our industrial potential had more than doubled in four years. An intensified public relations industry which had learned much from war propaganda—especially that bit about repeating the big lie—plus the torrent of consumer's goods poured out to a war-deprived American public, made us forget everything we had known (and are in the process of learning again) about the unreliability of the procedures of the commercial world. And so, what was good for General Motors was good for the country, and I do mean the entire country. Not just its economy and its government, but its churches, its institutions and, most shamefully, its institutions of higher education.

For in the past twenty years, there has been a radical merger of the marketplace and the university, and this is the third major factor in the intellectual quicksand. In a matter of twenty years, the university has flipped from its position as the only guaranteed, independent prober of the entire spectrum of thought, the one source that valued the ability to distinguish between the temporarily and the permanently significant, to a condition of being continually washed by the values of the marketplace, and constantly shifting with their ephemerality. In a letter in my collection of the poet Robert Graves, he dismisses summarily the importance of American universities, which, he contends, are part and parcel of big business. The near truth of his statement becomes more uncomfortable every year.

The reasons for this radical change, whose cost to society is immeasurable, are financial pressures, on universities, on their faculty, and the ability to get more and more money from government and industry, always at a price, ending up in dependency. And as always, the piper plays the tunes he is ordered to play. For our purposes, this is a crucial fact, since library automation began in, and is still predominantly practiced in, the colleges and universities, despite the MARC project.

Let me recapitulate quickly, before getting to work on Mrs. Avram's specialty as I have seen it. In the recent past, very powerful forces in our country's mentality have resulted in: (1) a massive retreat from reality, resulting in an unwillingness to think problems through to their ultimate conclusions. To George Orwell's *Doublethink* we have added *Half-think* as a standard methodology, and coupled it with a reaching out for emotional jackets into which we can slip ourselves snugly. (2) The euphoric feeling now connected with imitating industry. (3) The get-with-it-ness in the universities, now largely deprived of the mentality to question marketplace ideas. The total effect of these forces has been to weaken greatly our ability to distinguish between alternatives which are useful and alternatives which are useless. In sum, we are unable to think clearly about a whole range of important problems. Library automation, unfortunately, emerged right in the middle of these mental disabilities, and was severely crippled by them.

Now down to specifics. I assume that I am here because I wrote an article about the use of the computer in libraries for *College & Research Libraries* this spring.[1] The reactions to this article were marked to a high degree by the Springbok mentality that I find common among library automaters when they think about the reasons for or justifications of their projects. My critics assumed that the article was about library automation and computers, whereas it is clearly about the thinking that lies behind automation in libraries. It was attacked as a faulty scholarly article, undocumented, whereas it clearly is a satirical polemic, issuing the warning that accountability is here, the hero medals for computerization tarnished, and from where I stood, that it all looked pretty silly.

I argued that computerization was launched in libraries for personal and institutional ego reasons, or was pressed on the library by the ignorant, among whom I number (but not exclusively) electronics engineers, campus computerators, and top administrators. If my memory serves me well, it was foolish pressures like these that dragged the Library of Congress kicking and screaming into automation in the first place.

I argued that I have yet to see or come close to a library automation project that has been chosen as the best of carefully appraised alternatives on a managerial basis. I argued that although the computer can do nearly everything in the library (and it is a fascinating machine), it can do nothing, cheaper than alternative methods, that we need to have done. I argued that we were ignorantly imitating industrial research and development, which comprise our systems programming, and would have to make the industry come to us with solutions. I argued that we were wasting money on a faith the exact equivalent of a witch's faith in flying ointment.

I have gotten some interesting answers, in person and in public. About costs: admissions that the computer is not cost competitive, coupled with the view that we can't go on the basis of costs.[2] This is 1968 mentality; costs become the grinding fact more crushingly every day.

About ego motivation: "Mason should give credit to the downright heroism of research institutions that, in the face of high costs, are willing to try the untried to advance the state of our sadly backward art." I think he means catalogers—that sadly backward art—and he's saying that it takes a lot of courage to waste money.

About the industrial ploy: "Mason decries the added cost of automation without allowing for increased service speed and accuracy, which are the chief reasons for the successful application of modern techniques in business and industry." Perhaps Mrs. Avram will say a few words about the increased service speed and accuracy of automation.[3] The interesting thing about our creep after industry—which a friend of mine has characterized as the whore with the virgin PR—is that when we got with it, industry had already been wallowing in the computer for fifteen inebriated years. But hardly anything remains the darling of industry that long; now it is the laser, which I expect any day to be imported into the library for erasing catalog cards. Two years ago, with the squeeze on profits, industry found itself with a hangover from its binge of computerization, and has drastically cut back its commitments to computers. Data-processing vice-presidents are being displaced by accountants, and the chips are really down. There is a brilliant, thirty-page survey of the current industrial computer status by Dan Smith in *The Economist* for February 27, 1971, entitled "The Accident-Prone Miracle." Meanwhile, back at the library computer, we proceed with the gung-ho 1968 brave new world mentality, damning the torpedos, while our libraries wither around us.

About faith, it's touching, but painful: "Machines are expensive toys: no one knows how much they really cost. All the caveats that Mason issues have been well-known for years, but we still have faith that eventually, not tomorrow or the day after, but eventually the computer will make drastic changes in the library world."[4] Just buy this prayer cloth (as we have been doing), and if you believe, if you have faith, it will cure all the ills of libraries. Even from the Midwest, one cannot believe that this is the voice of the future.

The latest word comes from Gerard Salton, chairman of the Department of Computer Science at Cornell University, in an article replying to mine in *Library Journal* for October 15. This veritable gem catches the computer mentality, like a fly in amber, in its most unblushing pristine form, and reads like a caricature of itself. While admitting freely that library automation development costs are high, and operating costs higher than the manual costs replaced, he nevertheless insists that computerization of libraries is inevitable, because our large loads are piling up backlogs, which will get larger. In the future, automation will be economical.

My view is that backlogs are caused by misappropriation of university money which is in the computer center being wasted, when it should be in cataloging staff where it would be economical. If the computer does become cost effective in the future, we will go with it when it is cost effective. In the meantime, only the reckless waste money on computerized systems that cost more to do the same thing.

Salton then goes on to automatic indexing, which isn't working well, he says, but people are even less promising, and we will use it despite its defects because once we mechanize acquisitions, "there is no reason why the same file should not also serve for the cataloging and indexing processes at a relatively moderate cost." Added costs, as you know, are enormous, and no one has yet presented evidence that stringing operations together in an automated system reduces costs for the components.

178

Salton then goes on to examine at length retrieval of bibliographical data, which will inevitably proceed from the two former automation areas, and ends in the summary: "The managers of some systems report that their customers are highly satisfied. . . . Nevertheless, the current retrieval systems exhibit so many shortcomings that present operations are not likely to be maintained for long." Oh, well. Another million dollars down the drain! But you can't win them all!

The final computer application, which will proceed inevitably from the former three, is relevance feedback in a system of collection management and control, and by this point, Salton doesn't even bother to mention costs. Even Onassis doesn't think this loosely about spending money.

Mr. Salton looks from his photo like a very nice man, and I am confident that he can throw a wicked COBOL, but the line laid out in this article is not only old hat—it was first spewed at us ten years ago—it demonstrates a remarkable capacity to avoid valid thought. This very avoidance is what I find widespread among computerators and I protest it most vigorously.

The final word should be left to Jonathan Swift, in Laputa section of *Gulliver's Travels,* which is his satire on science written 250 years ago: "as they undertake, one man shall do the work of ten, a palace be built in a week of materials . . . to last forever. All the fruits of the earth shall come to maturity at whatever season we . . . choose. The only inconvenience is that none of these projects are yet brought to perfection, and in the meantime the whole country lies miserably waste."

REFERENCES

1. "The Great Gas Bubble Prick't, or Computers Revealed—by a Gentleman of Quality," *College & Research Libraries* 32:183-96 (May 1971). This was reprinted, for the edification of college presidents, in *Liberal Education* (October 1971), p. 394-412, and nicely corroborated in its main points by Daniel Melcher's article, of which I had no knowledge, when I wrote, entitled "Cataloging, Processing, and Automation," *American Libraries* 2:701-13 (July-Aug. 1971).

2. This is essentially Mrs. Avram's view, at a time when the New York Public Library is cutting service hours from seventy-eight to forty hours a week and closing three major departments.

3. "The MARC II magnetic tapes, intended to expedite the transmission of the cataloging information, deliver most of their data about twelve weeks late, and, according to one would-be-user, there are currently unpredictable errors of some kind in about every fifth entry . . . ," Melcher, "Cataloging," p. 708.

4. This sepulchral voice was once Jesse Shera. See *Library Journal* (Aug. 1971), p. 2408-09 and my reply in *Library Journal* (15 Nov. 1971), p. 3699.

LIBRARY AUTOMATION: A BALANCED VIEW*

By Henriette D. Avram

Ellsworth Mason's two recently published papers, severely criticizing
library automation, are refuted on the basis that he presents a biased view.
Many of his opinions are expressed as blanket statements which require
qualification to reflect the total picture. In addition, while admitting
to the failures and problems, this paper presents the positive accomplishments in a brief evaluation of the status of library automation in 1971.

In preparation for this paper, I read all the material Mr. Mason cited in his
recent article on library automation.[1] Although the experience was informative,
I was left confused. Mr. Mason gave the impression that the literature took a dim
view of automation. However, going through the same articles, I found, in general,
as many pro-automation statements as anti-automation statements, and I wondered
why he, too, had not found them. Apparently he chose only those points which
served to reinforce his position. We must assume that his purpose was to shake
up the library community to positive constructive action toward efficient use of
automation, for there is much to improve—much to accomplish.

Mr. Mason has made two principal thrusts: an attack on managerial practice in libraries and an attack on library automation itself and all it includes—the
hardware, the software, the individuals involved, all attempts to date, and the
cost. The first point can be dispensed with rather quickly. Any successful program has been supported by management. An administrator stands on his own
merits and the use of the computer in the system is irrelevant. Good administrators, if concerned with automation, will support the program by gaining an understanding of funds, time, and personnel required. They will look to a specialist
on their staff to advise them when they lack the expertise themselves.

On the other hand, if administrators do not augment their staff with specialists to avoid "being taken" or allow a project to be designed that mimics in
all details a manual system including any built-in idiosyncrasies, they are not
fulfilling their responsibilities. To a large extent, administrators must depend on
others for information. It does not follow that this dependence implies an abdication of their roles as decision-makers.

It appears to me that to bury one's head in the sand because we do not
fully comprehend the processes involved in mechanization is indeed indicative of
abdication of the role of administrator. We must face the fact noted by Mr.
Mason that a crisis does exist—that there are social and cultural changes adding
to and abetting the crisis, that there is the possibility of obsolescence of the
library as we know it today, and that manual methods fall short of satisfying
the basic objectives of providing service. The computer as a tool will not solve
all the ills of libraries; however, some remedy is needed, and if it isn't the computer, what is it?

Tom Alexander, one of Mr. Mason's citations, refers to a new book called
New Power for Management, in which Dr. David Hertz of McKinsey and Com-

*Reprinted from *Library Resources and Technical Services*, 16:11-18, Winter 1972.

pany, the management consulting firm, "predicts that a company that hasn't put its computers to work on higher order activities [than routine clerical tasks] by the early 70's will be wallowing helplessly in the wake of competitors who have."[2, 3]

Let us hope that today's library managers won't also be wallowing helplessly while the "information centers" take over.

Mr. Mason's second thrust is an attack on the computer industry and the use of the computer as a tool, both generally and specifically in relation to libraries. Here Mr. Mason is under a handicap for, although in his own words, he has "followed the development of computerization in libraries since 1960 and . . . took a course in programming to come current with the field,"[4] he cannot be considered an expert in the automation field. Therefore, he often misinterprets an expert's opinion or adds to the confusion with another nonexpert opinion.

Mr. Mason often blames the computer for problems that arise from other sources. In discussing the need to write tailor-made software for each application, Mr. Mason quotes Mr. Alexander again:

> In effect, each new task for a computer entails the design, development, and fabrication of a unique machine, assembled partly out of a box full of hardware and partly out of a box full of software.[5]

Basically, this is true, thanks to the genius of Dr. John Von Neumann, who is generally credited with conceiving the idea of the stored program. Mr. Mason seems to believe that this situation is undesirable. Is he perhaps suggesting that we revert to the hard-wired machine with its lack of flexibility?

Mr. Mason compares a computer without software to a car without a battery strong enough to power it. But he fails to note that a car performs only a single function of transportation. His analogy seems wide of the mark. Is Mr. Mason suggesting that we could define all library processes to such precision that a computer could be pre-programmed to perform them?

Mr. Mason addresses the lack of transferability of software from one institution to another. True, programs are designed and written to perform a specific function, according to a very precise set of rules. Computer user groups such as IBM Share have made programs for clearly defined tasks—for use on a specific hardware configuration—available to users for many years. The problem of transferability, for libraries, thus lies in defining procedures with sufficient commonality across libraries and with sufficient precision.

Realistically, what standards will libraries accept? Can they agree on objectives? To use the words of Bob Hayes in a letter to Mr. Mason in 1968: ". . . a package for serial control depends upon the procedure for serial check-in; this differs so radically from library to library that it is virtually impossible to standardize."[6] Perhaps Mr. Mason has forgotten those words of truth.

Mr. Mason condemns the computer for the difficulty in controlling the quality of programming. It is true that there are no standards of performance, but this lack is not peculiar to the computer field. Can Mr. Mason point to performance standards for reference work or cataloging? Nevertheless, although management cannot evaluate the efficiency of programs, a project director who is technically qualified can so judge. The computer field, like every other field, has competent people and not so competent people—and as a result, better and worse programs are designed and written. As time passes, furthermore, new problems come to light or new insight is gained into old problems, and a program is rewritten. This is the usual burden of progress in any endeavor and not a specific shortcoming of the machine approach.

Mr. Mason feels that librarians have been innocent victims gulled by engineers, systems analysts, and computer programmers. Without doubt, hardware has been oversold. Technicians have minimized the complexity of library automation; oversimplified the solutions required; proliferated abstract concepts concerning information retrieval—neglecting the fact that you can't retrieve anything until you have succeeded in inputting the data and efficiently organized the computer-based file for access to these data. All true, but let us for a moment look at the other side of the story.

Many library automation projects are directed by librarians with a good deal less experience in computer technology than it takes. Taking a course in systems analysis and a course in programming or several courses in both does not make a computer expert. Projects where the computer system design is performed without sufficient in-depth background experience are doomed to failure or mediocrity. Some librarians have gained sufficient insight into the technology to realize the extent of the expertise required and are taking action to hire qualified people for their staffs. Although we go to great lengths to provide training in technology for librarians, how many organizations provide background training in the complexities of bibliography for the technicians? Have librarians in the past ever had to describe a process, a procedure, or the content of a description in the minute detail that is required for computer programming? As Donald Knuth of Stanford says, in summarizing the application of computers in the field of mathematics, "Attempts at mechanization of mathematics are also very important, since they lead us to a greater understanding of concepts we thought we knew (until we had to explain them to a computer)."[7]

Mr. Mason emphasizes the cost aspects of the application of computers to libraries: ". . . my observations convinced me that the high costs of computerization make it unfeasible to library operations and that it will become increasingly expensive in the future"; "we now know that there is no clear evidence that the computer has saved industry money 'even in routine clerical operations.'" (The "even in routine clerical operations" is part of a statement made by Alexander which reads in full: "It turns out that computers have rarely reduced the cost of operations, even in routine clerical work. What they have accomplished is mainly to enable companies to speed up operations and thereby provide better service or handle larger volumes.")[8, 9, 10]

Mr. Mason admits to the serious financial situation in libraries, but offers no constructive suggestions. Rather, he attacks automation on the basis of its cost. Several of the projects described later in this section do indicate cost effectiveness. However, the validity of cost/benefit being the only justification for library automation must be questioned.

We may compare the cost of computer operations with staff costs required for a similar manual operation and measure cost effectiveness in terms of plus or minus dollar values. Comparing the output (service) of a computerized application with present manual services forces us to assign dollar rates to quality and speed of service, but the value of information, the contribution of a library, is beyond measuring only in terms of dollars.

It is a regrettable fact, however, that operating costs of libraries continue to rise, even though it is doubtful that there is substantial improvement in service. If we believe in the importance of libraries to the nation, then how to support them properly (with or without computers) is a national issue, and beyond the scope of this paper. What does concern us is whether computers can assist libraries in giving better service for the money expended.

Libraries have always and will continue to put material under control to provide services. What makes today different from the past is: (1) more material, (2) a shortage of trained librarians, and (3) rising costs. There simply are not enough people even if there were no funding problems. The machine offers the hope that we can concentrate professional cataloging expertise at one point only in the system. This is the attribute we must capitalize on. In a manual system, professional librarians are needed throughout all parts of the system. After all, the unit card does not file itself; and although it guides you toward making added entries, it does not make them for you. These tasks now require professional supervision. They could be performed by a computer in an automated system and unlike people, the machine will carry on its work in a uniform way; no variation will enter into the system.

Mr. Mason certainly is correct in criticizing much of what has been done in library automation but is wrong to draw the conclusion that all efforts are misdirected and doomed to failure. A poorly designed project does not prove that library functions cannot be automated; it proves that a disaster is a disaster. It is true that large amounts of money have been expended and there have not always been positive or meaningful results. It is questionable whether any effort breaking new ground in a complex environment has been successful in its first attempts. The literature on librarianship clearly exemplifies this fact. The *Anglo-American Cataloging Rules* of 1967, following upon the *ALA Rules* of 1949, 1941, and 1908, demonstrate the difficulty of "knowing all the answers" the first time.

Library automation projects can be considered a universe. One statistically evaluates the characteristics of a universe by drawing a random sample in such a way that each member of the universe has an equal chance of being included in the sample. If we drew a random sample of library automation projects and analyzed them, the sample projects would almost certainly yield a normal curve, with the majority of them falling into the "not conclusive yet" area of the curve and the extreme ends of the curve representing the failures and successes, respectively. It appears to me that Mr. Mason's sample was not random or that he selected his examples from the end representing failures. The failures certainly exist but so do the successes and projects that are not yet conclusive. Recognition of these facts leads to a more balanced evaluation of library automation.

We have not automated any library in its entirety—we may never succeed in doing so. To quote Herb Grosch, "There is a spectrum of feasibility, from the very easily do-able to the forever (yes, forever!) impossible."[11] Automating some of the intellectual aspects of librarianship, in my opinion, falls into the impossible end of the spectrum.

However, progress is evident in research and in the automation of specific functions. In some cases, great strides have been made toward a core bibliographic system. We are at last seeing research projects that conceptualize ideas that lead to advances and that are of an order of sophistication that at last matches the complexity of the problems. The work performed covers such areas as bibliographic searching, virtual scatter storage schemes, format recognition, etc.

More projects are operational, providing services and in some instances proving to be cost efficient. The Oklahoma Department of Libraries prepares weekly SDI listings from the MARC data base for sixty-six subscribers. Runs for most subscribers cost between $1.00 and $1.50 per week. The MARC data base storage and retrieval project provides selected MARC records in machine-readable form to libraries, thus saving the cost of conversion by the several institutions.

As Bierman says, "The same data base used repeatedly for a number of tasks for several different libraries can be economically and operationally successful. Visit MARC-Oklahoma and see!"[12] Developmental costs in Oklahoma have been kept to a minimum and have been carefully reported by Bierman.

The Ohio College Library Center (OCLC) has now implemented two projects: the off-line catalog production system and the on-line shared cataloging system. OCLC has fifty Ohio college and universities as members. Kilgour reports that "the computerized off-line procedure produces cards at less than half the cost of manual procedures. . . . The majority of the cost of computer produced cards is incurred by associated manual procedures not yet mechanized."[13]

The on-line catalog system, recently implemented at OCLC, provides bibliographic data, products, and location information. It is predicted that after two years of operation, there will be substantial savings to the member libraries if they extract catalog data from the system at the anticipated rate of 351,000 titles per year.

The Ohio State University catalog access and circulation system provides the user with bibliographic and availability information so that the user need not waste time pursuing a title not available. The preliminary estimate of cost savings to faculty in terms of time is encouraging. The University of Chicago Library automated system for technical processing also is operational.

In addition to an on-line book order and selection system, the University of Massachusetts serves as a technical processing center for twenty-eight state institutions. Initial apprehension on the part of the staff has gradually changed to an appreciation of the speed of access to information.

I could go on describing projects at some length. However, since this is an evaluation and not a review of library automation, these examples should suffice to indicate progress and to contradict Mr. Mason's blanket claim that "the computer is not for library use; that all the promises offered in its name are completely fraudulent; . . . that its use in a library weakens the library as a whole by draining off large sums of money for a small return; and that it should be stamped out."[14]

Librarians have performed admirably in their endeavors to control information, but long before the computer reared its ugly head, the lack of standardization and the problems incurred by such lack were obvious to them all. The potential use of the computer for bibliographic processing, the advent of shared cataloging, and the MARC project at the Library of Congress have provided the climate to increase our efforts toward standardization. There is a great deal of activity both nationally and internationally. The MARC structure is now a national standard and a recommended international standard. There is reason to believe that groups within the International Federation of Library Associations and the International Standards Organization will begin work on an international standard for the explicit codes and content of a bibliographic record in the not too distant future. The draft standard presented to IFLA this summer on a standard bibliographic description is close to adoption by the national bibliographies of Germany, the United Kingdom, and France. It will be turned over for discussion and hopeful adoption by all national library associations.

The Library of Congress distributes cataloging data in the MARC format to sixty-two subscribers. If one counts member libraries of the New England Library Information Network, OCLC, and the Oklahoma Department of Libraries, etc., there are really several hundred MARC subscribers. The regional networks we have long discussed are becoming a reality.

Cataloging-in-Publication records in machine-readable form will appear on MARC tapes four to six months prior to publication of the book. This means that the machine-readable record will be available to produce book orders long before the book is published. And, for those willing to do without the collation, catalog-related products could be ready long before the book arrives at the institution. As the project director of an automated system for a public library system has said: "The timeliness of this data can be characterized best as a godsend."

There is a growing awareness, both conceptually and in the design of several implemented projects, of the importance of a central bibliographic record complete enough in detail to be responsive to any need, and a realization that such records are fundamental to successful library automation. This is progress.

Although there may be no readily available evidence to support Mr. Mason's seventh truth: "Thou shalt save money as you multiply the separate operations that you computerize if you combine them by a systems approach"[15] common sense tells us that a systematic approach must pay dividends. It is important to automate in an orderly fashion instead of on an "ad hoc" basis so that when the various subsystems are implemented there is some assurance that they will eventually become parts of the whole with a minimum of disruption and redesign (thus saving money).

This has been stated by Warheit, Burgess, Avram, Veaner, and others.

It cannot be denied that there are issues in need of decisions, problems requiring solutions, and concepts calling for further development. For example:

1. There must be recognition that the bibliographic problems are more significant than the machine problems.

2. Bibliographic standards must be accepted largely as a means of achieving bibliographic control economically.

3. Insofar as possible, duplicate efforts should be avoided.

4. Libraries differ by type and size; therefore, the proposed solutions to problems must be evaluated in terms of the library needs.

5. The development of regional centers should be continued because this appears to be the only economically feasible approach.

6. LC name and subject authorities must be provided if libraries are to do local cataloging in a standard way. References required for established names must be provided for the production of book or card catalogs.

7. The problems of transferability of computer software must be addressed.

Victor Strauss might have been describing the status of library automation when he said about the publishing industry: "Right now we are standing, as it were, with one foot in the 19th and the other foot in the 20th century, our eyes gazing at the 21st."[16] Getting from here to there will require talent, hard work, imagination, risk-taking, patience, cooperation, and common sense. We must attack the problems that are feasible of solution leaving aside the more glamorous possibilities that are beyond the present state of the art or that require system capabilities that have not yet been developed.

REFERENCES

1. Ellsworth Mason, "The Great Gas Bubble Prick't . . . ," *College & Research Libraries* 32:183-96 (May 1971).

2. Tom Alexander, "Computers Can't Solve Everything," *Fortune* 80: 126-29, 168, 171 (October 1969).

3. *Ibid.*, p. 126.

4. Ellsworth Mason, "Along the Academic Way," *Library Journal* 96: 1675 (15 May 1971).

5. Alexander, "Computers," p. 171.

6. Robert M. Hayes, "Letter to Ellsworth Mason," *College & Research Libraries* 32:388 (Sept. 1971).

7. Donald Knuth, *The Art of Computer Programming*, quoted in *Computing Reviews* 12:cover (Sept. 1971).

8. Mason, "The Great Gas," p. 184.

9. *Ibid.*, p. 189.

10. Alexander, "Computers," p. 126.

11. Herbert Grosch, "Why MAC, MIS, and ABM Won't Fly (or, SAGE Advice to the Ambitious)," *Datamation* 17:71 (Nov. 1971).

12. Kenneth Bierman to H. D. Avram, private correspondence, August 24, 1971.

13. Frederick G. Kilgour, "Libraries—Evolving, Computerizing, Personalizing," *American Libraries* (at press).

14. Mason, "Along the Academic Way," p. 1675.

15. Mason, "The Great Gas," p. 189.

16. Victor Strauss, "Betwixt Cup and Lip," *Publishers' Weekly* 197: 265 (26 January 1970).

VIDEO TECHNOLOGY

Television is certainly familiar to everyone as a recreational and informational medium. It was the great technological hope of education in the 50s and 60s—a panacea for all the failings of education. This hope was not fulfilled.

Application of television to libraries has generally been rather limited. The use of remote access audio/video systems has received considerable attention in schools and academic institutions, while cartridge television appears to be a format generally looked upon with favor by libraries of all types.

The intent of this selection of articles is to create an awareness of some of the ramifications of television. Acronyms such as CATV, ITFS, and EVR are discussed and some specific utilization practices explored.

ITFS AS A DELIVERY SYSTEM*

By Francis Ryan

Since its inception in the early 1960s, Instructional Television Fixed Service (ITFS) has proved to be one of the most flexible types of television service for educators. Perhaps the greatest advantage of such a system is its capacity of four channels—allowing the operator to carry an optimal amount of programs to an entire school district or region. The operator or owner of the license has the advantage of a closed-circuit system although it covers many square miles of terrain. Because of this there is a certain amount of built-in flexibility to meet local needs on special occasions or at times to operate solely on a request basis for the school audience. As the size of an ITFS system increases there is a direct proportional increase in the problem of programing times. As with any broadcast type facility, especially in a school situation, it becomes almost impossible to satisfy all of the people all of the time. For example, it is much easier to program four television channels of instruction for 10 receiving locations in one school district than to try to program for 100 schools in a region comprised of perhaps 10 school districts. The former is difficult; the latter is almost impossible—or at least was considered so until this time.

Many of the current breakthroughs in technology—especially in the field of telecommunications—give us as educators the best of all possibilities. By meshing and mixing technologies with ITFS as the core, it is now possible to bring the greatest amount of information to almost all students for a minimal amount of taxpayer dollars. Sound too good? It's not as far-fetched as it may seem. It requires looking at ITFS from a different perspective. Instead of seeing it as a regular broadcasting system delivering four channels of instruction during a normal school day, take a look at it as a 24-hour delivery system to constantly

---

*Reprinted by permission from *AV Instruction*, 16:43-45, November 1971.

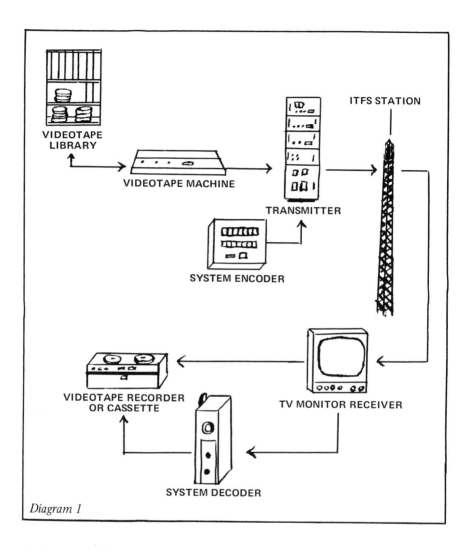

Diagram 1

feed the demands of local schools, teachers and even individual students. Don't view ITFS in isolation, but rather as the heart of a functioning system employing many technologies. Hold this in mind while I list and briefly describe some of these other facets of our integrated system.

- *CADA VRS* (Computer-Assisted Dial-Access Video Retrieval Systems)— It sounds like a lot, and technologically it is. More simply, it's a system that enables a broadcast or ITFS facility to activate unmanned videotape recorders at distant locations. VTRs set in a standby mode can be activated and turned off by an electronic signal, thus enabling the user to utilize TV spectrum space during down time. (Marketed by Display Systems Corporation—St. Paul, Minn. See Diagram 1.)

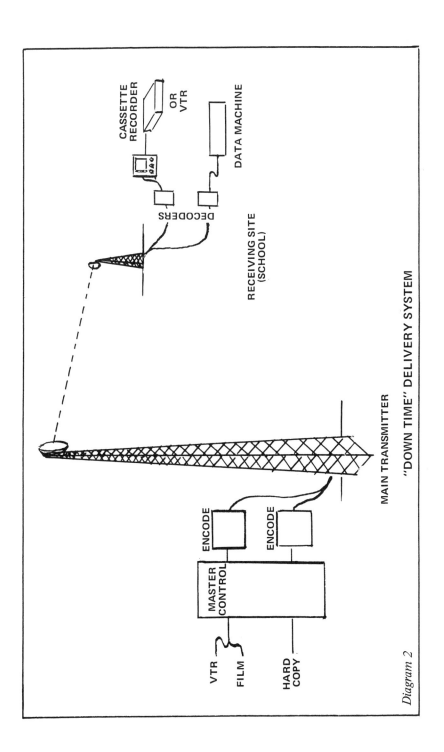

CASSETTE RECORDER

OR VTR

DATA MACHINE

DECODERS

RECEIVING SITE (SCHOOL)

MAIN TRANSMITTER

"DOWN TIME" DELIVERY SYSTEM

ENCODE

ENCODE

MASTER CONTROL

VTR

FILM

HARD COPY

Diagram 2

189

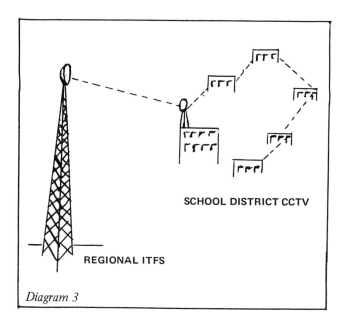

SCHOOL DISTRICT CCTV

REGIONAL ITFS

Diagram 3

- *Television Cartridge Systems*—Any type of the new video cartridge systems that are capable of recording and playing back audiovisual materials. The definition used here applies to those cartridge systems that use videotape only.

- *CATV* (Community Antenna Television)—In this instance, any number of locations connected by cable and using the same "head-end."

- *Hard Copy Transceivers*—Any of the new machines that are capable of receiving or sending hard copy data over existing cable or telephone lines.

- *Computer Terminals*—The newer variety that are used in classrooms by students—specifically, those with a memory disc that lend themselves to time sharing.

Okay—armed with the overall objective of DELIVERY and the above technologies, let's let our imaginations run wild. To preclude any notion that the aforementioned or what follows is simply the dream of a mad technologist, I'd like to interject that all of these systems are on the market and that they do work. Furthermore, every engineer and business representative that I have consulted assures me that they work and will work in combination. I have been involved with many of these systems using ITFS and they have worked with small scale experiments.

For example, in July of this year we here at the Diocesan Television Center, with the aid of several commercial firms, conducted an experiment with data transmission. It was a first for all of the companies involved and it worked.

190

We were able to transmit hard copy data at high speed (12,000 wpm) over our existing system. The copy received at the selected locations was perfect. One of the selected sites worked off a repeater situation and there was no loss in quality.

In addition, the data receiver located at a school installation lends itself to computerized instruction in that it can be equipped with a keyboard. But, going back to our original function of ITFS as a delivery system, think of the possibility of delivering teachers' guides, program notes, and even mail through a television system. By coupling the CADAVRS system with a data system, an ITFS station cannot only deliver programs during "down time," but also the hard copy materials (that are so often lost in transit) at the same time. (See Diagram 1.)

Another new dimension to an ITFS delivery system is CCTV and CATV. For example, several smaller school districts may connect all of the schools in one district together via cable. Normally, this would provide the particular school district with the capability of delivering 12 channels of instruction via cable into all of its schools. At this point in time, setting up 12 videotape recorders and the accompanying staff would be highly impractical. A more realistic approach would be to originate four channels at the district level, receive four from a regional ITFS system via one-head end (see Diagram 2) and allocate the remaining four channels to computer-assisted instruction.

In relation to privately owned CATV franchises held in various communities there is no reason why channel space allocated to education cannot be fed by a regional ITFS system (see Diagram 3). The additional equipment required for our existing ITFS system would be a receiving dish and "down converter" at

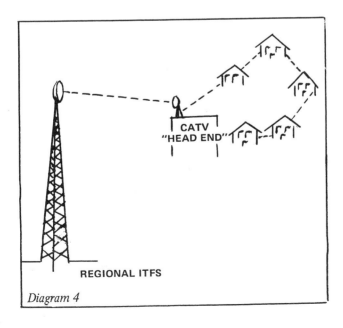

CATV
"HEAD END"

REGIONAL ITFS

Diagram 4

the CATV head end. The benefits from a combination such as this are many, especially in relation to school public relations, which we all need during these pressing times, and in reaching those students who are not attending school. They can tune in at home to a series that the rest of their classmates are viewing in school. The possibilities for adult education in this area are even greater.

I've only scratched the surface of ITFS as a delivery system. My sole objective has been to present the flexibility and even the economy of such a system or systems. In brief, the technology to accomplish these ends is now here. Do educators have the imagination and drive to carry these potentialities to reality?

CATV: VISUAL LIBRARY SERVICE*

By Brigitte Kenney and Frank W. Norwood

Community Antenna Television (CATV)—just another acronym? A way for those of us who live in remote areas to receive our favorite program? A way for enterprising businessmen to make money by bringing a service we want into our homes, for a fee? CATV is all of these, but it can become much more. It can become a powerful new tool by which librarians may reach both their "regular" library clients and those presently unserved, with special programming tailored to their needs. More importantly, it can become the means of interconnecting libraries for better delivery of information and documents.

What is CATV? Some of us, living in areas where television reception is poor because of our distance from the nearest station, or because of the mountains and valleys between station and receiver know all about how it works; others, living in mostly urban areas, may not. A brief explanation is in order. Television signals travel in a straight line and do not follow the curvature of the earth. TV signals may be blocked by tall buildings, hills, or other physical obstructions. The CATV industry has come into being because many people could receive only one or two channels, and sometimes those suffered from interference, or "snow." CATV operators erect high masts with sensitive antennas to pick up signals off the air, amplify them, and distribute them by cable to the receivers of customers who pay a modest fee, usually about five dollars per month. This allows a far broader choice of programs and brings in strong, clear signals where only weak signals, or none at all, were available before.

While CATV began in remote areas, usually in small hill-locked communities, it now serves virtually every state; more than 2,700 systems in the United States now transmit programs into 5,500,000 homes.[1] Some of the older systems are able to carry only a few channels in the lower portion of the VHF (Very High Frequency) band, while most modern systems can use all of the VHF channels, 2 through 13. Some systems are now being constructed which will carry more than twelve channels either by using dual cables so that the set can be switched from channel 2 to 13 on cable A, to channel 2 to 13 on cable B; or by carrying TV signals at other frequencies on the cable and "retrieving them" by the use of convertors mounted atop the homeowner's set. At the present state of the art, the cable will not carry UHF signals, so UHF stations are received and converted to a vacant VHF channel.

What makes CATV so different from television broadcasting (both commercial and educational)? One important factor is that more TV signals can be carried over the cable than can be made available over the air. In broadcasting, TV signals can and do interfere with one another so that in any given city no more than seven VHF channels can be assigned. Further, there are VHF frequencies suitable for TV below channel 2, between channels 6 and 7, and above channel 13, but these cannot be used for television broadcasting because those portions of the electromagnetic spectrum are assigned for other over-the-air services. On a CATV cable, however, the signals are enclosed, as water is in a

*Reprinted by permission from *American Libraries*, 2:723-726, July-August 1971.

193

pipe, and can be transmitted without interfering with other receivers not connected to the cable. Another important difference, the full value of which is yet to be exploited, is that cable holds the technical potential of being a two-way device. Given the proper amplifiers and terminal gear, messages could be sent both to and from the home.

Another important factor is that until recently CATV was strictly under local control; franchises are awarded by local government authorities to CATV operators. Each franchise is negotiated individually between the two parties; conditions laid down are usually binding for the length of the franchise. The Federal Communications Commission, under whose jurisdiction falls all broadcasting (i.e., use of the electromagnetic spectrum, which is considered as belonging to the people), has recently begun to take a long, hard look at CATV, because of its effect on broadcast TV stations. There is concern that commercial TV audiences may become diluted because of a wider availability of channel (and therefore program) choices via CATV. For example, under present FCC rules, TV signals from distant cities may not be imported by cable into the hundred largest markets in the United States.

Hearings are presently in progress before the FCC, which will influence the development of CATV to a considerable extent. Testimony has been given by many interested parties, asking that the FCC require CATV operators to set aside some of their distribution capacity for educational and instructional purposes. The Joint Council of Educational Telecommunications, and others, have suggested that 20 percent of the spectrum space on CATV systems, old and new, large and small, should be made available without charge for broadly educational uses, including not only television but eventually computer assisted instruction, facsimile transmission, and the like. In a number of cities and towns, educational interests already have free access to one or more channels on the local CATV system and CATV operators have, often as a matter of course, provided free "drops" (connection from trunk cable to receiver) to schools and other public institutions. Some CATV operators and school systems are generating new, local programming on otherwise unused channels on the cable. CATV has become not only a medium distributing existing television signals but an opportunity for providing entirely new program services. A recent ruling by the FCC encourages such "cablecasting," and will soon require that all CATV systems serving more than 3,500 subscribers engage in a substantial amount of local cable originated programming. Much of this is expected to be public service in character, including coverage of high school sports, city council meetings, and discussion of local issues. Cable systems may, if they choose, support such programming with commercial advertising.

As schools are now taking advantage of present and potential applications in their planning, so could librarians include CATV in their activities. Let us take a look at what could be done right now by and for libraries and with existing technology.

If a library had a channel set aside for its exclusive use or shared one with a school system, it could bring children's story hours, book talks, local programs taking place in the library (such as discussion groups, chamber music, adult education activities) into each home connected to the cable system. It could generate special programs for specialized audiences, such as the disadvantaged, teenagers, church and community groups, and the like. With videotape equipment becoming quite inexpensive, such program generation is within the reach of most medium-sized libraries or systems.

This is only the beginning, however, and a quite traditional view of library use of CATV. The true application lies in the future. The inherent quality of a sharp, clear picture via cable, which can carry all kinds of data on a very wide band, and therefore very fast, opens up possibilities for libraries hitherto thought impossible.

We believe that CATV will become perhaps *the* most important means for interconnecting libraries, as well as for connecting users to libraries. All kinds of information can be transmitted, from facsimile of the printed page to microfilm, from pictures to drawings, and from maps to voice communication. The possibility of two-way communication which is technically feasible now would allow an almost infinite number of applications. The Federal Communications Commission suggested some services in one of its documents:

It has been suggested that the expanding multichannel capacity of cable systems could be utilized to provide a variety of new communications services to homes and businesses within a community, in addition to services now commonly offered such as time, weather, news, stock exchange ticker, etc. While we shall not attempt an all-inclusive listing, some of the predicted services include: *facsimile reproduction of newspapers, magazines, documents, etc.*; electronic mail delivery; merchandising; *business concern links to branch offices,* primary customers, or suppliers; *access to computers: e.g., man-to-computer communications in the nature of inquiry and response* (credit checks, airlines reservations, branch banking, etc.); *information retrieval (library and other reference material, etc.) and computer-to-computer communications; the furtherance of various governmental programs on a federal, state and municipal level, e.g., employment services and manpower utilization, special communications systems to reach particular neighborhoods or ethnic groups within a community,* and for municipal surveillance of public areas for protection against crime, fire detection, control of air pollution and traffic; *various educational and training programs,* e.g., job and literacy training, preschool programs in the nature of "Project Headstart," and *to enable professional groups such as doctors to keep abreast of developments in their fields;* and the provision of a low-cost outlet for political candidates, advertisers, *amateur expression (e.g., community drama groups)* and for other moderately funded organizations or persons desiring access to the community or a particular segment of the community.[2] [Italics added]

It is easy to see that if we conceive of a multipurpose multitype of library network, many or all the italicized passages in the above statement would apply. If we are indeed convinced that the public library should become *the* community information center, backed up by other types of libraries with their specialized resources, we can then selectively distribute needed information wherever and whenever needed—perhaps becoming a modern version of "the right book to the right man at the right time." Conversely, this would hold true for the scholar who has need of a document or a piece of information located elsewhere; rapid transmission of the needed document will indeed speed his research. We can envision large microform storage libraries located in a few selected places, from whose vast stores desired documents may be distributed to someone needing them.

Inherent in this concept is the two-way communication referred to above. With relatively modest investment, both on the part of the home viewer—who would need a talk-back device (a telephone would do)—and the CATV operator—who would need to install equipment allowing him to distribute selectively rather than to the entire community—this two-way communication could soon become reality. With somewhat more sophisticated equipment, including a device providing hard copy (but costing considerably more, and therefore perhaps to be located only in the library at first) the user could have his document in hand, instead of projected on the screen. He might also install a small videotape recorder near his home set and record for replay whenever convenient. The ability to store and "hold" still pictures for reading exists now; this would be another necessary part of such a system.

Ultimately, the user would be able to interact with the network directly, similar to the kind of interaction now possible with computer-stored information via terminal. He could request, read, respond, and even alter information with the aid of a light pen, which transmits a signal a TV screen can "read."

Not all of this is possible right now, of course, but there is no question that such a system will gradually evolve as time and money permit. It should be pointed out that the cost of a CATV-based network would be far less than one based on existing telephone lines, where lines at present are far too costly to allow most libraries the use of even such simple devices as telefacsimile.

While the technical and economic parameters are likely to become considerably more favorable in the future, problems of equal or greater significance will have to be solved in the area of copyright lest we find that what is technically possible and fiscally feasible is also—regrettably—illegal. Long-overdue revision of the 1909 copyright statute has been hung up on the complex questions of present-day CATV and how the proprietary rights in the television programs of local and distant stations are to be accommodated when a CATV system brings the programs of Los Angeles stations to San Antonio, Texas. How much more complex, then, will be the vexing issues to be solved before a page of copyrighted text can be delivered to the user in ephemeral or hard copy form? This is not to say that our present dreams are doomed to disaster, but that if we wish to see them come true, we shall need to keep an eye upon copyright as well as upon cable.

If we believe that the future does indeed hold this kind of promise and if we accept the vastly increased user services possible with a CATV network as desirable, then what can we do right now to be sure that libraries will be entitled to their rightful share of the system? As we said before, franchises are awarded locally. This means that city fathers negotiate with a CATV company; whoever offers the most attractive "deal" to the city or town usually wins out. In the past, this was often a matter of money. We have seen countless CATV systems going in with little thought being given to educational or informational use, with little knowledge of technological developments. City fathers are usually not expected to be television engineers: therefore we have many cases where CATV can only distribute a limited number of channels and cannot expand to include two-way communication and other, newer developments. The educational community has only recently realized the potential of cable television, and often did not plead its case early enough to see to it that certain channels were set aside for its use. Lack of information has prevented open-ended franchises allowing for expansion; many run for a given number of years and terms cannot be changed.

There are certain steps librarians can take right now to inform themselves about the local situation and to convince other interested parties that libraries do indeed have a stake in CATV systems. The first step might be to find out where your community is in the development of CATV. Do you presently have such a system? Who holds the franchise? What are its provisions? For how long does it run? Who is the manager? Get to know him and show him that you are truly interested. Is the system owned by a small company or by a corporation which operates a number of other systems (a "multiple system owner")? What kind of a record does the company have, in your town and in other towns? Have channels already been set aside for educational purposes?

If there is no CATV system in your town, what are the plans for the future? Has the city government been approached by prospective operators? And most important, are members of the city government properly informed of all technical and social aspects of cable television? Are hearings being held? Who has presented testimony? What did it say?

The second, and very important step, is to find out who else is interested in educational and instructional uses of CATV in your community. Have you talked with your local school administration? How about the educational television station? Do you have closed-circuit television in the schools already? How about the local college or university? The YMCA? Other groups engaged in educational programs? Why not form a planning group of all interested parties? By discussing common goals and objectives, and then presenting a united front to city government in the pursuance of these, much more can be achieved than when we go it alone. Too, librarians are not likely to be ready with a full-fledged program of their own, and in some areas they may always wish to share channels rather than have one allocated solely to library purposes; in this way they can combine forces with others having mutual interests right now, and make their voice heard. Early creation of a planning group would serve another purpose; it could prevent needless duplication of services, given by various community agencies, and may have the added benefit for the library of making other agencies aware of the library's present and potential services via CATV, as well as its more traditional ones.

Another goal of a planning group should be to keep its members continuously informed about technical developments and results of FCC rulemaking so that they can present city government with the necessary technical information, as well as means of achieving stated goals of local programs. Some suggested readings are appended; there is a vast literature on the subject, much of it written in layman's language, which the librarian can read and provide to other interested parties.

There are those among us who say that before we plead our case for CATV, we must decide "what to put on the channel." They say that we are so enamored of technology that we forget the many problems yet to be solved before we can take full advantage of all that is available now. We agree—in principle. In practice, we must make our case now. There are only so many channels; and many, many interested parties are clamoring for them. If we don't participate in franchise negotiations, we are sure to be left out, probably forever. An analogy might be to say that we cannot support the funding of the "Networks for Knowledge Act" (1968) because we do not yet know what types of networks we want, or what we want to put on them. The time to act is now; planning must proceed apace, but it must not deter us from doing what has to be done.

To quote from a recent paper:

> Enlightened self-interest of those who plan communications networks requires, as does the public interest, that parochialism give way to broader vision, and that acute specialization be tempered with cooperation. Each new development in communications—new technology; new policy decisions . . . offer[s] an increasingly favorable climate for the development of library communications and other information networks. Library and information specialists can help themselves, and others, if they will seek to pool their interests and cooperate fully in the pursuit of the new opportunities which are now increasingly within our common grasp.[3]

NOTES

1. Unpublished estimate provided by Research Department, National Cable Television Association, Washington, D.C.

2. Federal Communications Commission Docket No. 18397, *Notice of Proposed Rule Making and Notice of Inquiry*, (FCC 68-1175), p. 5.

3. Frank W. Norwood, *Telecommunications Programs Affecting Network Development,* paper presented for the *Conference on Interlibrary Communications and Information Networks,* Warrenton, Va., Sept. 28-Oct. 2, 1970, p. 38.

BIBLIOGRAPHY

Joint Council on Educational Telecommunications. 1969. What Every Educational Media Specialist Ought to Know about CATV. *Audiovisual Instruction* 14(8):67-75.

Joint Council on Educational Telecommunications. 1968. *CATV: Data Base.* Washington, The Council, 1126 16th St., N.W. 4pp.

Kemeny, John G., et al. 1962. A Library for 2000 A.D. Martin Greenberger, ed. *Computers and the World of the Future.* Cambridge, M.I.T. Press. pp. 134-178.

Licklider, J. C. R. 1967. Televistas: Looking Ahead Through Side Windows. *Public Television: A Program for Action.* The Report and Recommendations of the Carnegie Commission on Educational Television. New York, Harper & Row. pp. 201-225.

National Education Association. 1971. *Schools and Cable Television.* Washington, NEA, Division of Educational Technology. 66p. $2.25.

Norwood, Frank W. CATV and Educational TV. *Audiovisual Instruction* 13(2): 1058-1061.

COMING THROUGH YOUR FRONT DOOR: PRERECORDED VIDEO CASSETTES*

By John G. Burke

Administering a library is often made significantly more difficult when technological developments surface, and libraries are forced to take some cognizance of their presence. More often than not, these technological developments ultimately come into the library through the back door, and it is only after extensive development elsewhere that they usually find their way into the library. This was the case, certainly, with automation, though not the case with a number of new developments in technology in book and film preservation. The introduction of prerecorded video cassette systems in libraries, however, will probably make its way into the library through the front door as a result of patron demand, for in the next few years a great many homes in the U.S. will be regularly receiving an advertising message somewhat along these lines:

> Imagine being able to choose your television programs—the time they are shown, the subject matter, the featured performers—being able to stop at any frame, or to go back and repeat what you've just seen. Seems too good to be true, but if all this appeals to you, get ready for the "paperback of the movie industry," the "big thing" in the home entertainment market for the '70s, the phonograph for the eye; and prepare yourself to select your own programs from a library of inexpensive tapes, playable over your own TV, in black and white or color.

It is undoubtedly true that prerecorded video cassette systems will become a big factor in the home entertainment market. *Newsweek, Saturday Review,* and *Barron's* have already predicted this development, and with industry now gearing up to produce and market these systems, the demand for the inclusion of both the hardware and software in the public library, and some college libraries, is just around the corner. A number of manufacturers are currently working on prerecorded video cassette systems involving a player about the size of the average tape deck, which attaches to the antenna terminals of any TV set and is able to play prerecorded tapes through the TV set. The Columbia Broadcasting System is now marketing a system to libraries, EVR or Electronic Video Recording. This is also the first system available to the public. The initial cost for the EVR hardware, which is manufactured by Motorola, is $795, and a tape library of one hundred films is available to libraries in a package program. Twentieth-Century Fox's entire feature film library will eventually be available on EVR, and the Popular Science Publishing Company is preparing a series on "How to Keep Your Car in Tune," and a series on camping entitled "The Outdoor Life." In addition to leisure and entertainment programming, EVR has also begun educational programming on prerecorded video cassettes. This type of educational programming may turn out to have as much importance to the development of library acceptance of prerecorded video cassette systems as the availability of feature length films.

---

*Reprinted by permission from *American Libraries*, 1:1069-1073, December 1970.

Two other commercial firms in the process of entering the market with video cassette systems are the Radio Corporation of America and the Sony Corporation. RCA's SelectaVision and Sony's Videocassette will probably appear on the market sometime in 1971. SelectaVision's target price is under four hundred dollars. One of the unusual features of RCA's SelectaVision is the use of a tape which is considerably less expensive than videotape or other existing film. RCA's target price for a cassette with a half-hour of running time is projected at about ten dollars. Sony's Videocassette, like RCA's SelectaVision, is capable of playing color programs, but Sony's Videocassette will use standardized videotape, and the system is projected to sell as low as $350.

In contrast to RCA's SelectaVision and Sony's Videocassette, Admiral's Cartrivision, a third entry in the videotape cassette market, incorporates a 19-inch television set and a recording and playback deck in one console. Not only can the viewer play prerecorded tapes, a portable video camera can be used to tape scenes for immediate playback through the tape deck without processing. By setting a special timer, the viewer can automatically record a TV program to be played back at a later time. Initially, Cartrivision's cost is projected at less than one thousand dollars, and it is expected to be ready for marketing in 1971. Admiral hopes to be able to sell tapes of feature length movies for approximately $25, and like Sony's system, the Cartrivision videotapes can be erased by simply recording over them.

If the manufacture of hardware for video cassette systems is just getting off the ground, the software aspect of the industry is out of its infancy. The film and videotape libraries in this country and abroad all have the capacity of being transferred to videotape or electronic video recordings in cassette size, and the range of this material currently being transferred to electronic video recording is staggering: training materials, basic chemistry, short and feature length films, occupational documentaries, popular lectures, performances of recording groups, and children's films are all making their way into this new medium. The first such package offered specially for libraries is now available from CBS/EVR in collaboration with the Film Library Information Council (FLIC). In this offer, EVR, Motorola, and the National Audiovisual Center in Washington, D.C., are offering a package of one hundred titles covering a broad range of topics selected from the National Audiovisual Center's catalog of films. The complete set of one hundred titles is being sold at a cost of $2,653.65. In connection with this proposal, Motorola will sell the EVR Teleplayer to institutions for $695, one hundred dollars less than the usual list price. This offer is based upon the participation of one hundred institutions, and the New York State Division of Library Development will oversee the evaluation of the systems in participating libraries. Equipment performance, user reaction, and library staff response will be measured. Joan Clark, audiovisual consultant for the Division of Library Development at the New York State Library in Albany, is serving as project coordinator for FLIC in her capacity as chairman of the New Media Committee.

As the video cassette revolution makes its way through the library world, the librarian will encounter most of our traditional library problems. First, and perhaps the most difficult problem to resolve, is the incompatibility of video systems. Of the manufacturers of electronic video recording systems which are now on the market or will be on the market in 1971, not *one* is offering cassettes that are compatible with another system. As the production of system hardware proceeds, the necessity for standardization of cassette size will be more demanding, but it will undoubtedly be some time before a situation develops in this field comparable to the present situation in audio recording tape cassettes. The decision to buy hardware, given the fact of mutual incompatibility, becomes then a function of the availability of the software complement. In this matter CBS/EVR does seem to be ahead of its competitors, though as the hardware arrives on the market, there will probably develop a group of software distributors which will specialize in providing all sizes of cassettes for the different systems. The problem of compatibility of cassette systems remains, however, until the industry can come to an agreement on standardization—and it is here that librarians presently have a clear professional responsibility.

Another problem which lies on the horizon for librarians is the implication which electronic video cassettes and other video systems have for library architecture. Viewing areas may be required in most libraries and these areas may not be compatible with the public meeting areas now considered a standard complement to the branch library building. An early decision will be required by libraries which purchase this equipment as to what accommodations should be made in the library to offer maximum service to patrons who come into the library to use electronic video systems. The educational as opposed to entertainment potential of the software also complicates this problem, for the material to be viewed may often be of interest only to a single person.

One of the major promotional rationales for the acquisition of video cassette systems in the library is that feature length films can be obtained at a cost significantly below the cost of obtaining a celluloid print of the film. The September 30th issue of *Variety*, however, reports that the Eighth Congress of the International Federation of Actors, which represents 27 actors' unions including the Screen Actors Guild and Actor's Equity, unanimously passed a resolution that performers appearing on video cassettes or TV programs and films in cassette form should be compensated on a system of "fees in perpetuity," with payment related to the exposure and economic return of the cassettes. It is at least possible, given this development, that the ultimate cost of a feature length film to a library might make its purchase in cassette form prohibitive. The advantages of large-screen film and the relative cost of renting a celluloid print as opposed to purchasing the film in cassette form all come into play at this point, and the circumstances of the individual institution will dictate the wisest policy to follow in individual cases. There is, of course, a great deal of film material out of copyright, and with these films one would not expect to encounter unusual charges for the purchase of this material in cassette form. It should be pointed out, however, that in copyright law this is an area in which there is little prospect for agreement, and unusual developments can indeed be expected as the full impact of this new medium makes its way through the entertainment industry.

Libraries contemplating a significant commitment to the purchase of electronic video recordings will also want to consider the future of cable television systems in their locale. In what is likely to be an equally unique delivery system for television programming, the public library could find itself in direct competition with a channel exclusively reserved for the presentation of feature length and short films. Librarians cannot escape considering cable television as an area in which possibilities for cooperation exist. At the same time, it is possible that cable television as an outlet for programming might pre-empt whatever role the library might have in the community.

The question of how best to serve the public in any community with electronic video recording will, to a large extent, be determined by the community. Initially, most libraries will have to involve themselves in the purchase of hardware, just as most libraries have purchased motion picture projectors to service their film collections. As the price of the hardware component for electronic video cassette reproduction decreases, there will be greater demand for institutions to devote more of their available budget to software. What standardizations there will be in industry and what demands will be placed upon the library to service this media revolution will evolve in time. In the meantime, public libraries as well as a number of college libraries will be pressured to join the video cassette revolution by staff, patrons, school systems, and even private industry. This presents both a challenge and a responsibility, for once again librarians face a new communications medium where the tenets of selection and the impetus for interlibrary cooperation will be seriously tested. Whether librarians as a group rise to this challenge and accept their professional responsi-bility remains to be seen. The issues raised by the introduction of prerecorded video cassette systems in libraries, however, cannot be avoided, for this new medium is coming through the front door of libraries now in the form of sales-men and in the demands of library patrons.

UTILIZING CLOSED CIRCUIT TELEVISION*

By Nelson Harding

Norwalk, with a school population of about seventeen thousand, has a closed circuit television system to twenty-six schools operating from a central studio in the Administration and Service Center. Every room has a television tap, and over three hundred sets are located in various buildings. Use of closed circuit television in relation to the library has followed three directions.

In-service programs designed for clerks and volunteers. Clerks and volunteers do the filing and mending and need an understanding of the Dewey Decimal System. To give the same course eighteen to twenty-six times was too time-consuming; to get the people to come to the center at one time was impossible; large group teaching of mending and filing was not practical. Small groups, located in their own school, could all be taught at the same time, via television, the necessary skills to do a particular job.

Arrangements were made to find out the day and the two most convenient times when TV sets, people, and a telephone could be synchronized. Quizzes, repair kits, and lists of needed materials were sent in advance of the programs in the numbers requested. Each program was written and rehearsed, with the librarian checking time and detail. The programs were given twice, live, with a direct telephone connection to the TV teacher so that questions could be asked about anything not understood. Short quizzes were given during the program and the answers were shown immediately. People involved were asked to repair books along with the TV teacher.

Evaluation was made in a number of ways. First, the clerks and volunteers were asked their opinions of the program. These same people were also tested on how well they could file, mend, and locate books. It was observed that filing and mending techniques have improved and there are more questions from clerks and volunteers on points they would not have known enough to ask about with the programs. A certainly positive evaluation of this program could be implied in the fact that the people involved have asked to have it repeated this year.

Teaching library skills to students. Secondary librarians make much the same kind of presentation as done with in-service programs. One librarian was asked to make video tapes of an orientation presentation she had made to several classes on using the *Reader's Guide.* The objectives here were to make the best possible presentation once, to save preparation time, and to make the programs available to teachers so they could use them at their convenience before embarking on a unit needing such a background. Students could then come to the media center better prepared to work. The librarian spent twenty-five hours preparing her scripts and, with the help of our graphic artist, preparing visuals. Again rehearsal time had to be scheduled and a script for the camera man and console operator developed. These programs are now included in the Instructional Materials Center catalog that goes to all teachers. No real evaluation has been undertaken except to know that the librarian who did the scripts

*Reprinted by permission from *American Libraries,* 1:165-166, February 1970.

is using the programs and at least one teacher from another school has made use of the *Reader's Guide* program.

Story telling programs. This was aimed at the lower elementary grades, with the original purpose of getting more people interested in our closed circuit system by involving them in the programing. We asked for volunteers from each school—a staff member or parent—to read a library book and then to tell the story. Our Superintendent, Dr. Becker, gave one of these programs. We tried to allow a volunteer to select any book as long as it could be found in most of the other schools. We needed two copies of the book for each program. One camera with a telephoto lens was kept on the book and another camera on the storyteller. Short picture books were used. This type of program took less rehearsal (two hours) and preparation than the others and was of great interest in the school from which the teacher came.

One teacher, Janet Bender, took our story time and changed the objective, improved the format and made it a valuable part of our catalog of programs. By spending as much as fifteen hours in preparation time, she developed pre- and post-program activities, brought in props, painted back drops, called it "tell-a-tale time" and prepared a series of stories. These programs helped to teach children by giving them listening and viewing skills. They provided the teacher with free time she would have used to prepare her own story hour, to use on other projects. Our evaluation has come from the fact that we do get many requests for these programs and the results of the activities can be seen on display in some classrooms.

With a closed circuit television system, we would recommend using a primary typewriter or larger print for words, using visuals in place of words wherever possible, using a four by three ratio when making visuals, and allowing plenty of rehearsal time. Do scripts that include lighting and camera angles, and make enough scripts for cameramen and console operator.

Problems or barriers that one might encounter could possibly be lessened by providing release time for teachers as you cannot expect volunteers to prepare programs. You might need professional help on such things as graphics, lighting, etc. The biggest problem even after you have a worthwhile program is: how do you get the teachers to accept another person in their classroom? The more people involved in making programs the greater is your chance for success. Start with volunteers, and if you can show some good programs being utilized, your Board of Education may give funds for release time and even summer workshop money to develop better programs. Norwalk's original equipment was purchased largely through federal funds but now the Board of Education supports the program totally from local funds. This includes rental of lines from the telephone company, a TV technicain, a TV teacher, and materials and supplies to keep up programing.

Harry A. Becker, superintendent of schools in Norwalk, has fervently and judiciously supported these programs since they started about two and a half years ago. His statement about the changes effected through closed circuit television should demonstrate what an inspiration he has been:

For quite a few years, the teachers and administrators in the Norwalk Public Schools have been seeking ways of making education more effective. When we stop to think about it, this is to be expected. We are living in a world in which technological changes are revolutionizing every industry and profession. Can education continue to be unaffected by technological changes? The obvious answer is no. Many of the technological developments can be put to very valuable use in education. We need good teachers and as many of them as we can get. It is important, however, that we provide teachers with all of the technological and human assistance possible so that they can be most effective.

Educational television can be one of the important mediums used. Through the miracle of television, our students can have opportunities and experiences that would have been impossible otherwise. We must not delude ourselves, however, into thinking that educational television is a panacea or that educational television will permit the elimination of teachers. Quite the contrary. Educational television can make important contributions, but it can also be misused. Educational television can never eliminate good teachers, but it can make it possible for good teachers to be more effective. As someone has said, the teacher who can be eliminated by television should be.

REMOTE ACCESS: AUDIO/VIDEO TECHNOLOGY

Today's remote access systems developed as an outgrowth of the language laboratory first developed in 1961 by Chester Electronics Laboratories. "Dial access" was the term used in the early years because of reliance on a telephone type dial as the means for calling for a particular program. Remote access simply means housing audio or combined audio/video equipment in a remote, centralized location, while listening and viewing facilities for users are located in various locations such as libraries and language laboratories.

This technology is rapidly penetrating the school and academic institution. While less expensive alternatives for audio and video utilization are available, this is a technology to be reckoned with. It is broadly applicable to libraries in general.

The articles in this section include both a comprehensive discussion of the system and a description of utilization practices in libraries.

THE REMOTE ACCESS AUDIO/VIDEO INFORMATION SYSTEM*

By David Crossman

Libraries and media centers have historically been facilities in which recorded information and, more recently, equipment needed to display that information, have been centralized for the convenience of students and other users of such information.

During the past decade a subtle but very important shift has taken place in the importance of local access to information. In the library applications of computer technology—in automation, in systems development and in information retrieval—we have seen a decentralization in the accessibility of information. The Medical Audiovisual Center in Atlanta, for example, now provides computer-based remote access to an enormous bank of bibliographic data relating to non-print material for the health professions.

Education, like so many other institutions in our culture, is very easily diverted by novelty. Since 1947, the profession has been preoccupied with the possibilities of television. Perhaps the most conspicuous example of this diversion occurred during the late 1940s and early 1950s when educational radio was totally scrapped in favor of television. In spite of the fact that the audio tape recorder was developed and introduced into the United States in 1947, its importance clearly took a back seat to the video image. On April 14, 1952, the Federal Communications Commission issued the now famous sixth report and order allocating 242 television channels for educational use.[1] This new interest in television caused a dramatic decrease in the applications of audio technology and particularly educational radio broadcasting. The unfortunate effects of this

---

*Reprinted by permission from *Library Trends,* 19:437-446, April 1971.

rush into television technology are still being felt. While television facilities, equipment and systems are today very sophisticated indeed, developments in audio technology, until recently, were comparatively primitive.

Much to the delight of those few faculty members who still have not purchased a television set, the world of audio is staging a renaissance. This situation has developed for two main reasons: 1) the cost of television systems has become so great that other alternatives are being sought, and 2) it has become increasingly apparent that a high percentage of television programming is being used for purposes far better suited to simple audio technology.

For the better part of the twentieth century, learning theorists have attempted to identify general learning characteristics to provide education with data upon which to make decisions relating to curriculum, the arrangement of the school day, instructional resources and the need for specialized physical facilities.

For many years cognitive theorists have been at odds with the behaviorist school. Certainly areas of agreement between these two schools of thought have left the profession with very little theory that can generally be inferred about the learning process. This substantial disagreement, however, has stimulated perhaps the most important trend in American education of the past decade.

We have finally come to the conclusion that it might be wise to concentrate on the many differences among learners rather than center all of our attention upon their far fewer similarities. As a result of this rather dramatic departure from conventional ways of looking at learning patterns and related instructional needs, the idea of individualizing learning has gathered strength.

Because of the flexibility such new patterns provide, the individualization of instruction has permitted experimentation with an almost unlimited number of learning resources. One of the most useful of these is the remote access information system.

Every four or five years a new piece of technology manages to sweep through the education community carrying with it excitement, enthusiasm, promise, apprehension, and usually considerable expense. Such a piece of technology is the so-called dial access system. The use of the term "dial" refers to the usual use of a telephone-type dial as the means of access to information stored in the system. During the past four years, however, the manufacturers of such systems have introduced push button equipment similar to the common touch-tone telephone, rendering the term "dial access" somewhat obsolete. A more generic term which embraces all such equipment, both audio and video, is "remote access information system."

The remote access information system normally is composed of a number of student carrel positions, each of which is equipped with a telephone dial or touch-tone pad, volume control and headphones. Carrel units designed for audio-active response for foreign language purposes are generally equipped with a microphone as well. Video systems also include a television screen. From a centrally located series of audio and/or video playback machines with associated switching equipment, an individual, by consulting a directory at his carrel, may request any program available through the dial or push-button control. Such systems have the advantage of removing audio and video tape from the hands of the user. This not only preserves the tape but enormously simplifies user access. Further, the number of programs that can be stored in such a system is limited only by the size of the system purchased. Generally speaking, equipment of this kind handles short programs—from five to fifteen minutes—more efficiently than longer programs. Where long programs are necessary, portable tape (either audio or video) equipment can be set up without tying up the switching potential of the remote system.

The remote access information system was developed as an outgrowth of the language laboratory. It was thought that students of modern foreign languages would be well served if the many audio programs which are needed for language laboratory usage could be put into a system from which any program could be available automatically upon request. Under the direction of F. Rand Morton, the first dial access language laboratory was developed at the University of Michigan in 1961 by Chester Electronic Laboratories. The initial success of this experimental installation has led to a proliferation of both audio and video systems during the intervening ten years. In a recent publication, *Dial Access Information Retrieval Systems; Guidelines Handbook for Educators*, by Gabriel D. Ofiesh at the Catholic University of America under a grant from the U.S. Office of Education, it is reported that by the spring of 1968, 121 systems had been installed nationwide with 56 institutions planning to purchase remote access equipment.[2]

Of particular interest to the librarian is an interesting change in direction that has been characterized by a broadened use of the remote access information system in a wide variety of subject matter areas. First conceived as a tool of primary use for the learning of modern foreign languages, it grew, predictably, to meet some of the needs of music and speech. What might not have been predicted, however, has been the extension of systems of this type into practically every subject area. Further, the primary locale of the user carrel has shifted from the language laboratory to the library.

With this change in locus and broadened utility has also come a change in rationale. No longer limited to foreign-language pattern drills, the remote access information system is now generally viewed as a means of providing information to an individual student on any subject at any level. It simply provides another medium through which audio and video information can be made available.

One of the rather inappropriate terms that became associated with the remote access information system has been that of "random access." In fact, some systems have become known as "random access systems," suggesting that any program can be made available to any student at any time. Most common of these installations is the four-track tape playback system. Utilizing four tracks on each tape machine, four separate programs can be accommodated on each machine; therefore, the purchase of ten machines yields a capacity of forty programs. This multi-channel utilization of each machine quadruples the program capacity of any system, but at the same time it reduces the random accessibility of each program. Obviously, any program in use requires the movement of a tape upon which are located three other programs. Unless a user is satisfied by entering a program at some point distant from the beginning, each of the three remaining programs is tied up until the first user has relinquished his program, which automatically rewinds the tape to the beginning of all four programs. At that point a second student may select a second program. In short, only 25 percent of any system of this type can be used simultaneously. The problems of accessibility, of which the multi-track problem is only one example, have led to at least three different programming arrangements: serial access, parallel access, and scheduled access.

Serial access is essentially an audio or video reference collection. A series of programs, generally under five minutes in length, are recorded on a single reel of tape and are indexed for electronic access, one program at a time. The use of one program of course renders all other programs on that tape inaccessible, in much the same way that a reader consulting an article in an encyclopedia renders inaccessible other articles in the same volume.

Parallel access partially alleviates the difficulties encountered in the multi-track arrangement described above. By anticipating the need for certain programs, multiple copies of individual programs can be placed on different playback machines. In this way more than one student can be accommodated simultaneously. Where program needs can be anticipated and where high-speed dubbing equipment is available, this method of providing multiple copies of the same program is quite practical.

Scheduled access provides yet a third possibility. Where extremely heavy use of individual programs is anticipated, timing devices can be installed which automatically play programs on a preannounced schedule; that is, a program for which heavy use is anticipated can be preset to be played repeatedly on any time schedule. In this manner students come to their carrels just prior to the transmission time and dial the timed program.

At Ithaca College in Ithaca, New York, a basic dial language laboratory has matured into the kind of configuration described above. Audio lines were run between the language laboratory, located in a classroom building, and the new library where, in a series of carrels, telephone dials were installed permitting access by any student in the library to any program available in the system. A further refinement of this idea at Ithaca has included the installation of microphone lines to a number of classrooms adjacent to the language laboratory area. By a telephone request to the control room, any instructor may record his lecture or presentation, or perhaps record the presentation of a guest lecturer. The recording, made in the control room, is then placed into the dial system for access at a later time by any student in the library who, for any reason, was unable to be present in the classroom. This mode of use has the obvious advantage of providing for students who are unable to attend class or for the professor who must be away from the campus. Further, the storage of presentations of this type permits repeated listening for added clarification and understanding.

In 1965, Oklahoma Christian College set perhaps the most ambitious goal involving remote access information systems. Convinced that students study ineffectively in their rooms, Stafford North, dean of instruction at Oklahoma Christian, undertook to provide each student with a separate carrel on the second and third floors of the new library. Each carrel contains a telephone dial which provides access to as many as 136 separate programs. The college now has constructed over 1,000 carrels and has placed terminals at numerous points throughout the campus, including several large group classrooms. Each student carrel in the library, in addition to the dial console, is equipped with a lockable compartment for personal property, a bookshelf, a typing "L," and a large work surface.

Power outlets were built into each carrel so that projection equipment or supplementary lighting fixtures can be used.

North feels that a remote access system can provide immediacy, pointing out that audio and video materials can be generated and made available far faster than print materials. He suggests further that an important quality of such systems is the ease and efficiency of presentation which they provide. There is no time wasted in setting up equipment, and terminal or dial units can be placed in locations to meet the needs of users. Unlike most reference systems, remote access terminals can be made available without providing staff, although some institutions report vandalism of terminal units in nonsupervised areas.

Another elaborate audio system has been installed on the campus of Ohio State University. The Ohio State system to a greater extent than perhaps any other has decentralized its terminals, providing access to the system in a number of different places throughout the campus. Special emphasis on the Ohio State technique should be made here since one of the main advantages of any electronic distribution system lies in its potential for decentralization.

The Ohio State facility was begun in 1960 as a result of experimentation in the romance language and speech departments. Paul Pimsleur, director of Ohio State University's Listening Center, reports that their first installation included 150 student listening stations from which students had access to eleven program sources. During the center's first year of operation, Pimsleur indicated that most users were students whose curiosity had been piqued by new equipment. Professors seemed unaware of the potential of the system and very few courses in the college of arts and sciences were structured in such a way as to be able to profit from the center. During the 1961-62 academic year, a shift in emphasis took place in the center. While up to that time it had been considered a well-equipped language laboratory, it gradually assumed the dimensions of an audio resource facility of an interdisciplinary nature. By 1962-63 the use of the facility had increased ten times.

Since 1960, the Ohio State Listening Center has increased its program breadth to involve 22 departments and 125 different courses. There are over 400 student booths in 37 different docations, both on and off campus. The equipment is available 95 hours per week. While Pimsleur indicates that most audio equipment has performed well, he advises that dial video equipment recently acquired has proved less than dependable. This caution has been expressed elsewhere in this paper.

Other more elaborate systems, some including remote access to extensive video programming, have been installed in libraries at Oral Roberts University in Tulsa, in the public schools of West Hartford in Connecticut, in the Beverly Hills Public Schools in California and elsewhere. In most installations visited by the author it appeared that audio equipment, in general, works very well indeed, but that those institutions which have invested in video distribution equipment are limited to very few programs, unreliable operation and expense that far exceed the utility of the system.

When planning is based upon an installation of approximately forty audio carrels utilizing an audio-passive mode (listen only), Ofiesh estimates that a reasonably accurate cost can be projected by calculating $500 per carrel position and $500 for each program source. The adding of video capability to any system can be estimated at approximately four to five times the cost of the audio system. Thus, an average audio system of forty carrels capable of storing forty programs, audio-passive, would cost approximately $40,000 plus an estimated $6,000 for installation, or a total of $46,000. A video system of the same capability would cost between $184,000 and $230,000—considerably more than many institutions have to spend.

A unique audio/video system is in the final stages of completion at the Oak Park-River Forest School District in Illinois. Utilizing high-speed, bin-loop duplicating machines, each student requesting a program has it duplicated at high speed from a master tape onto his own tape. In this way no student must wait more than a minute for any program, thus more closely approximating random accessibility than any other system now available. Late in 1970 the district completed the installation of a video disc system for the retrieval and display of still television images. These too are reproducible at high speeds.

In Pennsylvania, pioneering work in remote access audio systems was done at the Abington School District near Philadelphia. More recently installations, all located in the library, have been completed at Marywood College in Scranton, and the Shippensburg State and Carlow Colleges in Pennsylvania. At Shippensburg the carrels are placed in rows adjacent to the stacks. The control room is located nearby in a nonpublic area of the library with a glass wall overlooking the carrel area. Fifteen of the 100 carrels in the Shippensburg system are equipped with video capability programmed from a video tape recorder designed to store information in a serial access mode. At Carlow College the system is linked with a language laboratory in the library.

Other significant installations include those at Forest Park Community College in St. Louis, Missouri; Wayne State University in Detroit, Michigan; Southern Illinois University in Carbondale, Illinois; Brevard Junior College in Cocoa, Florida; Bucknell University in Lewisburg, Pennsylvania; and the State University College in Fredonia, New York.

If one looks at a fair sample of the various types of remote access systems now in use, several tentative conclusions can be drawn. First, those institutions that have planned carefully and thoroughly on the basis of their needs and have written specifications directly around those needs, invariably acquire systems more satisfactory than institutions which permit a vendor to make decisions for them. Second, quality audio systems work very well indeed. Access times for programs not in use are well within tolerance limits (frequently less than ten seconds), and audio quality can be excellent. Both Ohio State and Oklahoma Christian handle thousands of dial requests each week and report very high audio equipment reliability rates. Third, remote access video, while installed in some institutions, does not yet enjoy the reliability of audio and generally is more expensive than can be justified in an automatic retrieval system. The recent development of electronic video recording, which is a new and inexpensive way of recording video information on film, as well as the excitement now being expressed in the video cartridge,[3] promises to provide an economic and technological breakthrough in the accessibility of video information. At the time this article was prepared there were seven manufacturers competing for development of these cartridges: 1) Electronic Video Recording (CBS), 2) Selectavision (RCA), 3) Cassette VTR (Panasonic), 4) Cassette VTR (Ampex), 5) Cassette VTR (Sony),

6) Video Disc (Teldec), and 7) Cassette VTR (Arco). Several of the systems noted above use conventional magnetic tape. One (Electronic Video Recording) uses a photographic process combined with a flying spot scanner, and one (Selectavision) uses a holographic system which uses a special low energy laser and inexpensive vinyl ribbon for storing both video and audio signals. Fourth, it appears that future remote access systems will be combined with other methods of providing both audio and video information. Present systems permit a student to utilize information only at the carrel or terminal position.

In recent months much interest has been expressed in utilizing the one-eighth inch audio tape cassette in conjunction with remote access systems. Through the development of high-speed cassette duplication equipment it will be possible for a student to request a program from a central storage bank in the remote access system and to have it duplicated on a cassette. A contract for such a system has already been written for one western community college. Further, cassette players are now available in the less than twenty dollar range, making it possible for libraries to lend them and for student book stores to sell them. Such equipment is clearly not suited for music reproduction, but it is entirely adequate for speech. *Consumer Reports* noted recently that some cassettes now contain audio quality comparable to disc versions of the same recordings. Some, they report, were actually superior to reel-to-reel types.[4] The increases in cassette audio quality have taken place even faster than many predicted. In fact, several cassette equipment manufacturers are providing hardware that is capable of reproducing music of astonishingly high quality. The use of new chromium oxide tape has helped speed the availability of high frequency recording and reproduction.

It is clear that remote access information systems have proved useful to a number of institutions. It is also clear that carefully designed equipment functions with great reliability. However, it is important that any user of this type of equipment provides himself both with programming personnel and with technical assistance. Trained librarians can be taught to handle and edit audio and video tape without difficulty, but the maintenance of remote access systems requires an electronic technician. For smaller systems a technician can be available on call, but larger installations ordinarily require the services of a full-time person. While a detailed guide to system planning is clearly beyond the scope of these few pages, a few precautions are in order.

Where a new building is being planned, attention should be paid to the provision of conduit from control room space to each carrel location. Further, if the system is to be decentralized into other buildings, institutionally owned cable or leased telephone lines will be required. Where video carrels are contemplated, 115 volt AC power should be available. In any case, power is necessary in the carrel for the operation of many types of additional audio and video equipment. Care should be taken in the selection of headphone units. Soft cushioned dynamic headphones provide a high level of noise reduction and increase acoustic privacy. This type of headphone is the most practical for use in public service areas. Because of the noise and heat generated, special space should be provided for tape playback and switching equipment. Building planning must provide for adequate power, air conditioning, and acoustic isolation from other spaces. A false floor similar to the type used in computer rooms facilitates the wiring of equipment.

A remote access information system is a most useful complement to a developing independent learning facility. It provides a particularly efficient method for handling audio collections of all types and within the next few years, will be capable of providing for video information at affordable prices. It is expandable and can provide unlimited decentralization. Remote access technology is no longer just an experiment. In many institutions it is already an important dimension to newly organized individualized learning programs.

REFERENCES

1. "TV Allocation Report, April 14, 1952" (Television Digest with Electronics Reports, Vol. 6). Washington, D.C., Radio News Bureau, 1952.

2. Gabriel D. Ofiesh, *Dial Access Information Retrieval Systems; Guidelines Handbook for Educators*. Washington, D.C., U.S. Dept. of Health, Education, and Welfare, Office of Education, Bureau of Research, 1970.

3. National Association of Educational Broadcasters, *Television Cartridge Systems—What Are They Good For?* Washington, D.C., 1970.

4. "How Cassettes Compare with Tapes and Discs," *Consumer Reports,* 35:397, July 1970.

A RANDOM-ACCESS RECORD LISTENING FACILITY*

By Edward McIntosh

As part of the general education program at Radford College, Radford, Virginia, Music Appreciation is a course that all students are required to study. But like many other colleges, Radford has recently experienced rapid growth in enrollment, and as a result several special problems have arisen in connection with courses such as Music Appreciation. Among these problems is the matter of providing adequate space for specialized instructional facilities that is peculiar to the study of music. Space, of course, is a problem on every campus, but in this case it became so critical that the library assumed responsibility for providing quarters where the class could meet and listen to selected masterworks in permanently recorded form.

The decision to provide this service was not easily made, for in arriving at such a determination the library had to face several problems of its own. First, there was the matter of how to contain the noise; second, some way had to be found that would keep equipment from wearing out; third, a system had to be devised for storing records and related accessories; and fourth, the possibility of overcrowding had to be forestalled. The use of earphones solved the noise problem, but the matter of how to prevent the deterioration of equipment and recordings, as well as the question of overcrowding, remained unsolved. In attempting to overcome these obstacles, the library first provided small audio-visual-type phonographs that were equipped with eight station earphone junction-boxes. The recordings were kept on reserve at the circulation desk and were checked out for use in the listening room on a first-come first-served basis. Obviously, such an arrangement meant that record life was short and that the quality of any given recording could never be guaranteed; in addition, equipment maintenance became a problem as a result of general student use. Therefore, while the library and music department were doing their best to maximize learning opportunity, space limitations continued to make any arrangement difficult, and—as anyone could see—the situation was far from ideal.

A NOVEL FACILITY

In 1964-65, final plans were drawn for an addition to the college library. So that the finest possible listening facilities could be made available, a section on the second floor of the new addition was planned as a modern, random-access, record listening area. A room, 31 feet by 17½ feet, was designed for listening which could be serviced by an audio-control room 8½ feet by 19 feet; in addition, a listening annex for the use of music faculty and music majors was provided. The librarian was closely involved in the implementation of these plans, and as a result of cooperation and understanding among faculty members, administrative leaders, and library workers, an excellent, functional system went into operation during the Fall quarter of 1967.

*Reprinted by permission from *Library-College Journal,* 3:29-31, Winter 1970.

As now constituted, the student listening room provides for forty individual listening stations, or electronically equipped carrels. Each of these stations has an earphone headset and a master twelve-channel selector switch. Thus, the student can select any one of twelve different musical presentations by selecting the appropriate channel number. The control room now has six Garrard record changes and six Ampex model 602 double track professional tape recorders, with plans for additional recorders as time goes on.

In operation, each originating point consists of either the Garrard changer or the Ampex recorder. The output from each is fed to an Eico model HF-12A fourteen-watt high fidelity amplifier from which a branching cable runs to the same channel number on all forty selector switches. In this manner, each originating station feeds a given channel number on the student's selector switch, and two selector switches are available in the control room for monitoring purposes. An earphone set connects to the output of each station switch.

A novel, but very valuable, feature of the control room is the manner in which each tape recorder has its own record changer interconnected for dubbing. Because of this arrangement, it is possible to feed not only the normal channel from the changer, but the tape recorder input at the same time. The tape recorder allows monitoring of the recording a fraction of a second after it is made, and this can also be fed to the channel number served by the recorder, if desired. Therefore, tapes can be fed at the same time that students are listening to any given channel. Since no "off-line" time is needed for dubbing tapes, a considerable saving in time is possible.

ACCENT ON UTILIZATION

All of this advanced technology, however, would be little better than the older system if left on a first-come first-served basis. With this in mind, all persons interested in the equipment agreed that a strategy of utilization had to be devised. Accordingly, each of the twelve channels became an individual closed-circuit radio station which could program a selected musical composition at regular pre-determined times. Because few selections were found to be more than fifty minutes long, it became possible to schedule programs so that each channel could be activated every hour on the hour. The selections, and their assigned channels, are listed by instructor and posted on a bulletin board in the listening room. Each student merely checks the board, locates the channel to which his selection has been assigned, and notes the hour at which his program will begin.

Assume that a Bach selection has been assigned and that students can listen to the composition on channel five every hour on the hour. The bulletin board will make such information readily available, so that all a student has to do is occupy an empty listening carrel, put on the earphones, and turn the selector to position five. On the hour, the control room operator starts changer five and the Bach selection is heard at all forty carrels. Special arrangements are made for those selections lasting more than one hour. This is done by starting such programs either every one and one-half hours or every two hours and making note of this information on the student bulletin board. Finally, during times of extreme overload, given selections can be programed every other hour, but this is rarely necessary.

As part of this system, provision is made for recreational listening when one or more channels are not needed for the music appreciation course. In this case, any student may request that a recorded selection be programed on an unused channel. In addition, the listening annex provides standard high fidelity phonographs and one audiovisual-type tape recorder which can be used by music students and members of the faculty. When these are needed, recordings and tapes are checked out by the record room operator and taken to the annex for personal use.

The random-access record listening system installed at the Radford College Library has provided a much needed and highly advanced type of service to the faculty and students. Although this system has been in operation for only a relatively short time, it has already proven its worth and demonstrated its value.

DIAL, REMOTE AND RANDOM-RADICAL SOLUTIONS TO ORTHODOX PROBLEMS*

By Ted Johnson

School library vocabulary continues to change. In some categories, new terms actually do identify revisions in library operations. Some of the new labels and procedures are quite literally charged with electricity. Not simply the electric service of the light bulb and automatic eraser, however! Now electricity is driving computers and a multitude of film and tape machines in pursuit of a new generation of library services. It is possible today to visit many schools in which computers are being used to improve book processing, bibliographic, reference, and circulation services. More common than these pioneer programs are schools in which the library is more than a book and pamphlet center. Individual access by students to audiovisual materials is being permitted and encouraged in a steadily expanding number of schools. In a few of these schools, this service is provided automatically. By using a telephone-type dial, the student is able to call the film or tape of his choice from a remote storage point and view or listen to the item in a library carrel. Such remote access facilities are generating much of the new library vocabulary and receiving a major portion of the attention given library innovations today. Of even greater significance than the computers or the remote access systems separately, are the possibilities for combining them. In combination, these additions to the library promise radical solutions to basic problems in the use and storage of instructional materials.

Computer-directed remote access systems can provide a truly random access to instructional materials in a library setting. That is to say, such a facility can guarantee the student instant access to the material of his choice at all times. From the full range of instructional media, large numbers of students can make their selections at will and know their requests will be promptly honored. By capitalizing on the efficiency of the computer and the impact of audiovisual materials, remote access systems can help achieve the goal of making the school library truly the center of the program of instruction.

The first remote access system capable of providing random access to audiovisual instructional materials is now operating in the library of the Oak Park and River Forest High School. Developed through a period of two years, with the support of a grant under Title III of the Elementary and Secondary Education Act, this system demonstrates the potential of much of the newest library technology. The continuing development and expansion of this system should demonstrate additional lessons during the next two years.

The machinery in the system consists of three basic parts: 1) a central storage bank for instructional materials, 2) a computer control center, and 3) individual student carrels. The storage bank houses units of instruction on audio tape. These units are typically independent programs designed to enrich or supplement classroom activities for individual students with audiovisual materials. The computer connects the student with the requested material, and the carrels serve as individual study stations. By using the push-button control panel in his

*Reprinted by permission from *ALA Bulletin*, 62:1085-1088, October 1968.

carrel, the student can direct the computer to connect him with any lesson in storage. In 30 seconds, the program selected will be available to the student in his carrel. In this library facility, random access means each student has instant access to all materials in the system at all times regardless of the requests being made by other students. For the student, this means a new level of flexibility and convenience in access and service. For the librarian, the efficiency of service is significantly improved.

The retrieval system of the Oak Park and River Forest High School library can even assist the student at home. If the student's home is equipped with a standard touch-tone telephone, he can call the computer and direct it to connect him with any of the programs in the retrieval system. Thus, the largest communication system in the world becomes an economical tool for extending library services and makes random access retrieval even more available. Reference materials, instructional units, drill exercises, and the sounds of life and history housed in the expensive school library are placed at the student's fingertips, automatically, in his home.

At the present time, the numbers involved in the first random access retrieval system are small. There are now 25 student carrels providing access to 224 on-line programs from a total system library of some 900 taped programs. Program production is continuing, however, and the random access characteristics mean that an unlimited number of receiver points can be connected to an equally open number of programs. The existing Oak Park and River Forest system is modular in its design to permit expansion with maximum ease and efficiency. An additional 50 carrels are now on order, video service will be introduced in the fall, program development is accelerating, and a system of evaluation will be placed in operation in October. In the following year, audio and video service will be provided in the classrooms of the high school, random access to video will be implemented, and broadcast services will be made available to neighboring schools and colleges.

As was mentioned above, in the Oak Park and River Forest High School retrieval system, technology is being used to handle materials intended to enrich and supplement teaching and learning. All the materials for use in the system are being prepared or selected by members of the high school faculty toward this end. In some instances, this means acceleration materials for the math student who should move ahead of his class. It also means access to materials which are remedial in their nature or serve as alternatives for the math student who is stumped by a particular process. In another instance, the materials are designed for the advanced chemistry student who should be able to pursue much of his study under conditions of independent study. For the English student, the enrichment materials can be professional interpretations of the works of a wide variety of poets. In partial contrast for this same student, the enrichment and supplemental material may free class time of some mechanical or drill work which does not actually require student and teacher contact.

The foreign language student is presented with effective access to literary, dramatic, and musical insights into the culture of the language he is studying. Because the retrieval system includes a recording facility, this student can also work improving his oral proficiency of the language. For all students electronic retrieval of enrichment and supplementary materials means readily available library service and guidance materials which could not previously be secured on a random basis by individual students. The history student gains command over the sounds and sights of history to strengthen his use of the printed record. Eminent practicing historians are also on line with individual interpretations of the events of the past. Valuable laboratory time and greater control of the rate of his progress is gained by the biology student because of the access and convenience which the retrieval system provides.

These examples should serve to suggest a basic point. All areas of the curriculum can be served by a random access retrieval system toward the goal of enriching and supplementing individual work. The full list of possibilities is limited only by the creativity of the school program.

Implicit in the basic rationale of the system are at least four other goals. The impact of the retrieval system on the whole library program may well be the most important of these. As the above examples illustrate, remote access facilities extend the role and significance of the library in the basic program of instruction. The amount of service provided for the teacher and his students is increased. The choices and possibilities available to the student as he conducts his self-study programs are multiplied. The opportunities for librarians to participate directly in designing and implementing instructional materials are expanded. In other words, a more effective integration of library, classroom, and department programs is produced.

Another aspect of this integration of programs among departments is the sharing of resources by teachers and departments. Programs prepared by the architectural drawing teacher on the residential architecture of Frank Lloyd Wright make it possible for the art, history, and math teachers to share his special talents with their students. As another example, we can point to the slide collection of the art department becoming much more readily available to the history, English, and music students and teachers.

Beyond this integration are the goals of accomplishing a greater individualization of instruction and appropriate independent study opportunities, a new flexibility in handling the new diversity of instructional materials, and a major reduction in the mechanical problems confronting the teacher who takes full advantage of the new media. The library is, after all, the area in which the most individualized study done in school is performed. A random access retrieval system can be a worthy step away from the mass and uniform terms in which most libraries are built and operated. Such a system can also gain time, conserve energy, and reduce frustration for teachers and students in search of the right material at the right time.

The first random access multimedia retrieval system did not spring full-born from a wholesale catalog. It has very slowly and deliberately evolved from within the Oak Park and River Forest High School program with the support and cooperation of the U.S. Office of Education, the Illinois Department of Public Instruction, and leading corporations. In January of 1966, Gene Schwilck, then the superintendent, organized a faculty study committee to determine how new technology could better be exploited to improve instruction. The members of this committee had previously been involved in a variety of new curriculum developments all of which related to or depended upon a greater individualization of instruction, independent study, diversified library programs, and flexibility in the use of time and spaces.

220

A key member of this committee was Lura Crawford, head of library services. At the time the committee was constituted, Miss Crawford and her staff were busy developing subject-area resource centers as part of the Knapp Project's national demonstration. The lessons of these resource centers and Miss Crawford's consistent and effective testimony for the cause of a full-service library clearly indicated much of the direction for improving library technology.

After the educational requirements and functional specifications for a new retrieval system had been defined, several leading manufacturers were approached to determine whether the idea could be made a reality. From among the proposals submitted in response, that of the Ampex Corporation was selected as most nearly meeting the school's specifications. Since the time of the selection of this proposal, the role of Ampex has been that of a corporation creative enough to design for the future and ambitious and dedicated enough to commit and risk corporate dollars and other resources in a joint venture with schools.

Not even a razzle-dazzle new electronic system will produce the school library millenium, of course. By the same token, given the scope and significance of the frustrations which plague library services, we cannot afford to lightly dismiss the potential of such electronic systems. With careful planning, judicious assessment and honest implementation, and the technology of the dial, the remote and the random can be exploited to human advantage. These new tools, too, can relieve and liberate.

LEARNING HOW TO APPLY THE FIRST TRUE RANDOM-ACCESS LEARNING SYSTEM*

By Ted Johnson

The completed installation of the world's first true random-access audio/video system in early 1971 placed the staff of the Oak Park and River Forest High School in a unique position.

It was time to put into practice the theories discussed while the PYRAMID (Program Yielding Rapid Access Major Information Device) was undergoing stage-by-stage installation. To some extent, we could no longer afford the luxury of total conjecture. With the nearly $1 million instructional hardware system offering broader capabilities than any other system of its kind came the opportunity and responsibility of putting it to use.

In essence, the PYRAMID system is a computer-controlled library of taped audio and visual instructional materials which may be accessed from a number of individual positions or carrels (55 carrels receive audio, 20 receive audio and video) and may deliver audio programs by telephone (students may "call" the PYRAMID system and enter the number of the program they require from their home phones).

The first stage of the three phase system, originally ordered in spring 1967, was ready for use in the fall of 1968, providing 25 individual student positions from which 224 audio programs could be accessed. The lessons, ranging in length up to 15 minutes, included vocational guidance, mathematics, science, languages, English, history, and many other subjects. Students could listen to programs and record their own responses, then play back both. The carrels were equipped to allow students to record lessons on personal tape recorders to take out for further study or review.

The programs were intended to supplement rather than replace classroom teaching. Each program is provided individually and from the beginning. It is started, stopped and rewound to the beginning or any point in the lesson by push buttons provided in each carrel.

Phase two, which was completed in 1969, included the addition of 50 student positions in 10 pentagon-shaped carrels and a basic video capability which made pictures available to students for viewing on individual monitors. Picture sources included a film/slide multiplexing system, a VR-660 videotape recorder, and a live television camera.

The third phase, completed last fall, achieved the final goal of true random-access video by adding a library of 3,000 video images.

Any of the images, like the audio programs, may be directed to individual student positions and into large classroom monitors from the beginning immediately upon request, no matter how many other individuals are using the same material.

Any number of students are able to receive a program, even if it is "out" to several other users, because each request is met with a rapidly-made duplicate of a master program. Throughout the system, no program is dedicated to a

*Reprinted by permission from *A V Instruction,* 16:78-81, October 1971.

single user. A copy of audio and video material is provided for the exclusive use of a student within 30 seconds after he calls for the program. Hence, he may stop and repeat program material at his leisure without interfering with other students' use of the same program.

Although the sequence of video images is automatically advanced to match the audio program, the student may advance the video program or return to previously viewed images frame by frame, independent of the control inherent in the audio program.

INITIAL OBJECTIVES

The system satisfies the initial requirements specified when we originally planned for the addition of a random-access instructional material system to the school's instructional resources facilities, and obtained necessary support from the U.S. Office of Education.

These specifications included:

1. True random access to all stored materials so that all requests would be rapidly honored and materials would never be "not available now."
2. Access to both audio and visual materials.
3. Full control for each user over the selection and use of instructional programs.
4. Wide-scale access from a variety of locations, including individual carrels, conference rooms, classrooms, other schools, and private residences.
5. Efficiencies of a single, central storage and control facility.

Although the PYRAMID system was the first random access system providing all these capabilities, and requiring new applications of advanced technologies, we were able to establish realistic goals and achieve our requirements, partly because of a unique relationship with the manufacturer.

Through every stage of the development of the system, Ampex Corporation instructional systems engineers worked with us to identify specific goals and problems. Rather than being "told" what was possible, and what capabilities could be provided for the money, the staff of the school was "asked" to specify its requirements, and we worked with the manufacturer to find economical and technically satisfactory ways of meeting these objectives.

INSTRUCTIONAL MANAGEMENT PROGRAM

It has been the hope and intention of the administrative and library services staffs at the high school to plan intelligently the acquisition and application of new instructional systems. The proliferation of tempting, high-technology instruments of education makes difficult the wise selection of usable and well-integrated systems.

While each staff member has his own ideas about the appropriate functions of instructional materials, there is general agreement about the need to move in the direction of instructional management. Under an instructional management setting, a wide variety of learning resources, including teacher time, are available to each student on an individualized basis. According to this design, a recipe of resources may be prescribed for each student to maximize his or her educational experience, and to most efficiently use faculty time.

Accordingly, instructional resource centers have been in use by most departments of the school for many years. Youngsters studying biology, physics, music, art, English, history, language, mathematics, etc., may supplement class work and satisfy assignments in specialized labs that utilize instructional materials most appropriate for the course of study. Physics and math students have access to computer terminals allowing them to solve problems and gain experience with the tools of their discipline. Library sections containing slides, films and audio programs enable history and art students to broaden their experience with materials related to their courses of study. Audio programs, some permitting the student to record his responses for review along with the pre-recorded materials, provide an instructional aid that is tailored for the needs of language and music students.

The PYRAMID system, while not replacing individualized departmental labs, allows central storage for an abundance of material so it may be readily accessible by the general student body. In addition, the system acts as a common medium for a variety of materials—audiotapes, records, slides, movies, videotapes, and live programs.

The system's switching center directs specialized or general interest material to several locations. An audio/video program describing the history of the school with slides and commentary may be used in classrooms filled with new students at the beginning of the year, or may be individually accessed as new students come to the school during the year. Live or taped programs, such as television specials that have been recorded off the air, may similarly be shown in large television-equipped classrooms, and at one or more carrel positions in the library.

Of course, we still have much to learn regarding the efficient allocations of the mix of instructional material and teacher time. It will take years for educators to assess accurately the relative values of all potential formal learning experiences, and it will take even longer to determine the best individualized prescription for each student.

LEARNING TO USE PYRAMID

In preparing for these capabilities, our most challenging current necessity is that of learning to explore fully the uses of the PYRAMID system.

Since its current store of materials is designed to provide supplemental material, the most avid users of the system are those students who will seek to enrich their learning experience under any circumstances. And those who are uninterested in venturing beyond mandatory assignments have only a passing acquaintance with the PYRAMID carrels. Yet progress is being made in educating students about the value that can be obtained from the system.

Some students have reported that the PYRAMID system has proved a fast and relatively "painless" means of catching up after a period of classroom absence. Others have found that certain programs help them overcome learning problems by presenting material in a more understandable form than lectures. And a few programs are so engrossing that they have "turned on" students who are seldom stimulated by educational experiences.

While the classic problem of educating people to the use of new technology is being faced with respect to the students, it is perhaps more significant where the faculty is concerned.

There are a number of teachers who have eagerly implemented the PYRAMID system as a valuable source of supplemental information for their classes. There are also some faculty members with prejudices about computerized educational systems. The majority of teachers fall somewhere in the middle. They are enthusiastic about experimenting with new educational media, but uncertain about how the implementation of new technology may enable or force them to assume new and different roles in the educational process.

Their uncertainty is understandable. Broad and unplanned expansion of television and computerized facilities spurs the argument for larger class size, in some circles, and introduces the risk of reducing human contact in the learning experience.

But, as more teachers gain familiarity with the PYRAMID system, we believe that they will provide the creativity and intelligence needed to identify the proper and most effective tasks which can be delegated to the system.

The programs currently used in the PYRAMID system provide a representative illustration of the system's strengths and weaknesses.

Teachers with unstimulating classroom presentations will not excite students at the carrels merely by taping lectures. A student subjected to eye contact with a boring lecturer may stay awake in a classroom, but once shuttered in a carrel the student experiencing that same presentation will quickly give his mind free rein or simply fall asleep.

On the other hand, a carefully thought-out presentation that is well organized and makes clever use of visual material may be the best method for imparting certain information.

An audio/video program discussing the use of the apostrophe has developed many confident apostrophe-users—students who reached junior or senior level without fully understanding how to make contractions and show possession.

An audio program which presents an eyewitness account of the atrocities at Auschwitz has brought scores of students to the carrels who do not need the program for their classwork.

The most pressing current need is for greater variety and quality of programs. While hundreds of requests are made for the PYRAMID system's programs from carrels and home phones each day, the system is designed to handle far greater capacity. As improved programing interests more students in regularly using the system, a greater number of faculty members will become involved in using it. And the process of preparing materials for the PYRAMID is an educational experience in itself, since it compels the instructor to analyze and refine his skills.

The considerable preparation that went into designing and applying the PYRAMID system has paid off by easing the learning cycle for teachers unfamiliar with the system. The equipment provides continuously reliable operation so it may perform as promised, and abundant facilities are available at the school for producing instructional materials.

An instructional materials design department and an audiovisual department have produced most of the internally-made programs. Many student staff members of these departments are enjoying a particularly rich educational experience by their daily use of television and still cameras, illustrative tools and audio and video-tape recorders.

PLANS FOR THE FUTURE

As more students and teachers gain familiarity with the PYRAMID system, they become involved in the process of expanding and perfecting its capabilities. The computer maintains a running tally of program utilization, enabling instructional planners to determine the kinds of programs that are most popular. And expanding teacher participation broadens the variety of programs and audio/video instructional techniques.

A steadily increasing flow of information and ideas regarding the system and its use are necessary, for our goal is to gradually formulate an effective scheme of instructional management with the PYRAMID system as a key element. While attempting to maximize the PYRAMID system's use under present educational conditions, we also intend it to be thoroughly adaptable to future educational requirements.

There is little doubt that current pressures (among them economic ones which force educational institutions to provide more services without substantially increased financial resources) will make necessary rather drastic and unpredictable changes in traditional educational methods. Hence, the PYRAMID system has been designed not only to accept continually updated software, but also to permit constant rearrangement of hardware modules to satisfy an unpredictable variety of future requirements.

Pieces of the system, including the central processor, computer memory, master audiotape library, audio buffer and duplicating system, electronic switching module, video disc recorders, telephone linkage, and various individual and group receiving instruments, may be assembled in many configurations. The current capacity and flexibility of the modules, and thus of the overall system, far exceeds current requirements. For example, present hardware may easily be arranged to permit computer-assisted and even computer-managed instruction. The digital signals which presently are used to cue appropriate images during audio programs can also instruct the computer to require student response to reviews or quizzes during or at the end of instructional programs. Additional memory capacity would provide the capability for evaluating and remembering each student's answers, so a running record of each student's performance may be maintained.

Moreover, the present system may be adapted to accept branched learning programs providing highly personalized communication with each student during the instructional process. Under this system, if a student enters a wrong answer, the computer may assess the nature of that answer to determine which portions of the program the student needs to review. Throughout this process, a portion of the computer would pay strict attention to the student's needs and would carefully evaluate and record his development with respect to various subject matters.

Presently available peripheral devices would allow broad utilization of stored programs. Either television displays or teletypewriters may be used for two-way communication in computer-managed instructional processes. And performance evaluations as well as program copies may become the personal property of students through the use of teletype print-outs and cassette duplicating systems, which transfer an entire audio program to a student's personal blank cassette in seconds.

Will computerized instructional systems effectively free teachers from repetitive paperwork and allow them to be more creative? Can teachers and students learn to "relate" to televised instruction without losing their ability to interact effectively in human settings? Can advanced technology reduce the economic pressures now facing educational institutions, while increasing the quality of the learning experience? These important questions are not merely subjects for idle philosophical conjecture. Our use of the PYRAMID system brings us into contact with these questions each day. We are gaining experience in producing effective programs and involving more and more students and teachers in the process of utilizing the system. And we are learning that the more effectively we obtain and apply information about the random-access instructional system, the better we can use the system to improve the quality of the educational experience at the Oak Park and River Forest High School.

MORE COMMUNICATIONS TECHNOLOGY

Radio, the telephone, and telecommunications in general are discussed in this section. The radio has been overshadowed by the advent of television. The telephone, because of its practical everyday function is rarely viewed as a sophisticated technology. Articles in this section deal with utilization practices in the field and the potential of telecommunications for libraries.

THE LIBRARY ON THE AIR*

By Dorothy Day

Service comes first with the Louisville Free Public Library, and this includes its audiovisual department. Now twenty years old and still expanding, the A-V department, once just an experiment, has established itself as a vital part of the library system and functions as an intricate part of the community as a whole. Once considered a step-child in the hallowed halls of the printed word, the department has helped to make the library a true communications center for the whole community.

Like most public libraries of the 1940s, the Louisville Free Public Library started its "new" services with a nucleus collection of 16mm sound motion pictures and the first-marketed long-playing records. By 1950 the Federal Communications Commission had issued an FM radio license to the library for a 10-watt transmitter, and with limited personnel and short broadcast days the Louisville Library tried to flood the airwaves with "culture." Unheard of? Yes and no. School systems and colleges had been doing it for years, but certainly not public libraries.

The tiny group of listeners increased as FM receivers became less expensive and more numerous. The library even purchased a hundred radios and let patrons borrow them with a library card. Listeners found that uninterrupted programs were being presented with no commercials. The library did not even promote itself with spot announcements (a policy that has continued throughout the years). The programming, however, was designed to stimulate listeners to seek further information, and the library was the logical course.

THE WIRE NETWORK

With the collection of recordings and non-musical transcriptions accumulating, the library was able to create the "Wire Network." This was the name given to the system of closed-circuit lines rented from the telephone company that connected the library with educational and cultural organizations throughout the Louisville area. The growing collection of recorded material housed in the audiovisual department of the public library would be accessible to citizens

*Reprinted by permission from the November 1969 issue of the *Wilson Library Bulletin.* Copyright ᶜ1970 by the H. W. Wilson Company.

all over the area—in each of the branch libraries of the Louisville system any record in the A-V collection could be transmitted to either an individual listener or group of listeners merely upon request. The radio control rooms were equipped with extra turntables and, later, tape machines while the connecting agencies had installed the proper audio receiving equipment, usually a speaker in the branch auditorium and headphone outlets for individual listening in the adult section of the building. At the same time, the library offered the same services to all non-commerical cultural and educational institutions throughout the city. Many immediately subscribed to the idea, and within the year over forty lines to agencies were in operation, including lines to the University of Louisville, the city's junior high and high schools, the Louisville General Hospital, a church, and the Kentucky School for the Blind, in addition to ten library branches. The library provided the control room operation—personnel and equipment plus the record collection. Each agency rented the closed-circuit line from the telephone company and was responsible for the installation of receiving equipment and maintenance.

The basic premise that intrigued the other institutions was the idea of a centralized collection of recorded material which was accessible to each for the small monthly telephone line rental. In many cases the monthly charge ran lower than the cost of one phonograph record. Yet the services rendered by the library on the closed-circuit or Wire Network was unlimited, and the recorded material acquired by the library was growing astronomically.

Many sources of recorded material which were open to the library were not open to any other institution. For example, because of the library's radio station, WFPL, the library became a member of the National Association of Educational Broadcasters. Through this Association, the best educational productions were acquired for use on the library's station and also immediately placed in the A-V record library for request listening over the Wire Network. Other sources of recorded material were found for both musical and non-musical programs. We did not limit ourselves to U.S. productions; we discovered Offices of Informational Services in countries throughout the world producing programs in English who were more than glad to send them to non-commercial educational radio stations in the U.S. For example, the Norwegian Information Service supplied a 15-minute program each week which presented interviews with famous Norwegians, recitals or excerpts from concerts by Norwegian musicians, discussions of scientific achievements or historical celebrations. The French Broadcasting Corporation has been the most prolific in overseas materials. They have supplied regular series of French language lessons on several levels as well as many half-hour programs on French music and musicians. The West German Broadcasting Company has in the past produced language lessons, and supplies us still with German music festivals, programs on travel within their country, and charming seasonal events. Other sources of programs from which we are still receiving recorded material are the Canadian Broadcasting Company, Radio Moscow, the British Broadcasting Corporation, Radio Nederland, the South African Broadcasting Company, and the United Nations organizations. There are many, many more, too numerous to name in this article.

Therefore, in addition to commercial releases, the suppliers of radio programs from the world over increased the recorded material available to the Wire

Network agencies. To date there are well over 150,000 titles of recorded programs in the A-V library on subjects from fairy tales to nuclear fission. There have been few if any limitations placed on the subject matter acquired, for just as with any public library, the Wire Network must be ready to meet the needs of all the public.

The music collection comprises a large portion of the A-V library. Since the beginning of the long-playing disc, the Louisville Library has attempted to acquire as many releases of different musical compositions pressed as possible. The Schwann Long-Playing Record Catalog issued each month is one of the major sources of information about new releases. In order to supply music on the library's stations as well as have musical recordings available for request listening on the Wire Network, we have been attempting to add every new title of serious or classical music released. This does not mean every performance, for such an undertaking would be nearly impossible financially. However, the audio collection incorporates nearly every composition recorded from pre-baroque through contemporary.

The use of the audio collection has been phenomenal. The record collection in the audiovisual department is closed to the public as a non-circulating collection, but it is readily available at all times for immediate use on request. Students of the University of Louisville are now assigned recorded materials to supplement printed materials. The University built listening booths in their new library building to accommodate the students' needs. Each booth is equipped with facilities for receiving programs from the public library with direct voice communications with the control room in the A-V department. Students can call for their assigned programs from the listening area in the campus library, speaking directly to the control room operator. If, for instance, a student wishes to hear just an act from a Shakespearean play, he can make such a specific request. The students can avail themselves of assigned programs between their classes in the same way they would reference volumes in the building. Because of the amount of use, the University of Louisville has eight lines on the public library's Wire Network in regular operation, making it possible for them to receive eight different programs simultaneously. Some of these lines are in seminar and lecture rooms for collective listening. Programs are often used within classes by professors to supplement lectures and to stimulate discussions.

RECORDING LOOPS

There are also lines of the Wire Network that are just the opposite from those previously described. These lines are recording "loops." That is, the public library can record programs live from the University. Well-known authorities and famous personalities visiting the campus are recorded, with their permission, of course, and their voices as well as thoughts are placed in the A-V library either for immediate playback or for posterity.

It should be clarified at this point that the public library has a policy that governs the use of this audio material. Because of a great many implications, the library will neither make nor permit copies made of any of the recorded materials in this special A-V library. All connecting agencies adhere strictly to this

231

regulation and take full responsibility in supervising the Wire Network use in order to prevent any infraction of the policy.

"EXPERIENCES BY WAY OF THEIR EARS"

One of the most interesting uses of the library's Wire Network is that by the Kentucky School for the Blind. The teachers find that they can give their students experiences by way of their ears that they would otherwise never witness. Watching such a class of children as they listen to a dramatized event in history or fiction, one realized a satisfaction beyond words.

We in the audiovisual department have a number of cherished stories and events to recall when pressures of deadlines or irritations in work procedures begin to squeeze one's disposition. There is one associated with the Kentucky School for the Blind. Several years ago an instructor at that institution, who was herself without sight, was pursuing her studies toward a master's degree in literature. By phone she came to us for help seeking the necessary materials for her studies. We compiled and supplied bibliographies for her. In all her free moments she listened to the recorded readings, dramatizations, and discussions in her field. The day she received her degree, we received her final telephone call to tell us of "our" success. She attributed her achievement to our cooperation. Just in the line of professional duty? Yes, but what a satisfaction.

Various psychologists and psychiatrists have worked with mentally ill patients at the city's General Hospital observing their reactions to different types of music. Therapists have scheduled programs over the Wire Network to stimulate groups to participate in projects of discussion and other activities that would help in their mental rehabilitation.

Our Coordinator of Children's Work for the Louisville Free Public Library regularly records reviews of new children's books primarily for use within the library's system. Children's workers, both professional and non-professional, listen to these reviews over the Wire Network whenever they wish or duties permit. Those who are responsible for the selection of children's books in each agency find this monthly recording an excellent help, but above all a time saver in their schedules, on which many demands are made.

Another organization, not before mentioned, that has been served by the Wire Network ever since its inception is the Louisville Orchestra. The library has a recording "loop" to the orchestra's auditorium, over which we have made recordings of each concert, which are placed in the archives of the A-V department. The library was also able to record first performances of the contemporary compositions which are part of the commissioning program initiated by the Louisville Orchestra. Composers visiting the city are informed by the orchestra office of our archive collection and many, in turn, have come to the library to hear the first performance of their composition. Although we were very often unable to interview the composers, plans are under way for this in the near future.

Orchestra performers, the conductors, and students of music often request the replaying of live concerts and we can accommodate their request by the use of the Wire Network. Recitals of faculty and students from the Music and Preparatory School of the University are recorded upon request and become a part of the A-V library. One parent of a former music school student periodically requests the playing of her child's senior recital and by Wire Network she listens again to her aspiring heir as she sits in her neighborhood branch library.

In twenty years the Wire Network has proven itself and of course is no longer considered an experiment. Its statistics per month may run as high as 3,200 programs played and the recording of several dozen concerts and lectures.

Earlier I mentioned the 10-watt transmitter put on the air as the first radio station operated by a public library. Its power was many times increased as were the hours on the air. Air time was given to local boards of education for arranging pre-recorded curriculum-oriented programs that were and are scheduled for in-classroom listening. The supervisors, under the sponsorship of their boards, write teachers' manuals for each program which are distributed to the teachers within the area using the programs. The University has for many years used air time for special programs for out-of-class listening.

But the library's FM operation is not primarily given over to formal instruction. There is time for many kinds of informational broadcasts. By 1954 the library was receiving such a wealth of pre-recorded materials that there was hardly enough air time on which to present them. It was then that a local, community-interested, commercial radio station gave the public library another FM transmitter. Although its power was considerably stronger than the first transmitter, WFPL, the library decided to use this very generous gift not as a replacement but to put a second FM station on the air, WFPK. With two FM non-commercial educational stations the library could provide a far greater variety of material to its listeners. We could arrange the programming so that any time during the day a listener could tune in and hear classical music on at least one of the library's FM stations.

Repeated schedules made it possible for WFPL and WFPK not to be in competition in any way with local commercial stations, either with sponsors or for listeners. Also, our listeners found it to their advantage to have a station that repeated its programs. They could always be assured of catching one of our special lectures or music festival broadcasts and yet not miss their favorite television or radio show. Many listeners, especially our music listeners, state they like to rehear certain programs for a second and even a third time.

The two stations work very closely together and attempt to complement one another. For example, when we would run a complete recorded performance of a Shakespearean play, the music program director might attempt to schedule in the same week a complete recorded performance of an opera based on the play.

Naturally, seasonal programming is expected on any radio station, but the library's stations keep in mind community events and around these attempt to present programs that might lead to a better understanding and possibly a better appreciation of them. Concert personalities or groups performing works in musical and literary fields and appearing in public performance might have a better audience if these listeners previously had heard a broadcast concerning the topic, a performance of the group, or another work by the same writer. This is by no means an undercover way of promoting or allowing advertisements, but just another way of informing. We hope it will in some way stimulate that degree of intellectual curiosity in people. We believe that this has happened many times during the years that WFPL and WFPK have been on the air. On one of those days that seemed unusually difficult, a telephone call was received at station from a housewife who, in a hesitating voice, expressed her gratitude for what she had been hearing on the library's two stations. She said that her formal education had been short-lived, but as she did her daily chores she left her radio on one of the library's stations. She did not wish to give her name, but her final statement was one of the high points in the life of our station. She said, "Thanks to the library's stations, many new doors have been opened that I did not know existed."

The radio stations and the Wire Network work very closely together. Not only is the source of material the same but so is the equipment and the personnel. The transmitting operation is thus simplified, and at the same time the library can render greater service to the library user. As an example, listeners who have missed a program on one of the FM stations may request it for listening on the Wire Network in his neighborhood branch. Or the avid student of poetry, having heard a modern poet reading his own works by way of a recording played on the Wire Network, can request that the recording be included on the air in a future program for many to enjoy.

THE EYES HAVE IT

Radio has by no means been superseded by the visual media. As a matter of fact, there seems to be greater need for good educational programming using any media. Radio in the future will make decided changes by working with and not against the visual media.

The visual aspects of audiovisual can never be overshadowed by the audio. Since the very early days of the department films have been the principal source of program planning by many, including the library itself. Films have rendered the greater responses and the larger audiences. They have been instrumental in bringing people to the library who had never had the need or curiosity to enter the building. When the audiovisual department began to offer its services, new people were reached. This was especially true when free films were presented.

Over the years various types of programs have been planned around motion pictures, slides, and filmstrips. It became an immediate policy that only films within the collection of the library would be used on the programs, and in this way the library would be serving a dual purpose: first, the film showings would be a means of introducing to the public the kinds of motion picture subject matter available to them, and second, the film showings would be a public preview for new films purchased for the circulating collection. The audiences that regularly come to the several weekly film series certainly have encouraged the continuation of the programs. Film showings are planned for age groups from the pre-school to the older patron.

Films, radio, whatever—A-V is a fine, satisfying field to be in. There are many rewards, through the library, in keeping both our own and our patrons' eyes and ears open.

TELETEACHING–THE PARTY LINE REVIVED*

By Gerald McKay

Two generations ago it was possible to lift up a telephone receiver and keep fairly well informed on community happenings and new ways of doing things. This method of communication was reasonably effective, albeit unofficial and informal. Learning from one's neighbors has since been proven by research to be one of our best methods of communicating.

During the past winter and spring, we have used the telephone party line to hold 75 meetings reaching 300 groups in two-thirds of Minnesota's counties, at an average out-of-pocket cost of less than $30 per meeting. Although some of the meetings could not be called complete successes, a majority met the needs of the audiences, brought them information they could not get in any other way, and supplemented their regular programs.

We have much yet to learn about using the telephone as a new dimension in doing extension work, but we did finish the season with a wealth of experience that will help us be more effective next year in teleteaching. In addition, our experience may help others use the telephone as their new dimension in extension teaching.

Groups were selected by county extension agents last year as they planned their program of work. Our first telelecture was held in November, and the last one March 31. Subjects included 4-H leadership, horse care, dairy management, fabrics, floor covering, consumer Ps and Qs, veterinary medicine, and 4-H organization. In the horse care and veterinary medicine series, registrants were charged tuition; other courses were tuition-free. Courses consisted of either three or four weekly meetings.

All programs originated in the radio studio of our Department of Information and Agricultural Journalism office, where the telephone was connected through the radio broadcast console. This made it possible for sound coming into the studio to go through studio speakers so the participants didn't need to wear earphones. Regular radio microphones were also used, instead of the telephone transmitter. This was very convenient when we had two or three lecturers contributing to the program.

Each receiving station had a teleconference unit, enabling an audience of up to 200 to hear satisfactorily (providing the room had reasonably good acoustics). Each unit had a telephone transmitter to allow communication with the sending station. Groups varied in size from five to 120 people. As long as the receiving equipment functioned properly, it was adequate to do the job.

Up to 11 county groups listened simultaneously to programs. The number of groups for any given program ranged from one to 11, with an average of about five. Each call, except for single stations, was a conference call put through by a central operator in the city from which the program originated. It would have been possible to handle more than 11 groups at one time and still allow for feedback from each one. It would seem that 20 groups could be accommodated

*Reprinted by permission from *AV Instruction,* 16:85-86, May 1971.

with our kind of program. A number would be reached, however, beyond which much feedback would have been difficult.

Charges for the telephone company's part of our operation could be divided into three categories—installation of equipment, rental of equipment, and line charges. Installation was $25 per month per listening unit, and rental $35 per month. Line charges varied with distance from the initiating point and length of time the line was in service. Average line charges for the 296 groups were about $15 per meeting, and the time averaged about one hour and 45 minutes—although some went up to two and one-half hours. A network of 24-hour lines could have been used more effectively, but at a much higher total cost. If enough departments of the university or state could schedule a system which would use a major portion of the 24 hours, however, the cost per program might have been lower than our conference call system.

Programs were publicized locally, with the starting time emphasized. (Programs had to begin on time.) Stopping time was flexible. Lecturers usually continued until questions from the groups were all answered or interest seemed to be waning.

We found it very important for the speaker to carefully adapt his message to his particular audience. Usually a color slide of the speaker introduced him. We found considerable misunderstanding if the speaker didn't know his audience well and didn't gear his material to their background and needs. We also found the best audience interest when at least two people took part in presenting the material.

In most cases, no speaker talked longer than 20 minutes without a break for questions or local discussions within the groups. When segments of a presentation did exceed this, communication between the speaker and groups suffered. In all but one meeting, visuals were prepared for each speaker and sent to the groups ahead of time, where they were studied and presented by the group leaders according to the speaker's directions. Visuals included 2 x 2 slides, overhead transparencies, and samples of fabrics and floor coverings. A few mimeographed drawings or graphs were also used for one program. In one case we did not use visuals, and the group leaders indicated some dissatisfaction and a lower level of audience interest. If visuals are to be used, they should be planned by someone with audiovisual experience as well as the presenter, well in advance, and mailed to the group leaders several days ahead of the meeting.

Careful training of the person in charge of each group (usually an extension agent) is essential if he is to operate the receiving equipment effectively. There were some difficulties when new, inexperienced people operated the equipment. On a few occasions, the groups had difficulty in starting because their leader was not familiar with all the switches. Simpler equipment may be available in the future.

In our series of programs on horse care, the instructor visited each group personally for the first meeting, where he had an opportunity to get acquainted with and study his audience. This was effective, but would be somewhat difficult if more than a half-dozen groups were in the circuit.

Some evaluation was done by the groups after each series to help plan future use of the telephone. Admittedly, all of the series were not successful. Some could have been more successful if the instructor could have been present at the meetings. Since this was not possible, the telelecture as an alternative to no meetings was at least useful.

A survey conducted to determine total recipient reaction to all the series showed that 33 percent liked the method very much, and 60 percent liked it fairly well. Eighty-eight percent were using telelecture for the first time this past year. About 85 percent indicated they thought the amount of material covered and level of difficulty was about right. Ten percent had other opinions.

As far as the technical aspects of presentation were concerned, more than two-thirds of those questioned felt they were good technically, and very few had suggestions for improvement. Several comments stressed the importance of visuals in the presentations. A few indicated that material on the slides was somewhat crowded. A wide variety of subjects was suggested for possible future programs.

Some of the meetings were very successful and well received. Others might have been done better by another method. Evaluation of some kind must give direction for work in the years ahead. At this point, it appears that tele-lecture was worthwhile in our program, and will probably continue to expand and find greater use in the future.

TELECOMMUNICATIONS PRIMER*

By Joseph Becker

As greater emphasis is placed on the development of regional and national library network programs to facilitate interinstitutional services, a concommitant requirement emerges to understand and apply communications technology. A great variety of communications methods has been used for interlibrary communications in the past, ranging from the simplest use of the U.S. mails up to the telephone, the teletype, the radio, and even experiments with microwave telefacsimile transmission.

Of all the different kinds of equipment used by libraries for interlibrary communications, the one which has received widest acceptance for its practical value and immediate usefulness is the teletype machine. The earliest use of the teletype machine can be traced back to the Free Library of Philadelphia, which in 1927 used the teletype as part of a closed circuit system for communicating book information from the loan desk in the main reading room to the stacks and vice versa. Following World War II, an installation connecting distant libraries was established in Wisconsin between the Milwaukee Public Library and the Racine Public Library.

Racine's limited collection was considered inadequate to the demands of its patrons and its director, instead of increasing the book budget significantly, negotiated an access arrangement with the larger collection at Milwaukee via teletype. Daily messenger service was instituted between the two libraries to effect pickup and delivery of library materials.

The teletype machine enabled the two libraries to have the speed of the telephone with the authority of the printed word. This advantage continues today and can be considered mainly responsible for the proliferation of teletype communications for interlibrary loan. Teletype communications between and among libraries are beginning to emerge in both informal and formal network configurations. In addition to its obvious application to interlibrary loan, teletype has also been used to augment library holdings on a reciprocal basis, to provide for general communications with other libraries, to serve as a channel for querying union catalogs, to accommodate reference questions and services, and to handle internal communications.

Perhaps the most important benefit to accrue to users of library teletype service is the ability to communicate immediately with any other teletype user anywhere in the world. Thus, it becomes possible for any participant in the teletype network to communicate reference inquiries to information points outside the formal network. (A classified teletype directory exists which lists library subscribers in the United States and Canada.) As reference demands increase, it is likely that libraries will begin to make wider use of the teletype machine even though it may have been acquired initially for a more limited purpose. In addition, expanded uses in the future are a virtual certainty both because of the low cost of teletype operation and because of the technical improvements in the equipment itself.

*Reprinted by permission from *Journal of Library Automation,* 2:148-156, September 1969.

Although the advantages of other means of telecommunication have been known to libraries for many years, their utilization has been retarded by problems of cost and systems planning. However, in recent years, as libraries have made greater use of computers and as they have moved towards new programs of inter-library cooperation and resource sharing, interest in telecommunications in general has grown more intense.

The purpose of this article, therefore, is to provide a brief explanation of the fundamentals of communications technology in order to establish a basis of understanding for current and future library planning.

TELECOMMUNICATIONS CAPACITY

Telecommunications may be simply defined as the "exchange of information by electrical transmission over great distances." For the past forty years, the United States, through its commercial carriers, the Bell Telephone System and Western Union, has built an increasingly effective system of wires, trunk stations, and switching centers for the transmission of human speech from point to point. The telephone network is a technological marvel despite the occasional busy signal one gets on the line. However, with the increasing use of computers and television in science, business, and industry, this network is being asked to carry digital and video signals in addition to voice, and its facilities are fast becoming overloaded. In the library field one can observe the trend toward use of machine readable data and non-print materials. These are but a few examples of library data forms that one will wish to communicate between and among libraries.

Voice can be efficiently transmitted over telephone lines, but data, like the digital language of the computer or the video language of the television camera and facsimile scanner, need a broader band-width for their efficient transmission than the narrow-band-width telephone line can provide. Band-width is a measure of the signal-carrying capacity of a communications channel in cycles per second. It is the numerical difference between the highest frequency and the lowest frequency handled by a communications channel. The broader the band, the greater the signal transmission rate. The tens of thousands of bits which make up a computer message or TV picture, if sent by telephone, have to be squeezed through the narrow line over a longer period of time to transmit a given message. This consumes telephone capacity that would normally be used to carry other conversations. A good example of the problem can be illustrated with the "picture-phone." This is the telephone company service now being tested which permits a caller to see and hear the other person at the distant end. The two-way picture part of this dialogue requires more than 100 times more telephone transmission capacity than the voice portion. There are 100,000,000 telephones in the U.S. today. Thus, if only 1% of the subscribers had picture phones we would theoretically exhaust our national telephone capacity for any other use.

Fortunately, the problem of telecommunications capacity is not without solution. New channels of communication are being opened that do provide capacity for broad band-width exchange. The new technology of laser communications, for example, stands in the wings with a long-range answer. The word LASER stands for Light Amplification by Stimulated Emission of Radiation.

239

Its theoretical beginnings go back half a century, but fifteen years ago scientists working in high-energy physics learned how to amplify high-energy molecules so as to produce a powerful, narrow, coherent beam of light. This strange kind of light remains sharp and coherent over great distances and can therefore be used as a reliable channel or pipe for telecommunications. All other long-distance transmission systems tend to spread or disperse their signals, but laser beams provide a tight, confined highway over which signals can travel back and forth. A few years ago seven New York television channels, in an experiment, transmitted their programs simultaneously over the same laser beam. In terms of telephone conversations, one laser communications system could theoretically carry 800,000,000 voice conversations! The intense pencil-thin laser beam is so powerful and reliable that it can and is being used as a communications channel for space exploration. The Apollo 11 astronauts left a laser beam reflector on the Moon's surface to facilitate future communications experiments.

TYPES OF SIGNALS

There are three principal types of signals that telecommunications systems are designed to carry: 1) Audio—originating as human speech or recorded tones and transmitted over conventional telephone lines. 2) Digital—originating with computers or other machines in which data are encoded in the binary language. The data, instead of being represented as zeros and ones, take the form of an electrical pulse or no pulse. 3) Video—originating with TV recorders, facsimile scanners, or other devices which change light particles into electrical energy in the form of small, discrete bits of information.

Each of the three types of telecommunication signals is associated with a telecommunication channel that can carry it most efficiently.

Audio, of course, was designed to travel over the telephone line. However, it can be carried just as well over the broader band-width channels. Digital and video signals are carried over the wider band-width channels because of the great number of bits that must be accommodated per unit of time. Sending computer data or pictures over telephone lines is possible if data phones are used; they convert digital and video data to their tone equivalents at the transmission end and reconvert them at the receiving end. This is, however, a very slow process and from a communications viewpoint it is most inefficient. When reference is made to "slow scan television" it means that the video signal is being carried over a telephone line. Library experimentation with telefacsimile has by and large been restricted to transmission of the facsimile signals over telephone lines. An 8" x 10" page carried by telephone lines takes about six minutes, as compared to 30 seconds if it were sent over a broad band-width channel.

A telecommunications system used for library purposes will eventually need to integrate audio, digital, and video signals into a single system. This integrated media concept is an important aspect of the design of an interlibrary communications system but it is poorly understood analytically in today's practice. The idea of an "integrated telecommunications system" became practical only during the past few years and commercial and governmental efforts are underway to provide these unified facilities as rapidly as possible.

SIGNAL CARRIERS

A number of methods exist by which audio, digital, and video information can flow back and forth for information exchange purposes. These telecommunications facilities are furnished for lease or private line use by the commercial carriers. A dedicated system may also be installed for the sole use of a particular customer. For example, the U.S. government has more than one dedicated system: the Federal Telecommunications System (FTS), which is available for official use only by civilian agencies; and it has similar dedicated facilities for use by the military. Large companies, such as General Electric, Weyerhauser, and IBM, have exclusive-use telecommunications systems also. In all cases, however, private or dedicated systems are planned in such a way that they interface smoothly with commercial dial-up facilities—thus increasing the overall distributive capacity of any one system. As might be expected, the tariff structure for these combined interconnections is very complex. The Federal Communications Commission is reviewing the overall question of cost for voice and data communication and is also investigating the policy issues raised by the growing interdependence of computers and communications.

Technically speaking, there are five means by which audio, digital, and video signals may be carried to their destination and returned: by telephone line, by radio, by coaxial cable, by microwave relays, and by communications satellite. An explanation of each is given below and they are presented in ascending order of their band-width capacity.

Telephone Lines

The telephone as a means of communication is beyond compare. It is simple, quick, reliable, accurate, and provides great geographic flexibility. Quite often the telephone can supply all the communications capability required for an information system, especially when it is coupled with the teletypewriter.

A good toll quality telephone circuit has a frequency response of about 300-3400 cycles, which is adequate to supply good quality and a natural sounding voice. Regular telephone lines are referred to as narrow band carriers because of the low cycle range needed to carry human speech.

Radio Broadcasting

As the word "broadcasting" implies, signals are radiated in all directions and the omnidirectional antennas which are used in radio broadcasting are designed to have this effect. Frequencies used are 500 to 1500 kilocycles for AM (amplitude modulation), and 88 to 108 megacycles for FM (frequency modulation). The number of radio waves that travel past a point in one second is called the frequency. The number of waves sent out by a radio station each second is the frequency of that station. One complete wavelength is called a cycle. A kilocycle is one thousand cycles and a megacycle is one million cycles. Broadcasting, in general, is used as a one-way system. Any radio or TV set equipped to receive certain frequencies can tune in to a particular station or channel. Low-frequency systems, in the kilocycle range, require less power to

241

operate. The signals are propagated close to the ground and the effective radius of reception is small. With ultra-high frequency, vast distances can be covered by striking upper layers of the atmosphere and having the signal deflected to earth; this can happen more than once before the signal is received. High-frequency systems, however, are subject to atmospheric interference, which causes fading.

Coaxial Cable (and CATV)

A remarkable extension of the carrier art was provided by the development of the coaxial cable. Within the sheath of most coaxial cables are a number of copper tubes. Within each tube is a copper wire, supported by insulating disks spaced one inch apart. The name coaxial reflects the fact that both the wire and the tube have the same axis.

Coaxial cables can carry many times the voice capacity of telephone lines and are thus considered to be broad band-width carriers able to accommodate digital and video data with equal efficiency. The coaxial cable has the additional advantage that the electrical energy confined within the tube can be guided directly to its destination, instead of spreading in all directions as is the case in radio broadcasting.

To provide necessary amplification along the route, repeater stations are placed at designated intervals. Repeater stations are unnecessary, however, within a half-mile radius and many libraries, planning new buildings, are including special ducts to accommodate known or potential requirements for communication between computer units, terminals, dial access stations, etc.

The technology of Community Antenna Television (CATV) incorporates extensive use of coaxial cables. CATV operates very similarly to the way a closed circuit television system works. A company in a locality sets up a powerful receiving antenna capable of importing television signals from many cities hundreds of miles away. On a subscription basis (about $6.00 per month), it will run a coaxial cable from the receiving station to the subscriber's home. Subscribers benefit in several ways: 1) the incoming signals are sharper and clearer because there is no atmospheric interference; 2) a roof-top antenna is unnecessary; 3) more channels are available than a local TV station normally provides (some CATV stations already offer the potential of 20 channels); and 4) CATV stations have close interrelationships with Educational Television Stations (ETV) and by law are required to make available to subscribers at least one channel for "public service" and "educational" purposes.

The latter benefit has special implications for libraries. School libraries in a town or city where CATV is proposed might well inquire whether the operator is willing to provide a school library programming service.

It is hardly possible to predict what effect CATV and its coaxial cables will have on libraries. It is clear, however, that many homes will soon have coaxial cables as well as telephone lines, and this implies a new capability for bi-directional broad band-width information exchange. Attachment of a coaxial cable from a CATV trunk station to the home provides an electronic pathway 300 megacycles wide. The telephone line is only 4000 cycles wide. Since a megacycle is one million cycles, the relative practical difference in an operational environment is in the order of 40,000:1. It is this significant difference that causes some people to suggest that advanced telecommunications will someday bring newspapers and books into the home by electronic facsimile, along with computer information from data banks, individualized instruction from schools, and a much greater variety of educational materials.

Microwave

The term microwave applies to those systems where the transmitting and receiving antennas are in view of each other. The word is not very definitive but generally describes systems with frequencies starting at 1000 megacycles and extending up to 15,000 megacycles, a range which includes the ultra- and super-high frequency bands of the radio spectrum. Microwave is, therefore, without question, one of the larger broad band-width carriers. Microwave systems are used to transmit data and multi-channel telephone or video signals. Antennas are in the form of parabolic dishes mounted on high towers and lined up in sight of each other. These antenna produce very sharp beams to minimize power requirements. Since microwaves do not bend, transcontinental microwave systems consist of relay towers spaced at approximately thirty-mile, line-of-sight intervals across the country. Because of the earth's curvature, trans-oceanic microwave systems are hardly possible without a repeater station. It is this limitation which helped give rise to the development of the communications satellite.

Many state governments have, or are planning, private microwave systems for handling the mix of official, internal communications. Here again, state libraries might investigate the use of such systems for interlibrary communications.

Communications Satellites

The newest and most promising telecommunication development is the communications satellite. A communications satellite is an object which is placed in orbit above the earth to receive and retransmit signals received from different points on earth.

A communications satellite is launched by a conventional rocket, which sends it into an eliptical orbit with a high point, or apogee, of about 23,000 miles and a low point, or perigee, of 195 miles.

On command from earth, a small motor aboard the satellite is fired just as the satellite reaches the high point of its orbit. This action thrusts the satellite into a circular path over the equator at an altitude of approximately 22,300 miles. Subsequently, the satellite's orbital velocity is then synchronized with the speed of the earth's rotation. Thus, a satellite in synchronous equatorial orbit with the earth appears to remain in a fixed position in space. Three satellites can cover the globe with communications except for the north and south poles. Or the antennas can be squinted to focus exclusively on one country or on part of a country. Early Bird's antenna was positioned to cover Europe and the northeastern part of the United States, thus making it possible to link North America with Europe.

A satellite is not very large; Early Bird, which is still operating, is about seven feet in diameter. It contains a receiver to catch the signal, an amplifier to increase the signal's intensity, and a transmitter. Signals received from one earth station on one frequency are amplified and transmitted on another frequency to a second earth station. The satellite receives light energy from the sun, and its solar batteries convert it into electrical energy for transmitting power.

Communications satellites are, in essence, broad band-width signal repeaters whose height enables them to provide coverage over a very large area. They can be "dedicated"; that is, designed for a single class of service, such as television relay; or they may be multipurpose and integrate a mix of different signals at the same time. Generally, we tend to think of satellites as an extension of satellite broadcasting, mainly because most of their use up to now has been for television broadcasting. However, the enormous band-width capacity which they possess also makes them very attractive channels for two-way voice and picture applications for education, business, and libraries. Within the next decade, domestic communications satellites will be available as "switchboards in the sky" for just such uses.

CONCLUSION

Libraries, like other institutions in our society, have learned the hard way that the new technology must be treated as an opportunity and not as a panacea. The same is true of telecommunications. Before telecommunications can be applied effectively to interlibrary functions and services, many non-technical problems have to be solved. Librarians must answer questions such as : How shall we organize our libraries to make optimum use of the advantage of telecommunications? What segment of our information resources and daily library business should flow over these lines? Will our users accept machines as intermediates in the information exchange process? How can the copyright principle be safeguarded if libraries expand their interinstitutional communications? And, of course, how do we measure cost/effectiveness before moving ahead with an operating program? To provide answers professional librarians must become more familiar with telecommunications technology and principles.

BIBLIOGRAPHY

1. Becker, Joseph. "Communications Networks for Libraries," *Wilson Library Bulletin,* 41 (December 1966), 383-387.
2. Gentle, Edgar C. *Data Communications in Business: An Introduction.* New York, American Telephone and Telegraph Company, 1965. 200p.
3. Kenney, Brigitte L. *A Survey of Interlibrary Communications Systems.* Jackson, Miss., Rowland Medical Library, April 1967. 74p. Prepared for the National Library of Medicine under NIH Contract No. PH-43-67-1152.
4. *Library Telecommunications Directory: Canada–United States.* 2nd ed., revised. Toronto and Durham, 1968.
5. U.S. President. Task Force on Communications Policy. *Final Report.* Washington, D.C., U.S. Government Printing Office, December 1968.

THE FUTURE OF TELEFACSIMILE IN LIBRARIES:
PROBLEMS AND PROSPECTS*

By Harold Morehouse

INTRODUCTION

There have now been a number of attempts to use telefacsimile systems in libraries, either on an experimental or an operational basis. Sharon Schatz has described nearly all of them.[1] Unfortunately, most of us who have undertaken telefacsimile experiments so far have proceeded as though we invented the whole idea ourselves, and have not benefited enough by each other's experience. You may have wondered why there is evidently still no such thing as a permanent, operational library telefacsimile system in service anywhere. There is one, which I will describe later on. There have been a few other installations which were so intended, but they have all fallen by the wayside.

What are some of the problems causing these failures?

PROBLEMS

First of all, the equipment itself was not designed with library needs in mind. Hardly anything electro-mechanical ever is. Libraries may adapt some useful items of hardware to their needs, such as the Xerox 914 or an IBM Magnetic Tape Selectric Typewriter, but it sometimes seems as though we are doing something like using an electric dishwasher to wash our clothes.

For many years expensive telefacsimile equipment has been in daily use by newspapers and the communications industries. Lower-cost systems for general business use have been developed more recently, and only since then have we impecunious librarians become interested.

Unfortunately, most lower-cost equipment has been designed for the business letter and business forms, mostly typewritten. Resolution just adequate for elite type may be hopelessly coarse for the 6-point type faces in which many scholarly and scientific journals are printed.

Then we have the problem of cost. Businessmen may be able to figure out how much it is worth to their company to have facsimile copies of purchase orders received at the factory in Chicago from New York within hours after the salesman lands the order. But how many librarians can tell you how much a completed interlibrary loan request is worth, or how much more it is worth if you complete it the same day it is requested, via facsimile, than if you take two or three weeks to complete it?

We can estimate pretty well what a facsimile copy will cost under a given set of conditions,[2] but it is difficult to estimate its worth. It will be a rare system that will deliver facsimile service over any distance for less than $1.00 per page.

Technical considerations are interesting. There is much research in progress in an effort to break some of the technical bottlenecks.

*Reprinted from *Library Resources and Technical Services,* 13:42-46, Winter 1969.

One of the big items in the cost of telefacsimile is the cost of the communication link. This could be anything from the Bell System's Telpak "A," which has a bandwidth of 48 kilocycles, costing as much as $18 per mile per month, down to a single voice-grade telephone line, which affords about 3 kilocycles of bandwidth and might cost about $3 per mile per month for a leased line.

Between these extremes lie several alternatives. Some systems use a single voice-grade line; some use two or three or four which are "cleaned up," that is, better quality than voice-grade. We hear terms like data-grade lines, full duplex lines, half duplex lines, telephoto lines, schedule 2 lines, conditioned lines. Essentially, what the telephone man is talking about when he uses these terms is that when one leases, say, a half-duplex schedule 2 telephoto line, it does not buzz, hum, grow faint, produce static-like noises, or otherwise foul up whatever communication is coming across the line. The telephone man does not say buzz, hum, etc.; he says distortion, delay, quadrature, Kendall Effect, attenuation, interference, cross talk, etc.

The big, fast systems like the Xerox LDX or the highest speed Alden equipment need expensive connecting links. If the connecting link is a 250-mile Telepak "A" at $3,750 per month, with black boxes at either end, which may be called terminals, or interfacing equipment, at $450 per month each, this accounts for nearly a dollar per page at a volume of 5,000 pages per month, without even considering costs of the scanner, printer, labor, etc. At higher volumes of use, costs are lower.

Another problem, perhaps the most serious one, is the general failure of telefacsimile-minded librarians to pay a little attention to the question of the need for such a service. We always seem to assume that there is an insatiable demand for faster service and quick, ready access to the resources of other libraries. Maybe this is because such an assumption makes us feel important. Studies at the Institute of Library Research and the New York State Library have shown that this demand may be quite limited, especially when one proposes putting a price tag on the service.[3, 8]

Librarians sometimes seem to feel that price tags are undignified, and often think of their institutional money only in large lumps, like grants or appropriations or annual budgets.

In any case, it seems that we should spend at least as much time and trouble analyzing the needs of our library users, and how well our conventional services are working to meet their needs, as we do in dreaming up glamorous new services. As an example, the Houston Research Institute concluded in 1965 that telefacsimile for libraries made little sense because the actual transmission time (via U.S. mail) in existing interlibrary loan service accounted for only a fraction of the total delay.[4] Most of the delay was found to be inherent in the slow procedures at the borrowing and lending libraries. The results of the Houston Research Institute study indicate much less concern about technical difficulties or costs than about the slow and inefficient way in which librarians handle the requests.

PROSPECTS FOR IMPROVEMENT

Technical improvements are inevitable. With these improvements will come better performance and reliability at lower cost.

246

One area of technical improvement is in the connecting link. It is unlikely that the vast telephone networks of the nation are all going to be up-graded just to take into account the needs of a handful of tele-facsimile buffs. However, there is an ever-increasing amount of non-verbal communication being transmitted via telephone lines.[5] Besides Teletype, data in computer language are being transmitted from one magnetic tape to another one at a distance. Tele-facsimile itself is gaining ground in the world of business and industry. All of these factors tend toward making more readily available at lower cost, the special lines that most facsimile systems require.

Of course, there is one system designed especially for use over an ordinary telephone. This is the Xerox Telecopier. Since this equipment was tested at the University of Nevada when it was a brand new product in 1966, a number of improvements have been made.[6] Since the telecopier has some unique advantages in convenience and low cost, especially for low volume-of-use applications, this system should be tested again to see whether the improvements add up to better performance and reliability.

Other manufacturers, such as Datafax and Alden, supply equipment which can also use an ordinary phone line, but require a Dataphone. (A Dataphone serves as an interface between the telephone line and the telefacsimile equipment, at about $30 per month apiece.)

Researchers are working on techniques to reduce bandwidth requirements.[9, 10] Although these efforts seem to be concentrated in the field of television, some of the new techniques may have potential application to telefacsimile.

One very interesting development has been introduced in Holland and the United States. RCA and N. V. Philips' Gloeilampenfabricken have found a way to use a commercial television channel for facsimile transmission while the regular program is in progress.[11] A television image is transmitted in successive fields with a blank interval in between. This blanking interval lasts only for 1.3 milliseconds (a little over one-thousandth of a second), long enough to switch in the facsimile circuit, transmit a fraction of an inch of the printed page, and switch it out again in time for the next television picture field. It is possible to transmit an average printed page in 2.5 seconds by this method. RCA uses an electrostatic printout, while the Dutch firm uses a camera to take the image off the cathode ray tube.

A Japanese system using a cathode ray tube prints by running recording paper over the face of the tube.[12] A special fibre-optic face-plate projects a sharp image onto the paper.

There are some other encouraging signs on the horizon. The Alden Company has developed a proposal for a scanner which will copy directly from books.[7] (The configuration of this device is far from ideal, however, since opened books will have to be turned face down on a glass platen.) The great potential advantages of a book-copying scanner may seem obvious, but I will enumerate them anyway:
1. The telefaxed copy will be of much better quality. Legibility is bound to improve, since one will no longer have to transmit from a copy of the original. Staff members in the New York State experiment complained that they often transmitted illegible copy because they were working from faint or low-contrast copies.[8]

2. Speed will be increased. The time required to take the original to the copying machine, wait for free machine-time, copy the item, and deliver it to the scanner will all be eliminated.

3. Cost of making the intermediate copy will be eliminated.

The proposed Alden book scanner will also supply the advantages of flexibility in speed and resolution, according to the needs of the particular job. Some existing Alden equipment already offers this flexibility, with resolutions ranging from 96 to 166 lines per inch, at various speeds. If the cost and reliability factors work out, this book scanner will largely take care of the technical limitations we have been concerned about.

Western Union has designed a new facsimile system which, they claim, will transmit an 8½ x 11" page over a single telephone line in three minutes, half the time required by existing systems.[13]

Project INTREX is experimenting with a microfilm facsimile system.[14] This is an ambitious project involving automatic microfiche retrieval combining remote access computer terminals with an image-transmission system.

There is, to my knowledge, one working interlibrary facsimile system now operating in the world today. This is at Pennsylvania State University, which has some twenty campuses. Eight are already linked with the main library at University Park, and twelve more campuses will be connected soon. The Xerox Magnavox Telecopier has been used for a year and a half. A detailed report on this system would be very informative.

So the overall picture is encouraging. While the engineers are busily at work conjuring up technical breakthroughs, the librarians should be planning sensible applications for them. Valuable experience gained in the last few years, if put to good use, can benefit those who depend upon the resources of all libraries.

REFERENCES

1. Sharon Schatz, "Facsimile Transmission in Libraries: a State-of-the-Art Survey," *Library Resources & Technical Services,* 12 (Winter 1968), pp. 5-15.

2. Harold G. Morehouse, "Equipment for Facsimile Transmission between Libraries; a Description and Comparative Evalution of Three Systems." (A study prepared for the Council on Library Resources, Inc., CLR-314.) Reno, University of Nevada, 1967.

3. William D. Schieber and Ralph M. Shoffner, "Telefacsimile in Libraries: a Report of an Experiment in Facsimile Transmission and an Analysis of Implications for Interlibrary Loan Systems." Berkeley, Institute of Library Research, University of California, 1968. 137p.

4. Houston Research Institute, Inc., "Facsimile Transmittal of Technical Information." Houston, 1965. 45p.

5. R. T. James, "The Evolution of Wideband Services in the United States," *IEEE Transactions on Communication Technology,* v. com-14, October 1966, pp. 636-640.

6. Harold G. Morehouse, "Telefacsimile Services between Libraries with the Xerox Magnavox Telecopier; a Study Prepared for the Council on Library Resources." Reno, University of Nevada, 1966. 54p.

7. Alden Electronic and Impulse Recording Equipment Co., "Proposal on Book Scanner and Graphic Communication System." (Prepared for) New York State Library, Division of Library Development. Westboro, Mass., 1967. (Unpaged), illus.

8. Nelson Associates, Inc., "The New York State Library's Pilot Program in the Facsimile Transmission of Library Materials; A Summary Report," New York, 1968. 85p.

9. Thomas S. Huang, "PCM Picture Transmission," *IEEE Spectrum*, 2 (December 1965), pp. 57-63.

10. Thomas S. Huang, "Digital Picture Coding," *Proceedings of the National Electronics Conference*, 22 (1966), pp. 793-97.

11. "Filling the Blanks," *Electronics*, 40 (November 1967), pp. 305-306.

12. "High-Speed Facsimile Has Fiber-Optic Cathode Tube," *Product Engineering*, 38 (October 1967), p. 73.

13. S. A. Romano, J. F. Gross, and A. Portnoy, "Solid State Facsimile Transceiver," *Western Union Technical Review*, 19 (July 1965), pp. 104-11.

14. Massachusetts Institute of Technology, "Project Intrex; Semiannual Activity Report." 15 September 1967 to 15 March 1968 (PR-5). Cambridge, Mass., 1968. 56p.

MEDIA EVALUATION

Librarians are occasionally critical of the limitations of sources available for the selection of printed media. Librarians have real cause for concern about the problems inherent in the process of evaluation and selection of audiovisual media. The articles selected for inclusion in this section are generally addressed to a consideration of aspects of the evaluation and selection process.

THE EVALUATION GAP: THE STATE OF THE ART IN AV REVIEWING, WITH SPECIAL EMPHASIS ON FILMSTRIPS*

By Janet French

The problems posed by the formidable production of information today are compounded by an equally remarkable multiplicity of information carriers. Anyone wishing to search for, make use of, or transmit information is faced with a dizzying number of possibilities. Certainly the educator is among those suffering from what appears to be an excess of choices. Charged with identifying "appropriate" information carriers, he must bear in mind his agency's curriculum, the competencies and idiosyncrasies of both staff and students, the physical limitations of his plant, the financial limitations of his budget. He must then relate all these variables to the range of available materials. Even without considering any exotic equipment, the educator is still faced with a host of possible carriers and possible combinations of features: print and nonprint, sound or silent, motion or still, simple or complex. And he must decide whether he wants the material for individual, small group, or large group use, or some combination of these elements, since materials are not all equally adaptable to all these uses.

These are by no means the only factors to be considered. The selector must know that not all formats are equally suited to any given educational task. Wide variations in quality also exist in the handling of any given topic in a *given* medium. Even when superior materials have been identified, the person charged with selection cannot assume that his job is done. Either his information or its treatment may be outdated tomorrow by new discoveries, new approaches in the original medium, or a superior presentation in an entirely different format.

Under the circumstances it seems reasonable to expect that a main goal of educational selection agents would be to establish national services for the bibliographic control and evaluation of all widely used instructional materials. Trade books long ago succumbed to such controls in response to the needs of librarians. To a substantial degree, 16mm films and educational records are also subject to control and evaluation procedures. As the matter now stands, however, no comparable systematic evaluation services have been established for the other media.

---

*Reprinted from *School Library Journal,* March 1970, published by R. R. Bowker (a Xerox Company), copyright ᶜ1970, Xerox Company.

A "FRUSTRATING TASK"[1]

Is there a substantial need for a comprehensive evaluation of the neglected nonprint media? How useful are the currently available selection aids? What suggestions might be made for general and local evaluation procedures? This study attempts to answer such questions for that unpretentious but widely used medium, the filmstrip, for reasons noted below.

For those who believe that nonprint media represent a new order of things, it may be worth noting that filmstrips have been around for 50 years.[2] It would not be fair to insinuate, however, that most films produced during this long period of time have been especially good. In fact, the brevity and mediocrity of filmstrips as a class before the Sixties may well explain their past exclusion from critical consideration.

The situation today has changed substantially. Color has almost entirely replaced the old black-and-white format, and the average new film is almost twice as long as films produced in the Fifties. Sound has been introduced through the use of synchronized records and tapes, and while it has not been uniformly successful, it can at its best add a lively dimension of depth and excitement to the visual presentation. Most important, several producers new to the field have been using the medium with respect and sensibility and are making films of aesthetic as well as educational value. (Let anyone who doubts it see Guidance Associates' *Streets, Prairies, and Valleys: The Life of Carl Sandburg.*) Thier superior films may be helping to stimulate a general upgrading of standards. Certainly substantial improvements in both technical and instructional quality have been evident and this fact, coupled with the filmstrip's original virtues of inexpensiveness and simplicity, probably accounts for its present position as the most widely used of the nonprint instructional resources.

It would be foolhardy to try to unravel the precise relationships between new educational practices, improved materials, and increased allocations (now, disastrously, waning). All have contributed to a vast expansion of materials holdings. In 1966, the educational establishment bought $442 million worth of a/v materials and equipment.[3] In that year the filmstrips absorbed over $500,000 of the $16.5 million in ESEA Title II funds spent on a/v materials.[4] That this substantial investment has not been generated solely by Title II pressures is shown by the fact that in the past eight years there has been an increase of 1000 percent in filmstrip sales to schools.[5] More surprising, perhaps, but fully compatible are the results of an NEA survey made in spring 1967, which showed that of some 1,600 elementary and high school teachers polled, 81.2 percent were using silent filmstrips, a figure which surpassed the reported use of any other material including records.[6]

BIBLIOGRAPHIC CONTROL AND SELECTION

To what extent has the substantial investment in filmstrips and their evident popularity prompted the development of useful selection tools? It should be noted first that a basic catalog of recommended titles on the order of the Wilson or ALA (book) catalogs has never been produced; anyone contemplating the development of a filmstrip collection must be prepared to build it from

252

scratch. Help appears to be coming, however, from at least two sources. The dimensions of the selection problem for both backlisted and current titles take on sharper focus when viewed in relation to the more than 25,000 individual titles listed in NICEM's *Index to 35mm Filmstrips*, published by Bowker last fall. To be fair, it must be admitted that some of these are no longer in print and that others were designed for adult rather than classroom use. Yet, even if we tentatively eliminate several thousand filmstrips, the residue represents a formidable challenge to building a superior filmstrip collection.

The NICEM Index itself, despite the grandeur of its proportions, is a puzzling tool to use even as a simple finding guide. The only information on the bases for inclusion is that the entries represent titles recorded in the data bank of the University of California since 1958. The user has no way of knowing, therefore, whether the Index is intended to be a comprehensive list of all filmstrips produced in this country (or elsewhere) from any given date or whether an effort was made to trace all such productions or whether the list merely represents items submitted for entry by those producers who were moved to cooperate. If the Index is not a comprehensive guide, neither is it a simple key to current materials on the order of *Books in Print*, since the alphabetic title list is peppered with "out of print" entries. Even such basic bits of information as the total number of entries listed and the number of o/p titles in the list have been omitted: the only way to approach either figure is through page sampling. The Index may not seem worth such extensive carping, but it was produced with substantial fanfare and represents a much-needed step towards the bibliographic control of the medium. Unfortunately, it also represents the cavalier attitude towards media control and evaluation evidenced by many of the agencies presently engaged in either enterprise.

A fervor for systematizing is undoubtedly a distinguishing feature of librarianship. Responding to the accelerated growth of the nonprint media in school libraries, *School Library Journal*, a principal source of critical book reviews, launched a semiannual *Audiovisual Guide* in November 1967. In an editorial introducing it, Evelyn Geller accurately reflected both the needs of the field and a professional passion:

> We felt that the main obstacle to better incorporation of a/v materials has been the failure to impose on them the same genius for organization that librarians, dictating their need for bibliographic control and systematic evaluation, have been able to stamp on the book industry.[7]

She picked up the challenge by publishing this nonevaluative but highly useful subject index to the current output of media in the pre-K to 12 range. The list, systematically expanded since its inception, now includes films, filmstrips, 8mm loops, slides and transparencies, discs and tapes, study prints, maps and charts, and a few miscellaneous items. It offers some useful figures for comparison.

CURRENT EVALUATION: SLIM PICKINGS

In November 1967, 204 filmstrips and filmstrip series were reported in the Guide. This figure increased to 250 in April 1968 and spurted again to 291 in November that year. Thus school-oriented filmstrip production from January

1968 to February 1969, as reported by the major producers, came to 541 series and individual titles. (The total for 1969, as reported in the April and November 1969 *A/V Guides*, comes to 617, but we are using the 1968 figures for comparison.)

It is instructive to compare the 1968 filmstrip or filmstrip series reported— 541—with the number of filmstrip reviews published during the same period. Though for many obvious reasons such a comparison is on wobbly statistical ground, it still provides an indication of evaluative activity in relation to production. The "Index to Audiovisual Reviews," published at frequent intervals in *Audiovisual Instruction*, reveals a total of 230 filmstrip reviews identified in the index in 1968. While it is perfectly possible that many reviews were overlooked, it is also true that large numbers of the listings were repeaters—reviews in different journals reported for the same filmstrip series. Numerically, then, filmstrip reviewing activity is well behind production, though the output for school consumption is certainly amenable to complete coverage. The man on the firing line—the selection agent—not only lacks selection tools for backlisted titles, but faces an increasing disparity between total production and items critically reviewed.

Seven readily obtainable journals carry most of the reviews listed: *Educational Screen and AV Guide, Film News, The Grade Teacher, The Instructor, School Library Journal, Science Teacher, Senior Scholastic's* teacher edition, and *Social Education*. In addition, the ALA *Booklist* last fall launched its filmstrip reviews. Of these publications, *Educational Screen, School Library Journal,* and *Film News* offer the greatest number of reviews, the first two covering an average of six to seven filmstrips or filmstrip series per month, the latter publishing ten or eleven reviews per bimonthly issue. The rest publish their reviews on a rather irregular basis, averaging three or less a month. Considering both the quantity and quality of their evaluations, *School Library Journal* and *Film News* warrant consideration by the selection agent as prime sources of responsible reviews, but neither provides the volume of service necessary to keep pace with production.

Booklist, long established as a critical guide to current books, 16mm films, and reference materials, may provide a comprehensive source of critical evaluation. In answer to the question on the extensiveness of *Booklist*'s planned coverage, Paul Brawley, editor of the nonprint reviews, wrote a year ago:

> The number of nonprint items to be reviewed will be directly proportional to the quality of the items received. Every known producer and distributor of nonprint materials [e.g., in the first year, filmstrips and 8mm loops] is being contacted in an effort to preview and evaluate as close to 100 percent of the educational market as possible.[8]

However, general access to ALA's evaluations is not as broad as this statement implies since reviews are being published only for material which "meets our criteria of selection and therefore is recommended for purchase."[9] Though there are doubtless many good reasons for limiting the reviews to recommended materials, space being an obvious factor, *Booklist* has seriously abridged the usefulness of its projected service through this decision. The reader will not know whether titles have been actively rejected. Though *Booklist* does seriously qualify its recommendations, as a concession to the generally poorer quality of production in the audiovisual field, its cautiously worded criticisms militate against their effectiveness.

Less obvious, but of greater consequence, a publication's ban on outright negative reviews damages the whole industry by withholding from public discussion the feedback producers need to improve their films. Perceptive and carefully considered reviews, both positive and negative, perform an essential service: at their best they represent a kind of ongoing, in-service education for the selection agent, calling attention to considerations that might otherwise have been overlooked, identifying the flaws and merits of a film, comparing it with others of superior or poorer quality.

Despite the manifold advantages of publishing reviews which reflect a full range of opinions, at present only *School Library Journal* does so as a matter of policy. Considering the modest number of filmstrip reviews published in *SLJ*, it is obvious that both producers and purchasers are receiving very little information about rejected materials. This is without question one of the most serious deficiencies of current a/v selection tools and a marked contrast to the publication policies of the major book reviews.

A number of agencies have award programs for filmstrips they judge to have special merit. Of these, Educational Film Library Association's Blue Ribbon awards, given annually at the American Film Festival competition, are the most important; they have been described as being "in the same tradition as ALA's Newbery-Caldecott Award."[10] Though one may doubt that they are as significant as the Newbery-Caldecott prizes, their choices are worthy of attention. EFLA makes a descriptive list of contenders available in its annual publication, *American Film Festival: The Best Of 19–* .

HEARTS AND FLOWERS EVALUATION

While the end of any selection procedure is presumably the same—to identify the best material for a given purpose—the degrees of responsibility imposed on persons evaluating materials vary substantially. The person selecting materials for his own use obviously accounts to no one save himself, but as the circle of persons affected by an evaluative decision increases, so does his measure of responsibility. The judgment of the evaluator may affect only one group of students, if he is a teacher choosing material for his class, or it may affect a whole school or school district, if judgment is being brought to bear on purchases for the media collection. If the results of evaluation are made public, as in printed reviews, the number of persons and institutions potentially affected by the evaluation increases enormously and, to the same degree, so does the evaluator's responsibility to provide a carefully considered and informative review.

It is possible, of course, to become so overwhelmed with these responsibilities that a kind of mental paralysis sets in. In an article on materials evaluation, one author indicated both a total abnegation of her critical faculties and a denial of the existence of objective criteria:

> Ethics involve one's professional responsibilities to make an evaluation that is fair to both the producer and the consumer. It is anticipated that material receiving poor ratings may be used successfully by some teachers,

or for some children and, conversely, that materials receiving good ratings could be unsuccessful in many cases. There is also a general concern about the effect of the variability of teacher-pupil-classroom transactions upon ratings, recognition is given to the possibility that the time of day or the weather may play some role in the success or failure of a material, and that success with materials varies according to the ability of the teacher to use them creatively. Even under hypothetically ideal conditions, the variabilities of a pupil, teacher, and environment are such that evaluation of a material is by nature intrinsically qualified.[11]

Not too far removed from the impotence of this point of view, and quite as useless to someone seeking guidance, are the evaluators who feel a greater obligation to be kind to the producer than to be honest with the user. In her excellent *Manual on Film Evaluation*, Emily Jones admonished:

> In the past evaluators have tended to be overkind rather than overcritical. They have been trained in the theory "if you can't say something good, don't say anything." This was based partly on the lack of materials which made it necessary to accept mediocre productions provided they dealt with the subject called for. This is no longer necessary, and mediocre films should be judged as severely as mediocre anything else. No one wants to hurt the feelings of film producers . . . but the responsibility of the evaluator is to the user, and there is no point saying "The film may be useful with some . . . groups," when what you mean is "The subject is unimportant, the treatment is uninteresting, and it is impossible to imagine any group of normal intelligence sitting through it."[12]

Despite Miss Jones' reference to past practice, the hearts-and-flowers approach is still evident in many reviews. It seems likely, too, that the lack of adverse recommendations in journals that carry reviews is as symptomatic of the sentiments she describes as lack of space or the desire to push good materials.

The fact is that it is both possible and reasonable to establish useful guidelines to cover the important features of any given medium. There is no need to examine them here in depth since virtually every treatise on a/v materials includes a list of evaluative criteria. Suffice it to say that the technical aspects of a filmstrip, for instance, and an accompanying record or tape, admit readily to objective evaluation: they either are or are not clear and free from distortion, synchronized with the sense of the captions or script, or relevant to the apparent subject of the film. With regard to the content itself, the questions of whether the material is up to date and accurate also seem beyond the influence of the time of day, the weather, or the creativity of the teacher.

Perhaps when the evaluator considers the coherence or logic of the presentation, he has entered into the arena of subjective judgment, and certainly this is true with regard to whether or not he finds the film stimulating, imaginative, or effective. If the evaluator takes his charge seriously, however, there is no reason for him to apologize for his subjective responses. Quite the contrary, in direct proportion to his appreciation for the film medium and his understanding of children and teaching needs, these personal responses will comprise a valuable aspect of his evaluation.

Of substantial bearing, too, on the usefulness of an evaluation, is the evaluator's familiarity with the medium and, in particular, with comparable titles in the subject area. The old maxim to the contrary, comparisons are not odious, and a knowledge of similar materials will give the evaluator a concrete basis for his appraisal of the relative merits of two or more titles. Furthermore, where such comparisons are possible, the subsequent review, to be of maximum value, will indicate the order of preference and the reasons for ranking. While references to related titles are an expected feature of book evaluation, they are almost totally absent from media reviews. The need for this kind of guidance is pressing, however, in view of the vast outpouring of new materials, the duplication of coverage, and the lack of basic selection tools for recommended titles. Another factor which makes comparisons particularly important in film evaluation is the special vulnerability of the medium to obsolescence and the need to find satisfactory replacements for aging titles.

It does not suffice that all these considerations enter into an estimate of the material's value. If the evaluator expects others to use the results of his effort, and particularly if his review is to be published, it is essential that his written evaluation indicate clearly:

1. The material's physical features
2. Its content
3. Its possible uses
4. Its comparative merits
5. The strengths or weaknesses which led to the final evaluation

As Emily Jones warns, "The evaluator must keep in mind the fact that he is acting for someone else. . . . He is being the eyes and ears of a potential user."[13]

Perhaps it would be useful to cite—without comment—the total content of two typical reviews. Their usefulness, or lack of it, should be self-evident, though it may be worth noting that the first review purports to offer guidance to the purchase of an 18-filmstrip set priced at $108, while the second reviews a single film sold by the New York Times for $7.95.

REVIEW A

Here are some answers to the endless and always recurring questions: Why do we need maps? What's inside us? What makes morning, noon, and night? The strips can be used by either class or individuals doing special study and research. Pupils are encouraged to think about the questions and answers and to understand the explanations offered. The material is adapted to the learning needs of young pupils.[14]

REVIEW B

If the librarian, teacher, or group leader can bear exposure to yet another word on the "youth rebellion," this filmstrip should be provocative, for it poses the ultimate question: "So what happens when you're 31?" (Don't trust anyone over 30.) The introduction by Russell Baker, in the discussion manual, is worth the price alone and should be required reading for parents and young people on either side of 30.

The filmstrip captures the youth phenomenon, reinforced by expert shots of their native habitats, by charts that signify their staggering presence among us, and by the veracity of their own dulcet tones and sounds. The black and white prints are dramatic in their straightforward reportage; the sound track well-matched to them. Both sides of the record are audibly cued; Side Two, however, allows for discussion breaks after frames 25 and 54. The manual lists activities, discussion questions, and books and pamphlets especially for young adults.

Since it lends itself to discussion, *Generation* . . . may be used effectively by a library club, guidance department, church group, social studies class, or even a PTA "happening." It may give hope to disadvantaged parents.[15]

A question may fairly be raised about the length of the second review; a little judicious surgery would not abridge the value of its content. But if the main concern of either the evaluators or the journals carrying reviews hinges on their brevity, the whole undertaking becomes pointless. The substance of the reviews should be weighed, not against the price tag of the materials reviewed, but in consideration of the degree to which they accurately mirror their potential service to the users. Insofar as an evaluation fulfills this end, it is successful; insofar as it falls short, it represents a waste of time and money for the reviewer and the journal, as well as for the selection agent who stopped to read it.

IN-DISTRICT EVALUATION: AN AWFUL EXAMPLE

Despite the surface advantage of systematic in-district evaluation, the literature is full of cases of catch-as-catch-can practices euphemistically described as "evalution." Were these projects pursued as a fringe activity, they would still be a waste of energy; when they are employed to identify materials which are to be a central factor in the educational program, they are inexcusable. A case in point was reported in *Audiovisual Instruction* describing preparations for an individualized instruction program. With pride and fantastic naivete, the author reported:

About this time the teachers were ready to evalute instructional materials as they related to their objectives. The Audio-Visual Department called in the complete nonprint libraries of EBF and SVE, as well as the "quick-strip" library of Eye Gate for evaluation and possible purchase. For the next few weeks the teachers looked through catalogs of all the known producers of nonprint materials. [They] were free to . . . order for evaluation any nonprint materials which they felt might have merit for our program. . . . By April, after the evaluation of many hundreds of filmstrips, tapes, records, and programmed materials, the teachers were ready to start ordering instructional materials with particular instructional objectives in mind.[16]

Overlooking the fact that the main suppliers reported are more noteworthy for the size of their catalogs than for the consistent quality of their products, the description of this project's "evaluation" procedures reads like a catalog of unsupportable practices. Nowhere is there any suggestion that criteria were established or adopted for the media under consideration, or that the teachers were given training in their implementation. One of the principal hazards to sound evaluation is that the skills and understandings necessary to the enterprise are so often underestimated. In-district selection practices appear to be based, time and again, on the assumption that the teacher who uses the material is, by virtue of that fact, fully equipped to judge it. Unfortunately, for systems operating under such assumptions, the use of a material does not of itself promote or guarantee expertise in its choice. A cardinal tenet of *any* evaluation process is that it should be preceded by careful indoctrination of the participants so that they fully understand the selection criteria and the nature of the responses required of them.

If the designer of this undertaking failed to appreciate the need for criteria, he performed as poorly in providing guidance in identifying materials for preview. With a very large staff and a great deal of time it might be feasible (if not desirable) to call in "complete libraries" of the major producers; but the present tidal wave of production will soon make such innocent unselective approaches to evaluation an impossibility. Given the size of the author's task force—12 teachers—and the time allotted for evaluation—three hours a week for about six weeks—their reported activities are nothing less than preposterous. In the time available to them they are described as having examined "the catalogs of all the known producers of nonprint material," previewed "the complete nonprint libraries of EBF, SVE and Eye Gate," and evaluated (apparently to their satisfaction) "many hundreds of filmstrips, tapes, records, and programmed materials." In view of the fact that the average filmstrip runs about 15 minutes and one side of an average LP a half hour, this reported evaluation activity can serve the profession solely in the capacity of an Awful Example. In the absence of any real commitment to guide the evaluation process and participate in it, in how many other districts have media specialists promoted—or at least accepted—similar debacles?

RESPONSIBILITIES OF THE MEDIA SPECIALIST

If these harried pseudoevaluation programs are not to become—or remain—general practice, media specialists must take on their full responsibilities for the selection of materials. They must develop or adopt valid criteria for evaluation and train other media specialists and selected classroom teachers to apply them to materials being considered. They must know both the physical aspects of the media and their content, and they should know which materials and producers are most likely to meet specific needs.

Responsible selection agents will try to bring order and purposefulness to evaluation, seeing it as an ongoing process, not a series of crash programs. To this end they will develop selective lists and systematically reevaluate their holdings to maintain a collection of genuine merit. Insofar as possible, they will structure each evaluation project so that evaluation can take place in the context of comparison—both of the viewpoints of the participants and of the materials themselves. On the other hand, they will *not* be cajoled into previewing massive portions of a producer's catalog, a practice which reduces the possibility of careful comparisons and tends to create a sense of obligation to the producer or his agent. Occasionally this arrangement gets an added fillip through the offer of a bonus if a certain number of items are purchased. Such inducements, when accepted, virtually paralyze any genuine evaluative effort.

The media specialist will make use of the selection tools available to him and encourage the development of better ones. I admit they are not now and probably never will be wholly satisfactory. Yet they provide a means of identifying promising materials, some of which might otherwise be overlooked, with far more hope of success than simple faith in the descriptive listings of a catalog or Herculean assaults on complete libraries of materials. The present lack of selective catalogs or adequate reviews suggests that persons responsible for buying media have never seen the need for such selection tools. If this is so, it follows that they have either failed to understand their responsibilities as selection agents, or they have failed to assume them.

That is really my main point here. The media specialist cannot properly take responsibility solely for the *form* of the materials he administers; he is equally responsible for its *content*. The teachers and others whom he draws into selection will have, at best, a fragmented acquaintance with the media collection. It is the specialist who must be familiar with it *all*—its strengths and weaknesses, the gaps that need filling, the material that needs replacing. He must be aware of what is available in the collection if he is to advise on its use. He must know what promising new materials are on the market and what superior materials appear on the backlists if his selection procedures are to be anything but exercises in serendipity. Of all the persons involved in selection, he alone is responsive to the total curriculum; he alone is knowledgeable about the complete collection and the needs of all its users. It is his responsibility, therefore, to initiate the selection process, guide its functioning, and see that it is brought to a satisfactory consummation.

At this juncture it may be worthwhile to consider the mystique of group evaluation. In 1957 Paul Reed wrote unequivocally:

> Selection of material should be based upon the judgments of those who are to use them. Group judgments are superior to individual judgments. Teacher judgments are best when they are based upon actual experience in using the materials in classroom situations.[17]

In 1963 Edward Schofield, addressing a symposium, quoted this statement almost word for word.[18] In 1968 Carlton Erickson used it verbatim in his handbook *Administering Instructional Media Programs*. It may, of course, be perfectly true, though none of the exponents offers supporting evidence, and precisely how the "best" selections might be determined is difficult to conceive. What is apparent is that in 1957, when Mr. Reed enunciated this doctrine, the dimensions of both media budgets and production were modest enough to contemplate in-district selection programs which strictly adhered to it.

It may seem heretical to suggest this, but the fact remains that group evaluation is neither the only nor necessarily the best approach to media selection. It should seem reasonable to suggest that the results of group evaluation can only be as good as the training, motivation, and experience of the participants. It is therefore a practice qualified in value and one which can readily degenerate into a parody of genuine evaluation: witness the example quoted earler. Furthermore, considering the logistics of enormously increased production and demand, evaluation procedures which involve large numbers of volunteers (not to mention those impressed into service) may prove to be a luxury better suited to the infancy than to present dimensions of media production.

Regardless of who participates in the preliminary events, the media specialist remains the central figure in the selection process, not merely its agent, and the final ordering of priorities is his to make. Responsibly conceived, his selections will be based on the merits of the material available, the nature of his collection, the needs of his users, and the size of his budget. A decision to buy or not to buy based fairly upon these considerations will represent the proper culmination of the evaluative process.

REFERENCES

1. Margaret Rufsvold, "Guides to the Selection and Evaluation of the Newer Media," *Audiovisual Instruction*, January 1967, p. 11.

2. NICEM, *Index to 35mm Educational Filmstrips.* Bowker, 1969, p. v.

3. Evelyn Geller, "Media Mix at Midpoint," *School Library Journal*, November 1968, p. 11.

4. Geller, "The ESEA Title II Report for 1966: The Difference It Made," *School Library Journal*, April 1968, p. 70.

5. Diana Lembo, "A Stepchild Comes of Age," *School Library Journal*, September 1967, p. 54.

6. "Instructional Resources in the Classroom," *Audiovisual Instruction*, March 1968, p. 284.

7. Geller, "Small Ways out of Chaos," *School Library Journal*, November 1967, p. 19.

8. Paul L. Brawley, Letter, February 27, 1969.

9. *Ibid.*

10. Lembo, *op. cit.*, p. 55.

11. Margaret H. Moss, "Evaluation as a Responsibility of the IMC Network," *Exceptional Children*, December 1968, p. 304.

12. Emily S. Jones, *Manual on Film Evaluation.* Educational Film Library Association, 1967. p. 5.

13. *Ibid.*

14. Irene Cypher, "Filmstrips," *The Instructor*, October 1968, p. 162.

15. Lembo, "Screenings," *School Library Journal*, September 1968, p. 65.

16. Thomas J. Ogston, "Individualized Instruction: Changing the Role of the Teacher," *Audiovisual Instruction*, March 1968, pp. 244-45.

17. Paul Reed, quoted in Carlton Erickson's *Administering Instructional Media Programs.* Macmillan, 1968, p. 70.

18. Edward Schofield, "Competencies Needed by School Librarians for Selecting and Organizing Materials for Materials Centers," in *The School Library as a Materials Center*, edited by Mary Helen Mahar. U.S. Office of Education, 1963. p. 21.

OTHER REFERENCES

Brown, James W., and Kenneth D. Norberg. *Administering Instructional Media Programs.* Macmillan, 1968.

ALA Bulletin, January 1969, p. 56.

Mahar, Mary Helen. "Equalizing Educational Opportunity," *ALA Bulletin,* February 1969, pp. 226-230.

Meierhenry, W. C. "National Media Standards for Learning and Teaching," *ALA Bulletin,* February 1969, pp. 238-241.

Educational Screen and AV Guide.

Film News.

Grade Teacher.

Science Teacher.

Senior Scholastic, Teacher Edition.

Social Education.

EFLA. *American Film Festival: The Best of 19– .* Educational Film Library Association.

NOTES FROM A SEMI-DARKENED ROOM*

By Diana Lembo

Nonprint media have become important in our programs because they are valued by our technological society. Traditionally, American education has been committed not only to conserving the proven values and techniques of the past, but to incorporating those of demonstrable worth that our society develops. This of course is one of its main functions. Society has placed administrators, teachers, and media specialists in the uncomfortable position of judging and adjusting, and refining the confusion of terms that generally accompanies this type of adjustment. No one suitable term, neither "non print" nor "non book," adequately categorizes our society's many ways for presenting ideas.

But, more urgently, we must examine what technology means to and has done to our youngsters. Youngsters value media in any and all combinations, just so long as they carry out their job well. The kids have no historical bias about technological developments. So, regardless of our acceptance of changing carriers of knowledge, they are making a rapid incursion into American education.

As I have researched and written my doctoral thesis on the history of DAVI, it has become obvious that the philosophy behind the *Standards for School Media Programs* had to appear formally somewhere in education at this time. It may have been an accident that school librarians helped to develop it, but they have now realized they must expand their training to embrace the developments in the field. They are already well trained in bibliographic control, evaluation and selection, and the use of books. More than anything else, these same skills are desperately needed in the media field, and situations now demand that we use them. First, the technical developments in media and each new generation's exposure to them outside of school has reached the point where a school environment without them is anachronistic. Secondly, and equally important, our atmosphere of augmented and widely distributed mechanization, electrification, and amplification is in some very real and physical ways making a youngster's perceptions quite different from those we have come to expect from ourselves.

If I understand the young's many-faceted message, it says, in part, "I am not you; I am not frozen into your modes. You may be the movie-made child that Henry J. Forman wrote about in the Thirties or even *The Moviegoer* who was the 1962 National Book Award fiction title by Walker Percy. I, however, am more open to feelings because I am a movie, transistor radio, stereo, cassette tape, portable TV, computer-terminal shaped person."

As the song goes, *I Am a Rock. . . .*

This music, this shriek of pain from our visually and aurally supersaturated younger generation is tragic and moving. It has great emotional appeal. Sound, and in particular a strong beat, generally makes a direct sensual appeal. And don't miss the incriminating statement in that song—books shield you from life, divorce you from feeling.

*Reprinted from *School Library Journal*, February 1970, published by R. R. Bowker (a Xerox Company), copyright ᶜ1970, Xerox Corporation.

The blues and rock music carries the revolutionary message of the young. They don't need books to transmit it as previous generations did. They are in revolt against the inhumanity of life—and they equate this quality with the machines they use and the books they read by the bushel basket. This willingness to consume while condemning indicates great confusion. In many ways, theirs is a terribly touching, naive, and brutally exploited movement. As their hero Peanuts has observed, "We have met the enemy and they are us." Above all else, the youngsters are not willing to be the enemy; they are determined not to become feelingless, or worse still, to leave their feelings unexpressed to others. Although these youngsters share with us the universalities of the human condition, they differ sharply in their almost unconscious dependence on media, as well as in their perceptions.

As media have improved technically, a paradoxical situation has developed. The latent emotionality in the projected image and amplified sound has become overt. This has tended to increase the subjective response in those who are ill equipped to deal critically and objectively with ideas. It has, in fact, contributed to an anti-intellectual position. Over the years, we have done a creditable job in teaching our students critical skills to use with ideas in books. *But we have failed to give them the skills they need to deal with other media.* They cry that education is not relevant. One reason may be that while media presentations have stirred their emotions deeply, their lack of a counterbalancing objectivity leaves them powerless to function rationally within an established order. Their decision to "drop out" is irrational to us, but the only logic possible to them.

If we are going to help restore some semblance of balance to the educative process, or, if you will, humanize it, we must use media and at the same time recognize their potential. Instead of the extreme positions of Bergson's subjective type of criticism, "I like it, therefore it's good," or Marianne Moore's intellectual insistence that a good picture must be ". . . lit with piercing glances into the life of things," we might try to achieve that balance of which William Butler Yeats sings:

God grant me from those thoughts
men think
In the mind alone;
He that thinks a lasting song
thinks in a marrow bone. . . .

It is only through a vital balance of reason and emotion that each human being can construct a valid picture of reality for himself.

By now you may think I'm not fond of books. Quite the contrary, they are my mode. But I am fond of ideas wherever I find them. I am a fan of the flicks, a sometime blues and rock record buff, and a voyeur in other assorted media—one of course being what used to be called the still picture, since I am a filmstrip reviewer.

As a reviewer and editor responsible for the filmstrip reviews in *SLJ*'s Screenings, I have found that the general principles of evaluation and good reviewing are much the same for the various media, with some provision made for the nature of the medium. Professionals who can judge printed materials critically are best able to extend these principles to other media, amplifying them to embody the technical criteria that apply to the film medium in general and to filmstrips specifically. Knowing a/v materials and filmstrips and their use is valuable, but more vital is knowledge of one or more curricular areas. Teaching experience or familiarity with teaching methods is valuable. And familiarity with retrospective filmstrip titles is invaluable. The critical comparison of titles; the familiarity that permits varied suggestions of use, in curricula, with classes, by individuals, or in special situations—these are the *sine qua non* of critical reviewing, whether for a publication or for building up individual collections.

POINTERS FOR PREVIEWING

Before viewing a filmstrip critically, preview it for its visceral impact. This is not always easy because one's mind generally objects to being disconnected from the action, and perhaps you can't be wholly successful. But it's not a new or earth-shaking technique. It can be and is used with books. Nevertheless, it is a vital step in my reviewing process, because the first adjective that best describes my emotional reaction answers my most basic question: "Will anyone watch it and Who?" Determining the maturity and interest level of audience appeal is my main concern. If it coincides with the producer's intent, which I search for next, we're at least off to a promising start. Whenever I'm in doubt, and occasionally to keep myself on the "growing edge," I rerun it with an appropriate school class, assorted neighborhood young adults and children, my own who presently represent three generations across the "gap," teacher friends, library school students, and other assorted guinea pigs.

At the second screening, it is time to identify and record those factors that make the strip a poor to outstanding example of the filmstrip art. Regardless of its eventual rating, however, I try to keep in mind that even a poor example may have some special or worthwhile feature. Not all the books on the library shelves are great literature. Many are pedestrian. But they may be needed to accommodate the variety of individual differences and our ways of dealing with them. It is equally necessary to remember that a "35mm dreadful" should be examined as closely as an excellent one, both to explain why it is poor and to look for any redeeming segment and use for it.

In many ways, media reviewing is like book reviewing. Media should be evaluated by the same general criteria one uses for books, such as accuracy of information, scope of the subject matter, comparison with others in the field, and the like. Other considerations of both content and format, however, differ somewhat by medium. In film or filmstrip reviewing, the format or technical qualities of the visual and sound components assume some prominence. (These considerations of technical quality and content are condensed and listed in my article in the September 1967 issue of *School Library Journal.*) Here I'm going to list some points to watch for in what we may arbitrarily call the *content* area, to distinguish them from the important craft or technical elements, such as graphic, camera work, et cetera.

They are:

1) The objectives should be clear and the organization inherently logical. This is often accomplished by the story line or narrative as it unfolds in the sequencing of the frames. It may also be done more unconventionally without

a script by relying on implicit visual literacy through the camera work.

2) The ratio of the number of facts to the number of frames should be appropriate to the intended audience. A gradual rate of accumulation of facts, provided they are interestingly presented, seems effective with most learners. *The English Literature Survey* series (see review, *SLJ* , January 1968, p. 57; *LJ*, January 15, p. 277), for example, condensed so many facts and concepts into so few frames that it marred an otherwise good filmstrip of high technical quality. Nevertheless, the strips could be suggested for summary and review or even as background material for other purposes, like a book talk.

3) The main idea or facts should be presented in several ways. Repetition is a bulwark of the teacher's trade and, if not abused, is extremely rewarding. Rarely, however, can a filmstrip afford more than one repetition for a main point, and even then the secret of success is to keep it fresh by some faint disguise. This can be done in a standard way by repeating the same verbal symbols against a different picture clue, or the reverse. Some 16mm films use the identical frame or clip repeatedly in split-second timing to achieve a special effect— e.g., the internalization of a thought or memory.

4) The filmstrip should be believable. This is a complex element which can be achieved with numerous combinations of technical effects, such as color, art work, photography, sound or the absence of it, size, pacing, detail, etc. The successful blending of these factors determines this quality. Many people, for example, will not accept color shots that accurately represent natural color. The processes of reduction or enlargement and the framing of the picture intensify the requirement of the human eye for more brilliance and color to approximate the original. Yet too much makes the scene or object patently unreal; a delicate balance is required.

5) A measure of authority or confidence in the film must be established. This is sometimes done by including recognized and respected roles or the well-known people who occupy them. The strip *This Honorable Court . . .* (reviewed in *SLJ*, January 1968, p. 57; *LJ*, January 15, p. 277) uses this technique successfully by introducing a Supreme Court Justice in the flesh—photograph and voice. Another basis is the viewer's ability to identify with what he perceives. As one reviewer wrote me recently, "I wish producers would aim at something with which both white and black urban youngsters are familiar." Some do, but perhaps not enough to be representative.

6) There should be a smooth merging of picture and word, whether printed in captions or spoken. A horror is one with both captions and sound, unless it has been done deliberately à la Peter Max; one may reasonably expect old footage doctored up or, worse still, a poor understanding of the film art. The strip *Temples, Mountains, and Gods* (reviewed in *SLJ*, February 1969, p. 56; *LJ*, February 15, p. 852) is a fairly good example of this *faux pas*. It does not contain old footage. In fact, without the record it is an extremely good captioned silent strip, with fine photography and layout. It also has a competent resume technique in the final frames. It would be fair to suggest that the strip could be recommended without the use of the record, which is excess baggage.

A reverse condition of this characteristic, which is even more tiresome, is the situation where a fine and useful recording accompanies a poor filmstrip that is little more than a distraction. The series *Folk Songs, 1700-1864 (SLJ,*

March 1968, p. 123; *LJ*, March 15, p. 1297) exhibits this affliction. The records in this series are noteworthy; they make a good collection of American songs of historical significance sung by prominent folk singers. The strip, however, is poorly done and peculiarly reminiscent of an old nickelodian-type movie without being sufficiently "camp."

When you come across a filmstrip that follows these general rules, it is lively and interesting. It can also in a sense be a work of art. *The Reckless Years* comes close. So does *John Henry, an American Legend* (*SLJ*, March 1968, p. 123; *LJ*, March 15, p. 1297), with its dramatic appeal, fine art work, and fidelity to the spirit of the legend. One youngster I know has watched it at least five times in private screenings.

Still another example is *The Three Robbers* (*SLJ*, September 1967, p. 65; *LJ*, September 15, p. 3133), which captures the satiric humor of the original story and enhances it because of the enlarged image. My overriding criterion for the second screening then is that the idea is best conveyed when all these points are in easy balance.

Other characteristics unique to the film medium demand consideration. They are: color, sound, and motion. For years the stricture was placed upon filmstrips that when motion was needed to portray something, a motion picture was a better medium to use. Lately, with techniques that regulate the tempo by manipulating sound and pacing, the filmstrip can successfully convey motion, and if expertly done, can literally deceive the human eye. Once this technique is refined and perfected, only one true distinction will remain to the viewer, and this will have nothing to do with the mm width of the film, whether 8, 16, 35, or the 4½ that has often been proposed. Rather, it will be dependent upon the size of the projected image. The reduced size of small-screen projection tends to lessen the viewer's identification and emotional involvement, the large screen to noticeably increase it. Television obeys the same rule. If it's "larger than life," one is more willing to suspend belief and lose himself in the presentation. If it's smaller than life-size, one tends to maintain the invisible barrier that says your body cannot enter. Under the latter circumstances our minds seem able to concentrate on an analysis of the perceptions more easily. As an example of this, witness the frank criticism one often hears as several boys in a lighted school workroom view a newly arrived film that they are projecting onto a wall a few feet away. (Not viewing in a darkened room is another factor, of course.)

It is enlightening to compare filmstrips that have similar subject content for their color, sound, and tempo. Here are six you may want to examine. For a comparison between black-and-white and color, look at two sound strips about youth and conformity, *The Generation Under 25*, produced by the *New York Times* (*SLJ*, September 1968, p. 66; *LJ*, September 15, p. 3234) and *Dare to Be Different* (*SLJ*, September 1969, p. 62; *LJ*, September 15, p. 3156), produced by Guidance Associates.

A comparison of any title in the series *Scandinavia and the Low Countries*, McGraw-Hill (*SLJ*, September 1967, p. 53; *LJ*, November 15, p. 4237), and either *Venezuela* or *Peru* in the Congressional Digest series *Basic Economic and Social Development: Two Case Studies* (*SLJ*, November 1967, p. 52; *LJ*, November 15, p. 4236). All are in color and treat social and economic progress, with silent, captioned strips.

Tempo is more difficult to compare fairly. *Eskimo Prints* from the National Film Board of Canada series *Canada's North* (*SLJ*, May 1968, p. 64; *LJ*, May 15, p. 2098) is an excellent example of the silent, color, self-paced filmstrip that has inherent emotionality because of its aesthetic beauty. Compare it to the tempo so artfully worked into the color strip *Lines* in the Warren Schloat award-winning series *The Art of Seeing* (*SLJ*, September 1969, p. 62; *LJ*, September 15, p. 3156) to observe the influence of regulated pacing.

Last, take another excellent filmstrip view of American society, *The U.S. House of Representatives*. Both this and Guidance's *The Reckless Years* (*SLJ*, January 1969, p. 51; *LJ*, January 15, p. 279) are in color. Both, using sound, have a tempo. One evokes a greater emotional response. There may be several reasons for this. What's your verdict?

PRINCIPLES OF FILM EVALUATION FOR PUBLIC LIBRARIES*

By Stanley Dunnetski

Library collections of 16mm motion picture film are being used more and more by organizations and groups from all walks of life to provide information, education, and recreation. A tremendous growth in the use and need of film has taken place in the immediate past. The reasons for this growth are many: the effective use of television as a form of mass communication, current trends in education which emphasize the use of visual aids as teaching devices, and the need to aid and inform the disadvantaged as quickly and successfully as possible as an adjunct to the War on Poverty Program. The problem which confronts libraries across the country is supplying top quality films on a variety of subjects to meet the demand of the various groups using them. It is a particular problem when we consider the cost of a single film and gauge this cost against the quantity of films produced each year. In order to establish a balance between budget allocations and film quantity, highly selective and discriminating standards of film evaluation for purchase are mandatory. Four factors are primary in evaluating film: content, treatment, utilization, and need.

Content is the statement and point of view presented in the film. The librarian must decide if the thesis of the film is presented accurately, honestly, and lucidly. A film which presents too much material will leave the viewer confused by the amount of information confronting him, while a film which presents too little material will leave the viewer dulled by the lack of communication. We must remember that a film which is overloaded with information cannot be rescreened as chapters in a book can be reread, for film is a mass experience whereas reading is a personal one. A film must make its point clearly, easily, and succinctly.

A tremendous quantity of film catalogs, brochures, and leaflets are received annually by film librarians. It is from this material that we make our selection. Each film listed and described by its producer sounds as though it were the best and most essential film made on the given subject and necessary to every collection. Sometimes this is true, and sometimes it is not. When an announcement of a film appears which seems relevant to a particular collection, a preview copy of the film should be requested and screened. This is the only way to select the newest and best films. Preview media are an aid in cataloging, preparing film notes, and gathering other opinions about a given title, but no film should ever be purchased without the librarian having seen it. This is the only means by which the librarian can honestly evaluate a film.

Once we have established and evaluated the content of a film, we must examine its treatment. This is perhaps the most difficult area to examine, for no matter how objectively we try, a certain amount of subjectivity and personal taste influences us. This area is also difficult because it is the treatment—that is, the use of film effectively—which separates this medium from all others and makes of it a distinct form. Our study of book evaluation in terms of character, structure, plot, description, and style must be replaced with the study of

*Reprinted by permission from *Illinois Libraries*, 49:89-92, February 1967.

movement, camera angles, color, mood, music and editing. We must, in a sense, become cameraman, director, writer, technician, and producer.

Movement is the essential quality which separates motion picture film from all other forms of communication. It is the librarian's job to evaluate how effectively movement is used to highlight and present a point of view in the film. For example, let us consider the movement in a discussion scene between two people. Does the camera simply focus on the participants for long periods of time as they speak, or does the camera move? Does the camera change position and angles on the face, focusing on profile, closeup, eyes, etc., to highlight the spoken word of the participants? If the camera remains stationary and we simply view the two people for a long period, we will become restless and bored despite the fact that what they are saying is important or beneficial to us. In other words, the content is fine, but the treatment of the situation is poor.

A knowledge of film technique is not gained overnight. This requires a great deal of study in terms of reading about film and film technique and in the actual viewing of films. The more films one sees, the better and quicker his critical evaluation becomes. The proper evaluation and selection of films is as much of an art as the proper selection and evaluation of books. It requires time and practice.

Particularly in large library systems, films are used by a variety of groups and organizations for a variety of purposes. It is essential to know your patrons before passing judgment on a film. At the high cost of film today, the librarian must keep an eye out for film which can serve the multiple needs of multiple groups. Once he begins to purchase with a specific, single group in mind, the collection will become singular in types of film titles in addition to types of groups served. For example, a purely classroom film on economics would be of use to school groups and is generally produced with this audience in mind. If this film were purchased, we would be serving one specific group. On the other hand, this film will not be of interest to women's clubs, church groups, business organizations, etc., because it was specifically designed for schools. A general film on economics, however, done cleverly and artistically, would be useful to any and all of these groups, because of its educational, informational, and recreational value. When we buy the general economics film, we are able to serve a great majority of our patrons rather than one segment.

We must also be careful of buying specific areas of material which are not serviceable or usable in terms of a general field of interest. For example, in the field of art one should not buy films which cater to the taste of only one group as would be the case in purchasing films only about the French Impressionists. First, this means that one would or should buy films dealing specifically with all other periods of art. Here we come face to face with the problem of budget. Can we afford to buy individual films dealing with particular periods? Second, when we buy a special film with a particular point of view, we are servicing only one segment of film patrons. What is actually needed in this instance is a film which presents a comprehensive survey of painting so that we can furnish needed material in one film, and at the same time meet the needs of many groups with this single title.

A most important factor in deciding upon the purchase of a film is an objective look at the need for such a film in the collection. It is often possible to

270

see a film which meets our standards of content, treatment, and utilization. Yet is the film really needed? Here we must evaluate the collection of films on a particular topic and determine whether or not that collection is sufficient to serve the patrons using it. We may have, for example, a new and excellently produced film on Africa fresh from our preview list. On the other hand, we may already have six or seven very good titles on this subject in our collection. Are these present titles circulating and to what degree? Are patrons requesting more films on Africa? Does this newly previewed film add substantial material that is not included in the other African films? When the librarian can objectively answer these questions yes or no, he will purchase or not purchase the specific film in question.

Through the course of a year, the film librarian previews perhaps hundreds of films. Many are good and some are excellent, but again we must remember the need. Often we see beautiful and moving films, films of humor and sadness, films experimenting with new techniques and theories, films of almost every broad heading in the Dewey Decimal Classification scheme. Despite our personal feeling and liking for a particular film, we must consider the need of such a title in the collection, and often bypass our own feeling and purchase a film that will be used. By the same token, we should not purchase a film which is in any way inferior to our standards even though the need for such a film is great. A poor or inadequate film on a given subject is far worse than no film at all. For a poor film can be as damaging in the dissemination of knowledge as an ill-prepared reference book or history. A film librarian can never accept quantity over quality, and quality comes only from the proper and objective evaluation of films.

Motion picture film review media serve as a guide and a source to the film librarian. Particularly useful are the *Film Evaluation Guide* published by the Educational Film Library Association, *The Landers Film Reviews* published by the Landers Associates, *Educators Guide to Free Films* published by the Educators Progress Service, *The Booklist and Subscription Books Bulletin* published by the American Library Association, and the *Educational Media Index* as produced by the Educational Media Council. Of special use for current reviews are the EFLA evaluation cards published by the Educational Film Library Association, which keep the *Educational Film Guide* current. Each of these publications will aid in the selection of films. However, there is no adequate substitute for actually viewing the film itself when selecting and evaluating 16mm motion picture titles.

REVIEW AND EVALUATION CONTROL*

By Richard Darling

One element in the Montgomery County Public Schools' library instructional materials program is review and evaluation. This activity, coordinated by the Review and Evaluation Division of the Department of Instructional Materials, involves more than 600 members of the professional staff of the school system, organized in 60 committees, with additional work done by individual evaluators, all of whom have the job of reviewing more than 30,000 items of instructional material each year to sift out those of inferior quality and those inappropriate to the school system curriculum. The logistics and record-keeping jobs necessary in a review program of this scope are very large indeed. The staff of the division must organize committees to do the reviewing, secure materials for review, maintain control records throughout the evaluation process, and issue lists of materials recommended for school use. In the process, they perform an enormous number of tasks of a clerical, and often repetitive, character. A brief description of the activities of the Review and Evaluation Division will provide a picture of the range of its services.

The major reviewing job is done by the sixty committees, which are organized by subject and by grade level. For example, there is a committee for elementary school mathematics, and one for secondary school mathematics, one for social studies kindergarten through third grade, one for grades four through six, and in the secondary level, committees for geography, American history, world history, and so on. These committees include classroom teachers, librarians, and the appropriate subject supervisors in their membership, with a majority of school-based teachers. Membership on the committees, with the exception of the supervisors, is voluntary. The staff of the Division must secure volunteers for committee service, a recruitment effort that includes an invitation to all teachers and librarians to serve, recommendations for persons to serve on committees secured from principals and other administrators and supervisors, and special invitations to the members of the previous year's committees to serve again. Since a county policy forbids teachers to serve on more than one review and evaluation committee, the staff must check to be sure that each teacher who volunteers for a review and evaluation committee is not already serving on another committee. A file of committees and their membership is maintained by the school system personnel department, but it must be checked manually since it is not, at this time, in machine-readable form.

After the committee file has been checked, the Division prepares letters notifying each committee member of his appointment, and prepares committee membership lists for the use of the committee chairman, the subject supervisor, the personnel department, and the Review and Evaluation Division itself. In order to provide for each of the uses to which this list is put and to make available the information most frequently requested concerning the committees, the committee list must include a listing by committee, an alphabetical listing by

*Reprinted from the *Drexel Library Quarterly,* 5:104-109, April 1969, by permission of the publisher. ᶜ1969.

the names of the members, and a list by the names of the schools in which the members ordinarily teach.

The second job of the division is to secure the materials for evaluation. These materials are secured in two ways. Many of them come through automatic sampling from trade and textbook publishers and from producers of audiovisual materials. Others must be requested from publishers and vendors as a need for them is identified. Requests that materials be evaluated come from many sources. Often the committees, looking at the curriculum and its needs, identify topics for which additional materials are needed or identify specific items which they believe may fill an identified need.

Other requests come from principals, teachers, and librarians in the schools. Any member of the school system professional staff may request that material be evaluated. When the Review and Evaluation Division receives requests, it orders the requested items for review from the appropriate publisher or vendor, often for a 30- to 45-day review period, at the end of which the material must be returned.

The Division must maintain careful records on each review item. As materials arrive unsolicited, a clerk prepares a control card so that each step in the evaluation process can be recorded to avoid duplication in ordering and in evaluation and to insure that "on approval" materials are returned by the correct date. The Division must also prepare evaluation forms for the use of the reviewing committee. Entering the correct bibliographic information on evaluation forms at the outset eliminates checking and correcting at a later stage in the operation.

The material and the evaluation form are then supplied to the appropriate committee at its next scheduled meeting. If an item was requested by an individual staff member, he is also notified that the material has been secured so that he may examine it, and the item is identified for priority handling. An exception to the committee evaluation is made in the case of trade books. So many are published each year, particularly in certain subjects, such as language arts and social studies, that it has been necessary to provide an alternative route for their evaluation. Trade books may be evaluated by any member of the professional staff. The school librarians act as liaison between the schools and the Division of Review and Evaluation, securing the books from the central office and coordinating reviewing activities within their own schools.

Committee responsibility includes all types of instructional materials: 16mm motion picture films, 8mm film loops, disc and tape recordings, textbooks, trade books, slides, charts, maps, globes, transparencies, pictures, models, sculptures, specimens, tests, and so forth. Through their efforts, it is decided what materials will be purchased for central inventory and what materials will be recommended for individual school purchase. Each item of instructional material must have the approval of at least three members of the committee, except textbooks and programmed materials, which must have six, including that of the subject supervisor. The three approving reviews of trade books may include one or two reviews in professional journals in lieu of reviews from staff members.

For those materials to be purchased for central inventory, the task of the Review and Evaluation Division is a simple one. It simply forwards one copy of the evaluation to the Instructional Materials Center, sends a copy to the subject supervisor, and files its own copy. Its job is complete. But for textbooks, library books, maps and globes, and other instructional materials, which are purchased for individual school inventories rather than the central inventory, the Division must disseminate the information that the materials have been recommended for county use. To do so, it publishes four lists of recommended materials, the "List of Approved Library Books," "List of Approved Textbooks," "Approved Maps and Globes," and the list "Filmstrips, Workbooks, Transparencies, Kits, Charts, Etc." annually, and, for two of the lists, issues periodic supplements which are cumulated into the next annual volume. Two of the annual lists are prepared by manual methods, and two are produced with some measure of data processing.

The smallest of the four lists is the "Map and Globe List." Since all maps and globes, except expendable outline maps, are purchased centrally as equipment items, the purpose of this list is somewhat different from the other three. It is intended to provide a standard indicating the number and types of maps recommended for each subject and level where maps are used, and to provide sufficient information to enable schools to request that appropriate maps be purchased for them. It is prepared manually and is arranged by type of map or globe, and by subject for historical and literary maps. At present this list has no index.

The second list prepared by manual methods is the "List of Approved Library Books." The basic arrangement of this list is alphabetical by title, with a second section in which the same titles are grouped by broad subject categories and, within those categories, alphabetically by author. The library book lists are issued at intervals throughout the school year and are combined in a single cumulated volume at the end of each year. The lists need an author approach and would benefit from close subject analysis in addition to, or in place of, the large subject grouping. Since the camera copy for printing the library book list must be typed within the Division, any expansion of the list would require additional clerical personnel and would greatly increase the cost of the lists. Improvement of the list, therefore, waits for data processing.

The list of instructional materials other than books and textbooks is produced with punched cards. The list is arranged by curriculum subject groupings and, within the subjects, by type of material. There is also an index by vendors. For each item listed, the following information is given: (1) grade level; (2) title; (3) date; (4) vendor; (5) whether color, or black and white (if appropriate); (6) the unit by which it is ordered; (7) cost; and (8) unique item number. The information for grouping the items and the information included in each entry is taken from the evaluation form. After the form has been returned by the evaluation committee, the staff of the Review and Evaluation Division checks it for accuracy, makes any needed corrections, and forwards it to the Mongomery County Public Schools Department of Data Systems. Data Systems key punches cards directly from the evaluation forms and returns a print-out arranged in the format described above.

During the course of the year, the Division prepares supplements to the basic list, usually every other month. The supplements are prepared in the same format as the basic annual volume and by the same methods. The supplements are merged, by machine, into the next subsequent annual basic list.

Throughout the year, the Division maintains a "Master List of Corrections" from which the Department of Data Systems updates its file of punched cards. In early December, the staff forwards the correction list to data processing, which makes the corrections needed. From the corrected cards, a print-out, arranged by vendor, is prepared and forwarded to the Division of Procurement, which supplies updated prices wherever necessary. This print-out, with the appropriate changes, is sent to Review and Evaluation for any last minute changes and corrections and then returned to Data Systems. After incorporating price and other changes, Data Systems provides a print-out in the format of the final list. This print-out is forwarded to the Publications Services Division, filmed and printed, a foreword and cover are added, and the list is distributed to the schools.

Unlike the list of other instructional materials, the textbook list is recorded on magnetic computer tape. The list is arranged by specific subjects in the curriculum, and within subjects is grouped by grade level and by a classification indicating whether the book is to be considered basic, supplemental, or for teacher's use only. The list includes two indexes, one by title and one by vendor. Use of computer tape instead of punched cards makes it possible to include a wider variety of information than on the instructional materials list. The data include: (1) grade level, (2) type, (3) title and author, (4) publisher, (5) copyright date, (6) binding (paperbacks only), (7) indication that the book is an anthology, (8) learning group, (9) reading level, (10) disability grouping (such as: braille or large print), (11) special comments, and (12) cost. While there are many new additions to all the other lists each year, the number of new titles added to the textbook list is limited, and many are deleted. As a result, only the new titles are added to the computer tape from an evaluation form. The form is planned, however, so that it provides all the information needed for entry in the list. The majority of changes in the list are taken from a transaction sheet which is used for deletion of titles and changes in copyright date; changes in price are also entered on the tape record.

The following procedures are applied:

1. Print-out by subject area is sent to Subject Supervisor. Books which sold less than ten copies must be deleted by completing a transaction form.
2. Any errors in titles or vendors must be made on a transaction form according to number (numbers appear in the Textbook List).
3. Evaluation forms for new titles are checked in "R & E" for accuracy according to the standards set up by R & E and Data Systems.
4. Evaluation forms of new titles and transaction forms are forwarded to Data Systems. This information is recorded on magnetic disc.
5. A print-out, according to subject area, of old titles which are to be retained and new titles is sent to each subject supervisor. Any corrections on this list must be made on a transaction form. Transaction forms bearing corrections are sent back to Data Systems where final print-outs of the Textbook Lists are made.
6. The print-outs are sent to the print shop.
7. Textbook Lists are delivered to the schools by April 15th.

Anyone familiar with the potential of computer services will have recognized already that our use of data processing techniques is limited and that it fails to take advantage of much of the capability it offers to reduce manual labor. We are currently in the process of developing a program which, we believe, will give us much fuller realization of the help the computer offers.

When our proposed plan goes into operation, the computer will enter the picture at a much earlier point. When an item of instructional materials is requested for evaluation, the correct bibliographic information will be supplied, the data entered in the computer, and the computer will produce the request for the item to be sent to the vendor. At that point, it will be possible to begin exerting control over the processing of that item. Those items, particularly trade books, which are received on a sampling basis will be entered in the computer upon receipt.

The computer will produce the evaluation forms, machine-readable, to be used by the committees and individuals who review the materials, and will enter approved items, automatically, into the appropriate list of approved materials. It will also be used, probably weekly, to produce lists of materials due to be returned to the vendor that week. Since the information will go into the computer on a regular basis, we shall also be able to issue more frequent supplements to the basic lists, and with far fewer man hours of manual labor.

The staff has made one additional proposal, that cataloging and classification of all items, other than textbooks, be done prior to review and evaluation. If this approach proves to be practical, and it has been done on a pilot basis for library books successfully, the possible arrangements of each list become greater. Not only can each list be arranged by broad subject categories, but also by specific subjects in a classified list. The ease of rearranging the lists by computer will also make it practical, for trade books, to add an author list to the present subject and title lists. It will also be possible to merge materials from the different lists to create multi-media order lists by subject.

The Review and Evaluation Division looks forward to having other, unrelated lists, provided through computer services, such as a vendor list and the committee lists, as well as lists for internal use only. The latter would include monthly lists of materials not recommended.

The most exciting prospect in this plan, however, is that it provides a basis upon which a whole system can be built. With classification and cataloging information for each item already in the computer record, automating acquisitions and production of catalogs for school libraries becomes a relatively simple matter. Since Review and Evaluation is the foundation of our entire instructional materials program, its automation provides the basis for the system.